APRON STRINGS

Carroll R. McKibbin

CENTRAL COAST PRESS

San Luis Obispo, California

ISBN 1-930401-46-9

CENTRAL COAST PRESS
P.O. Box 3654
San Luis Obispo, California 93403

Also by the Author

Lillian's Legacy: Marriage and Murder in Rural Iowa

In Pursuit of National Interests

Choices in American Government

A New Agenda for American National Security, **editor**

County Officials of Central Nebraska: Attitudes and Attributes

Political Parties

Advanced Public Administration

Introduction to Public Administration

Order Information

Signed copies of this book can be ordered by mail through CRM Book Distributors, P.O. Box 1526, San Luis Obispo, CA, 93401. Please enclose a check payable to "CRM Book Distributors" in the amount of $24.95 for the book, plus $5.00 for taxes, postage, and packaging. Email inquiries should be sent to cmckibbi@calpoly.edu

Orders by credit card can be placed with The Novel Experience bookstore by calling 805-544-0150 on a 24-hour line or by faxing 805-544-0165.

Dedication

This book is dedicated to the brave men of Guthrie County who sacrificed their lives in World War II so we might live ours in freedom. They were my heroes then. They are my heroes now. Their names are provided below with respect and reverence.

ANDERSON, JOHN W.
ARENDS, GERALD L.
ARENDS, LESLIE J.
BALL, JOHN
BATEHAM, ELLSWORTH J.
BAUER, HENRY J.
BEAN, RAY T.
BECK, MERLE L.
BENTON, RAYMOND J.
BLAUBAUGH, GEORGE F.
BLOMQUIST, HAROLD
BUTTLER, RALPH J.
BUTTLER, RICHARD C.
CAMPBELL, CHARLES L.
CARMICHAEL, JOHN
CONWAY, ROBERT
COOPER, ROBERT P.
CRIPE, KENNETH
DECKER, NED
DICKEY, DONALD D.
EGGER, DEAN J.
EMMONS, CALVIN L.
EVERSALL, GEORGE R.
FILLMAN, RICHARD D.
FLEAK, BOB C.
GARNES, LOREN W.
GEPHART, DONALD E.
GRANDBOUCHE, LEROY D.
HALL, CECIL E.
HALL, GALE H.
HAMBLETON, GENE L.
ISEMINGER, JAMES E.
JOHNSON, PAUL F.
JOHNSTON, BILLIE R.
JORGENSEN, MELVIN O.

JORGENSEN, WARREN L.
LYDON, LEONARD C.
MAHLER, EVERETT L.
MCCLELLAN, ESTEL R.
MCNARY, CHARLES E
MCQUEEN, DELMAR A.
MILLER, JAMES A.
NAUGHTON, EARL B.
NEWMAN, RALPH R.
NICKEL, KENNETH L.
PARSONS, KENNETH W.
PENNINGTON, STEWART R.
RAINS, JOSEPH E.
RASMUSSEN, HARLEY N.
RENSLOW, VERLAND D.
REYNOLDS, ROLAND E.
RUTT, DONALD T.
SAUCER, EARL F.
SEARL, RALPH D.
SEELEY, WILLIAM A.
SMITH, GEORGE
STAMMER, JAMES C.
STEPHENSEN, WARREN R.
STILES, JOHN D.
STOY, EARLE
TROTTER, GEORGE
TYSON, EVERETT V.
WADDELL, MAURICE E.
WESACK, EVERETT H.
WILSON, CLAIBORNE J.
WILSON, DALE R.
WILSON, DANIEL S.
WILSON, JOHN M.
WILSON, MARION E.

Acknowledgements

Authors write manuscripts. The talents and efforts of many people are required to produce a book. I am grateful to everyone who helped make *Apron Strings* possible.

Bill Charlesworth of Central Coast Press guided the publication process with skill and good cheer. Vanessa Schneider of the Sarah Jane Freymann Literary Agency provided support and encouragement. Carl Rowley designed the cover and enhanced photographs with remarkable originality.

Myrt Cordon, Joel Oswald, Anne Peterson, and Barbara Wolcott, each with a different perspective, applied the blue pencils of editors with style and grace.

Photos and related materials were supplied or loaned from a number of people: G.M. Barnett, Jr., Delores Beck, Doris Brainard, Fred Campbell, Ida Sanger Coffman, Gifford Covault, Dan Cronk, Howard Ely, Iowa State Historical Society, Bill Ludwig, Darrell McKibbin, Leonard McKibbin, Ned Moore, Jr., Donna Pete, Darcy Robson, Pat Sleister, and Darlene Tague. I regret not all submitted materials could be used, but I am grateful to all of you for making them available.

A number of people supplied useful information and advice: Scott Gonzales, Debbie Menning, Bob Secoy, Hugh Secoy, Pat Sleister, Roger Underwood, Bob Williams, Robin Wohlers, and many members of the SLO NightWriters organization who supplied critiques to my efforts. A special thanks to all of you.

I spent a lot of time with Bill Ludwig and my brothers, Gary and Darrell McKibbin, recalling and laughing over times past. I appreciate all the information they provided in putting this story together.

My wife, Lynn, delayed meals, re-ordered her schedule, and kept the house quiet while I typed at my computer keyboard. I am blessed by her patience and support.

Contents

Chapter 1

Paying Respects

That morning began like any Friday. Mr. James, milk bottles clinking against his metal carrier, passed beneath my bedroom window whistling "Remember Pearl Harbor." I turned on my side and watched slivers of dawn glittering through the tall pines that rimmed our yard. Snuggled deep between warm flannel sheets, I listened for the sound of Mom's kitchen radio and WHO-Des Moines.

Our usual radio day started with Herb Plambeck rattling off corn and hog prices in Sioux City and Omaha. Not this day. Instead of endless rounds of numbers, I heard a church song I knew well – or so I thought. "Bringin' in the sheeps, bringin' in the sheeps," I sang.

"The word is 'sheaves,' " Mom had corrected.

I took her word for it, but stuck with what I understood. Words caused me problems.

"What did you learn at school?" Mom asked one day.

"I learned about bowels," I responded proudly.

"Bowels?"

"Uh-huh. I know 'em by heart: A-E-I-O-U."

Mom laughed then. She wouldn't now. Church music was serious business. Why wasn't she listening to "Jerry and Zelda," her favorite morning program? The town whistle sounded its seven o'clock reminder and awakened the 2,000 people of Guthrie Center who occupied a square mile among the rolling hills of Southwest Iowa, fifty miles west of Des Moines. Alex Dreier and the war news came on at seven. This day, Mom replaced Mr. Dreier with "Rock of Ages."

I smelled frying bacon and boiling coffee. Did my nose also bring the good news of an apple pie? Mom baked a lot of pies, but never in the morning. I watched her, always in the afternoon, scalloping crust edges with nimble fingers, adding a floral design with a fork handle, and slipping the round pie dish into the oven with an encouraging, "Get in there and get all brown."

If Mom was fixing an apple pie, it was out of turn. Her three sons had different favorites, so Mom rotated the selection: lemon meringue for Darrell, her eldest; chocolate cream for Gary, who went by "Gab"; and apple loaded with cinnamon for me, the youngest at five. I had the last round. Gab would be mad if I got two turns in a row.

Normally, I would be getting ready for another day of kindy-garden, but school was dismissed this Friday. The teachers were making the hour-long trip to Des Moines to attend a meeting. I looked forward to a day free of lines: lines to keep Crayola coloring inside, lines to put letters on, and lines for going and coming from recess.

Gab stirred in the bed an arm's length from mine.

"Do you know why Mom is listening to church music on the radio?" I asked.

"Huh? Oh, she likes that stuff."

"Not during the week. She listens to Jerry and Zelda and then Alex Dreier and the war news."

"Maybe she's getting an early start on Sunday."

Gab's mumbled thoughts didn't help much in explaining Mom's change in routine, but at least he didn't notice the apple pie. I needed to find out what was going on downstairs. Besides, it was almost time for the "Uncle Stan and Cowboy Ken" radio show.

Barefoot and still in my pajamas, I straddled the banister and slid to the foot of the stairs by the front door. A line of cars was parked across the street in front of the Elys. Today was not Sunday, the day for family visits. Why were so many cars parked there, including a long black one with curtains on its side windows?

I checked on Father O'Sullivan through the bay window opposite the stairs before continuing to the kitchen. The pacing priest walked back and forth on his porch, hour after hour, reading from his black-covered book. Gab and I spied on the Father, usually through a vine-covered trellis on the front porch, waiting for the day when he took a fall.

Our porch had a railing. Father O'Sullivan's didn't. He never took his eyes off his book and teetered on the edge of disaster on every round. Gab and I wanted to be in on the excitement when the priest took a nose dive. On this day, while some things seemed different, Father O'Sullivan kept his footing and continued his sentry duty in the work of the Lord. I moved on to the kitchen.

My suspicions about the pie were correct. Through the oven window of Mom's Westinghouse, I saw dark brown juices bubbling through her crust cover artwork. A rich apple-cinnamon aroma teased my nose and stirred my taste buds.

Mom was not wearing her usual floral house dress with buttons down the front. Instead, she wore a high-collared black dress and a white apron. I ran to her and hugged her legs. "Good morning, Mommy."

She bent over and gave me a love pat on the back. "Good morning, sweetie," she replied.

Mom's mood had changed from the day before when, after removing the racks to clean the Frigidaire, she boosted me inside to watch Mr. Yahoody turn on the light. The door closed me into an instant of darkness before Mom opened it again and the light came back on.

"Did you see him?" she asked.

"Yeah . . . I kinda think so."

Mom laughed then, but not today. Her thoughts were elsewhere. Why was she making a pie, wearing black, and listening to church music? This was not the time to ask.

Mom was also making a green Jello salad. I knew what was inside – pears. Jello salads helped me learn colors. Dark red meant fruit salad, orange meant carrots and pineapple, and green ones, like Mom was making, always had pears.

I wanted to change the dreary mood. "Mommy," I asked. "Can I listen to Uncle Stan and Cowboy Ken?" She tuned the small white Airline radio on the stove to 1040-WHO.

"Good morning, buckaroos, this is your Uncle Stan." "And," said another voice, "this is Cowboy Ken." I stood before the white enamel stove at eye level with the radio. From this perfect position, I could watch and smell the baking apple pie, and Uncle Stan's Magic Eye could see me when it came time to count hands for the dressing contest.

"Okay, boys and girls, let's all get around and get dressed this morning. That's right, let's help our mommies out while Cowboy Ken sings the dressing song. And when you're all done, remember to hold a hand in front of the radio so the Magic Eye can count you. The girls have won three days in a row. Let's see if the boys can do better this time."

Mom kept the Magic Eye tally for me, writing the numbers on a calendar by the radio and circling the days the boys won. We lost the day before by one vote because I arrived too late to be counted. I wouldn't let the boys down today. Not dressed and ready, as the rules required, I kneeled in front of the stove, out of view of the radio.

"Okay," Uncle Stan announced. "The Magic Eye is ready to count the girls. If you are dressed and ready to go this morning, little ladies, get those hands high in the air . . . that's it . . . and the Magic Eye is counting . . . 30-105-167-211. Okay, now it's the guys' turn. Get those hands high, boys."

Uncle Stan did say "hands." I raised both of mine to radio level from my hiding spot.

"The Magic Eye is counting," Uncle Stan challenged. "Okay, the boys have 27-102-158-212 . . . that's it boys and girls. Looks like the little fellas pulled it out today by a single hand. Congratulations, guys! Now be sure and eat your Pep breakfast food, and don't forget to tune in again tomorrow."

Feeling clever for outsmarting the Magic Eye, I took my assigned place at the table. Mom, Dad, and Darrell each had an entire side of the white porcelain table. Gab and I shared the side in front of the stove. Everyone except me had a chair with chrome legs and a red plastic seat. I sat on a white stool covered with red gingham oilcloth. Until recently, I sat on a Sears and Roebuck catalog. Now, elevated to the status of schoolboy, I refused that symbol of infancy.

Dad sat down across from me. Bib overalls strained at the straps against his barrel chest. Popeye-size forearms extended from the rolled sleeves of his coarse blue work shirt and locked on the table at the elbows. His grease-grained mechanic's hands gripped a fork and a butter knife. Dad came to the table to eat.

I was relieved when other family members took their seats. I was uncomfortable alone with my dad. He didn't talk much, and I never knew what to say.

My thoughts returned to the mystery of the day. Sooner or later, either Mom would fill us in during a davenport session or Gab would track down the information and pass it along. Good news from Mom arrived in the blink of an eye. Bad news weighed her down and made her cry. The more time that passed, the more I assumed something bad had happened.

Darrell, like Dad, said little at the table. He was a high school student and budding scientist when I entered kindygarden. He had the tall, gangly build of a young Abe Lincoln. Half of his head was scarred and hairless from a family tragedy never discussed in detail and mentioned only as "the fire."

My mother also had scars from "the fire." The skin on her throat and chest, spreading downward to the unknown, had the texture of a cantaloupe rind. She bore her physical scars well, referring to the burned skin of her throat as a "necklace." Her internal wounds went deep, however, and never recovered from that day when she caused an explosion that nearly killed her and her infant son.

The continuing and eerie stillness of the breakfast table weighed on me. Even the talkative Gab remained silent. A joke was in order. I had heard a good one about a fence being built around the city park to keep the trees from "leaving."

"D'ya know they're building a fence around Mitchell Park?" I blurted.

"Why on earth are they doing that when there's a war on?" Mom responded.

"To keep the trees from getting out," I announced proudly.

I expected to hear laughter. Instead, I got a table-round of quiet, puzzled looks.

"That's dumb," said Gab.

I filled my bowl with Kellogg's Pep, not out of loyalty to Uncle Stan and Cowboy Ken, but because I wanted the cutout war plane on the back. I had a Spitfire, a P-47, a Messerschmitt, and a Zero. I needed a RussianYak to complete my collection.

Mom sipped at her coffee and stared into space, Darrell prepared his usual raisin bran, and Gab, who loved chocolate anything, ate Cocoa Wheat. Dad, as usual, was busy. I liked to watch him eat.

Aunt Edri, the family Emily Post, told me, "Don't eat like your father." I didn't understand why. He was so efficient at the table. Dad looked like Gene Krupa in a drum solo. His hands were everywhere: stabbing a boiled egg off a serving dish and jamming it down his mouth, spearing a gristly morsel from his private jar of pickled pigs feet, pushing a link of sausage through his non-stop grinding teeth. Dad moved through food at the table like a hay baler devouring a windrow.

Dad and Darrell sometimes talked about car repairs at the table, using words I didn't know. I understood Mom's sewing business better than Dad's garage work. I knew more about corduroy than carburetors, more about rickrack than radiators. This quiet morning, Dad stood, wiped his hands across the seat of his overalls, removed his greasy denim jacket from the kitchen door knob, and left for work.

Dad's presence, his do-not-bother-me, and above all else, do-not-ask-for-money attitude, created household tension. In Dad's absence, we could return to Mom's world of Mr. Yahoody and giggles and hugs. This day, however, Mom remained silent. I didn't know how to relate to her when she was sad. I finished breakfast as quickly as possible.

"I'm done, Mom. Can I be excused?"

My mother hesitated, and then turned my way. "Okay, run

and brush your teeth . . . don't change into your play clothes just yet."

Why, I wondered, shouldn't I get into my play clothes? Mom usually worried about me not wearing my everyday things.

I had recently learned to brush my own teeth. I liked being treated like my older brothers, but Mom's instructions to brush with one hundred strokes presented a problem. I couldn't count past the number of my fingers and toes. Fearful I would lose my grown-up status if I told the truth, I confessed nonetheless.

"Mommy, I don't know how to count that far."

"You can count to twenty, can't you?"

"Uh-huh."

"Well, count that far for each finger on one hand. Okay?"

Mom's numbers were getting complicated. She said to chew each bite fifty times and to look both ways twice before crossing the street. And now she required one hundred strokes of a tooth brush. I lost count on the chewing and teeth brushing, and she never knew the difference. She monitored my street crossing from her kitchen window. I couldn't snitch on that.

The arrival of more cars at the Elys reminded me something was happening across the street. Mom's mood and my morning routine had moved my thoughts elsewhere. I climbed the "wooden hill," as Dad called the stairs, to the room I shared with my two brothers. Gab and I had two places for privacy and free-from-adults fun. One was the front porch swing, the other our bedroom. I found Gab standing next to his bed, his head tilted backward, trying to balance a rubber ball on his nose.

"Gab, d'ya know what's wrong with Mom?"

He stopped his balancing act and frowned. "No, but it's not your turn for pie. How'd ya get her to do that?"

"I dunno. I didn't say nothin'."

"Yeah, sure, you little brownie."

"What's a brownie?"

Gab's face twisted with impatience. "Ya know, a brown-noser."

"No, I don't know. Are you saying something mean to me again?"

"Look, it's buttering up someone to get in good with 'em."

"Why wouldn't we wanna be in good with Mom? . . . D'ya know why she's wearing a fancy dress?"

"She's probably goin' shopping."

Gab always had an answer. Right or wrong, good or bad, sometimes funny, sometimes wise, I could depend on my brother for a response. I was often baffled. Not Gab. He was three years ahead of me in school and had everything figured out.

I stretched out on my bed and looked at the light bulb hanging above. The shadow of the cord followed the crack in the plaster wall. "Did ya watch Father O'Sullivan this morning?" I asked.

"Yeah, thought he was goin' a couple a times. You just about missed out."

"D'ya know why all the cars are parked at the Elys? There must be some doin's going on over there."

"Probably a meeting of those ladies that don't like people drinkin' beer. Mrs. Ely runs that outfit."

I sat up in bed and turned toward Gab. "D'ya know why Mom don't want me to change into my play clothes?"

"That's so ya won't run off. Something's up."

"What?"

"I dunno. We'll find out soon enough."

I relaxed on the soft warmth of my bed. The taste of Mom's homemade salt and baking soda tooth powder lingered in my mouth. The overhead light bulb swung gently in the cool morning breeze. My mind wandered.

"Gary Gene and Carroll Ray, come downstairs and seat yourselves on the davenport," Mom called.

"Seat yourselves on the davenport" and the use of our middle names meant Gab and I were about to be told something Mom found important. It had happened twice before. The first time, Mom told us she had to go to the hospital. "Checking into the hotel," she called it.

I understood why Mom's two-week trip to the hospital was serious. Her absence was a hardship and a heartbreak. The other session on the davenport made no sense to me. I felt Mom's concern, and I was always excited about being included in grown-up matters, but what she had to say didn't seem very important.

"I'm just going to come out and say it," she started. "Your Uncle Bud is a woman."

That was it? What a letdown. I thought "Uncle" was Bud's first name. I had lots of aunts and uncles. The uncles had short or little hair and bulges around their waists. Aunts had long hair and bulges above the waist. Beyond that, I made little distinction between aunts and uncles. Sometimes Mom said, "I'll be a monkey's uncle." If Mom was a woman and an uncle, why not Bud?

The uncle business was confusing. On Decoration Day, we placed flowers on the graves of two of Mom's brothers, Jesse and Gayle. She said they were my uncles and died when they were little boys. I didn't understand how little boys could be my uncles when the others were all grown-up men, at least until now. Uncles were hard to figure. Some were little boys and dead; some, as rumor had it, drank too much; and at least one was a woman.

Uncle Bud and Aunt Edri had a car named "Penny," a black

cocker spaniel called "Dinah," and a coffee table dish filled with gum drops. They traveled to far away cities like Omaha and Chicago, subscribed to *Holiday* and *Colliers*, had a filled bookcase, and ate avocados and shrimp cocktails. At home, we had no pets, no candy, no magazines, no books, no fancy foods, and a Hudson Terraplane that seldom left its garage.

All the fuss over who was an aunt and who was an uncle, and who was a man and who was a woman didn't register with me. Besides, my pals and I were still debating whether girls had peters.

I accepted the news about Uncle Bud with relief and without question. I hoped the news of this day would be as trivial.

Gab and I sat side-by-side on the maroon davenport Mom reupholstered and awaited her arrival. Our images reflected in the large fitting mirror that covered the cellar door and faced us from across a linoleum floor patterned with cream-colored flowers on a maroon background.

Viewing Gab in the mirror made me envious. His feet touched the floor. Mine didn't. His blond hair was cut in the short and masculine burr fashion. I had curls Mom adored and I tolerated. My brother and I both wore round, metal-rimmed glasses. His were gold and mine dull silver. Gab said my glasses were made of old Spam cans, while his were the real thing. His front teeth fit together neatly, and he had long fingers that Mom called "piano hands." My teeth had a gap wide enough for a straw and my stubby fingers were stunted with chewed nails.

People called Gab "all boy" and referred to me as the "family baby." He knew how to cuss and get into trouble. I could not do the former and seldom lapsed into the latter. Gab was "daring-do" and on his way to manhood. I was "daring-don't" and fighting my way through curls and babyhood.

Mom closed the bathroom door behind her and approached the davenport. She had added a black hat, kind of a baseball cap without a bill, to her outfit. A black net veil covered her face. She stood before us.

"Luella . . . ," she said. "Luella has lost her father, Mr. Knapp. We must go to the Elys and pay our respects."

Mom pulled her veil up and dabbed at her eyes with a lacy handkerchief. "You boys go get into your Sunday school clothes."

I could feel Mom's distress. She worried a lot when people were lost. I had been lost twice, once in Younker's Department Store in Des Moines and once at the county fair. Mom cried both times, but smiled and hugged me when I showed up. I figured she would feel better when we found Mr. Knapp.

Back in our bedroom and getting dressed in our good clothes, I questioned Gab. "Who is Mr. Knapp?" I asked.

"That's the old man that lives across the street at the Elys."

"How could he get lost? He moves pretty slow."

"Sometimes old people forget. Maybe he couldn't remember how to get home."

I sat on my bed and pulled on my brown socks. "Why do we have to wear our good clothes to look for him?"

"That's in case he went into a fancy store. You know, like Mom makes us dress up to go to Des Moines."

"Why do we have to pay to look for Mr. Knapp?"

"That's probably to help out with car expenses. Gas is hard to come by with war rationing."

Gab and I reported back to Mom dressed in our Sunday school clothes. A mandatory inspection followed. That meant five minutes of finger curling my hair, an inspection of my ears for "potato patches," a look under my chin to see if I had a "dirt necklace," and a spit bath with her moistened hankie as she wiped something – I never knew what – from my face.

With the inspection finished, Mom walked toward the kitchen. "Come along," she said. "I want you to carry the food."

Did this mean, I wondered, that our search included a picnic?

"Here, Gary, you can carry the Jello salad and, Carroll Ray, you can carry the apple pie." Mom handed Gab a square Pyrex dish with wax paper across the top. She handed me a round dish. I knew what was under the embroidered towel. I could smell the apple pie, feel the warmth of the dish against the palms of my hands, and sense the opportunity to eat my favorite dessert slipping away.

Apparently, we were paying for respects with food. Mr. Ely sharpened lawn mowers in his backyard. Maybe Dad had his lawnmower sharpened and we were paying for it with an apple pie and a Jello salad. I saw Dad throw his jacket on the kitchen floor and complain: "Didn't make a damned dime today. Don't know how I'm gonna buy groceries this week."

I took Dad seriously and ate extra portions for supper that evening. Perhaps, so I thought, Dad is out of money and has to pay off Mr. Ely with food. If we have to do that, why not give them some Spam and save the pie? Besides, if we are doing them a favor by looking for Mrs. Ely's dad, maybe they could call it even and we can keep the pie.

Mom guided us toward the front door. The front entrance was used only for special occasions. Obviously, Mom considered the hunt for Mr. Knapp something important. Before opening the door, she paused and looked us in the eye. Her list of "do nots" followed.

"Do not wander off, you hear? Stay right next to me. Do not talk and do not ask questions. Just keep still. Someone will take your dishes and give you a number so we can get them back later. Just put the numbers in your pockets and give them to me when we get home. We will walk on the sidewalk and down Father O'Sullivan's drive instead of taking the short-cut across the parking. It doesn't look right to walk in the grass in your good clothes, and you might get grass stains on your pants."

Mom's list of "do nots" was, as usual, too long to remember and too complicated to figure out. Her instructions didn't sound anything like those for a posse in a Hopalong Cassidy movie. But I would stick close to her. That I could remember.

Mom, with one hand on Gab's shoulder and the other on mine, steered us out the front door and down the steps to the sidewalk. We turned right toward Father O'Sullivan's house. Where his driveway met the sidewalk, Mom hesitated and turned toward the priest who, as always, was pacing and reading on his porch. Father O'Sullivan stopped! I had never seen our black-suited neighbor do anything but walk back and forth. He held his book at his side and turned toward us.

" 'Tis a sad day, Mrs. McKibbin."

'Twas for me. I was wearing itchy trousers and tight shoes, giving away an apple pie in payment for something or other, and facing a life of hardship because Dad had run out of money.

Mom turned her head and looked at the priest. "Yes, Father," she said. "It is a very sad day."

Father O'Sullivan had spoken six words, a record number. He opened his mouth to say more: "He's gone home now."

That was good news. Mr. Knapp had found his way back. So why were Mom and Father O'Sullivan talking about sadness? As I saw it, if Mr. Knapp had gone home, then the search could be called off and we could return home with a pie ready for supper. I awaited those instructions. They didn't come. Instead, Mom nudged us down the concrete drive and across the street. Mrs. Vincent, the local judge's wife and a talkative neighbor, waved to us from her porch swing without a word. Mom nodded and returned a faint smile.

An eerie presence had invaded our neighborhood. Something had sucked away the normal gaiety. Even the return home of Mr. Knapp had not changed the atmosphere. Hopping robins, cooing pigeons, and tall pines bending in the wind had given way to the unexplainable. The contrast of the usual and unusual puzzled me. Mom was sad and listening to church music, baking pies in the morning and not talking to them, and wearing a black dress and making Gab and me wear Sunday school clothes on a Friday. Father O'Sullivan stopped his pacing for the first time ever and spoke to us. Mrs. Ely's dad was lost, we had a debt to pay, and Dad was about to go broke. The pieces of the puzzle were not falling into place for me.

We arrived at the Ely house. The blinds were pulled and the drapes closed. A two-starred banner honoring members of the household serving in the war hung on a window near the front door. The Elys had two sons, Howard and Lawrence, in the army. We didn't merit a banner in our window. We had no one in the service. I was envious of those who did. Mom worried Darrell would have to go into the army. I worried he wouldn't. The McKibbins only had bib overalls for uniforms. We needed khaki ones.

When paying a visit to a neighbor, Mom opened the door, stuck her head inside, and hollered, "Anyone home?" Not this day. Mom knocked gently. Norma Ely, a young woman who worked in Des Moines, opened the door. When she was home on weekends, she sometimes joined us for Saturday breakfast. Mom would give me a quarter and send me to Ferguson's Bakery to buy a dozen oval-shaped pineapple rolls. Apparently, Norma came from Des Moines this day to help look for her grandfather. She wore a black dress similar to my mother's.

"Thank you for coming, Hazel. And thank you for bringing the boys," Norma said.

"It's good you could come home, for your mother's sake.

With Howard and Larry away in the service and Elbert in Virginia, it's a blessing you could be near," Mom replied.

"Please come in."

I visited the Ely home often. On those occasions, the console radio, with its rounded top and skinny legs, blared baseball games in the parlor where we stood. Mr. Ely sat listening to the Cubs while keeping his rocking chair in constant motion. Dazzling sunshine flooded the room from the facing solarium. Not now. The contrast deadened my senses. The radio stood silent, the rocking chair empty and motionless. A dozen faceless, hushed people, as wooden as their chairs, sat in the shadowy parlor. An occasional sniffle or nervous cough dented the heavy silence. The nameless group faced the dull glow of the solarium.

I didn't know what was happening and couldn't ask. I kept my head bowed and my eyes down. By avoiding eye contact, I hoped to gain time to think without revealing my ignorance. I kept my eyes away from Mom's. If she cried, I would too.

A pair of hands with bulging veins and brown spots slipped the apple pie from my grasp. Another hand gave me a slip of paper with a number on it. I placed the paper in the pocket of my sport coat. With my duties fulfilled, I reached for the warmth of my mother's hand.

The atmosphere of the Ely home was not what I expected. Search parties in movies were enthusiastic and full of action. This group was gloomy and sniffling.

An upward glance caught Mrs. Ely arriving out of the shadows, erect and formal. I thought she looked like Ethel Barrymore. She, like most everyone else, was wearing black. I had never seen so many black clothes. The world had turned from Technicolor to black and white. I felt like a neon sign in a dark alley in my snazzy beige sports coat with its plaid panels.

Mom released my hand, much against my will, and grasped those of Mrs. Ely. "He's gone to a better place," Mom said.

Mom talked as though she knew the location of Mr. Knapp. Anyplace would be better than the dreariness of the Ely house. I wanted to go home.

"Please come with me," said Mrs. Ely.

I took Mom's hand and, still looking downward, followed her feet the few steps from the entry into the solarium. Her feet stopped. A shudder ran down her arm and into my hand. I saw a row of flowers in pots lined and draped with colored foil and neatly arranged on the varnished floor. Behind the flowers were the legs of several chairs. I raised my view and saw an ocean blue metal box resting on the chairs. The box was as shiny as Dad's polished Hudson Terraplane. A half-lid on the box was open, exposing a sky-blue satin lining. Beneath the lid and above the edge of the box, the side of a man's face with a shark fin nose appeared. His skin was the color of Mom's pie dough and contrasted with his rouged cheeks and lips. I tightened my grip on Mom's hand. She responded with an extra "it's all right" squeeze. I didn't feel all right, but I caught on. This must be Mrs. Ely's father. He wasn't lost, and he wasn't going anywhere.

"He looks so natural," Mom said to Mrs. Ely.

He didn't look natural to me. He looked dead.

I tilted my head downward and out of view of Mr. Knapp. My eyes blinked, my lower lip quivered. Crying would embarrass Mom, and I could tell she was also fighting tears.

"Can I touch him?" Gab asked Mrs. Ely.

Gab's daring question stunned me. Why would he, why would anyone, want to touch a dead man? All I wanted to touch was the door knob. I wanted to go home. I wanted Mom to put finger curls in my hair, wash potato patches out of my ears, and tuck me in and tell me everything was all right.

Mrs. Ely nodded her consent to Gab's request. He stepped forward, arched his arm, and reached into the casket. He leaned over and sniffed. I shrank backward against Mom, hugging her leg through her crinkly crepe dress.

When Gab finished his inspection of the dead man, he stepped back and grasped Mom's hand. I was glad it was hers and not mine after what he had touched.

I was numbed and dismayed. I had not known, had not seen, had not thought about the end of life. Nor did I want to. I wanted to run and escape this horror.

Mom turned toward the front door. She released the hands of her sons and again cradled those of her friend. "He's happier now," she said.

My mother's knowledge and wisdom were reinforced by a lengthy list of proverbs, including: "Seeing is believing." Mom and I had seen the same lifeless form, but our conclusions were far different. She talked of a happiness I had not seen and could not understand. Happiness was a big hug from Aunt Edri, an ice cream cone at Ferguson's Bakery, or listening with the family to "Fibber McGee and Molly." Smiles and laughter went with happiness. Our trip to the Elys included none of that.

We three left the Ely house with Mom firmly grasping the small hands of her everlasting life. I was beginning to wonder about mine. Death seemed temporary and life renewable in movies. Brian Dunlevy got killed in one war movie and returned in another, looking as fit and healthy as ever. At Sunday school, we learned Jesus came back to life.

I had paid a high price for respects. I lost an apple pie, endured the dismal mood of the Ely home, and began to wonder about eternal life. I would have questions for Gab when we got home.

My senses jump-started as we crossed the street. St. Mary's

pigeons cooed louder, the robins in our yard hopped higher, and I breathed in the fragrance of our pine trees. I looked toward our house and its peeling paint. I couldn't get there fast enough.

"Go put your play clothes on," Mom said when we walked in the front door.

I needed no reminder. I wanted to run, to jump, to shout. I forgot about the apple pie and looking for Mr. Knapp and paying off family debts and Dad's financial doom. Clad in jeans and a T-shirt, I raced about the yard, somersaulting and cartwheeling about, and then moved to the porch swing for some quiet moments of reflection.

I wanted to soak in Father O'Sullivan's reassuring routine. I no longer wanted our neighbor to fall off his porch. I didn't want anyone hurt, and certainly not a man with connections with God.

Gab joined me in the swing. "What did Mr. Knapp feel like?" I asked.

"Ya know that waxy, slick stuff Mom covers the jam with when she cans? It feels kinda like that, except it's cool instead of warm."

"Did ya know we were gonna see a dead person?"

"Sure. They have funerals for 'em at the church, so if we're wearing Sunday school clothes it means we're gonna see a body."

"I don't see dead people when I wear my good clothes to Sunday school."

"Of course not, dummy. It's when ya put on church clothes during the week that ya see a dead person."

Gab had a point. It was Friday. "Why did we have to pay to see the body?"

"It's kinda like the county fair, where ya have to pay to see weird things. You know, like the bearded lady we saw."

I took a peek through the vines to make sure Father O'Sullivan was still busy before returning to my questions. "Gab, why were people just sittin' around at the Elys without saying nothin'?"

"Haven't ya noticed how the sicker people are the quieter the talk? People blab a lot about colds. They only whisper about cancer. And when someone dies, they just clam up."

Gab, pleased with his ready explanations, grasped his hands behind his head and leaned back in the swing.

"What about everlasting life?" I continued. "I thought if I went to church I got to live forever."

"Oh, that. That's just to sucker you into going to Sunday school."

"Why did they say Mr. Knapp was lost when he was dead?"

"People say 'dead' when it's someone else's family. If they're your own family, they get lost."

"Is Mr. Knapp coming back to life like Jesus?"

"Nope."

Chapter 2

Steeple People

The end of Mr. Knapp's life stirred doubts about my own. At Sunday school, I learned believing in Jesus led to everlasting life. And I believed. I belted out "Jesus Loves Me" every Sunday. I racked up enough silver stars on the attendance chart to fill the Milky Way. My commitment to the Lord was loud and fully recorded. And now, with the image of Mr. Knapp's lifeless form lingering in my mind, I began to wonder if the church was holding up its end of the deal.

I never suspected the Methodist Church would try to fool me. I had thought the same of the 7-Up Company, but both betrayed me in the span of a year. First, it was 7-Up. I drank their pop because green was my favorite color. The bottle was green, the soda tasted green, and I was satisfied until that unhappy day when a waitress at Cronk's Cafe poured a bottle of 7-Up into my glass. A clear and sparkling liquid foamed over the ice cubes. "It's not green!" I shrieked.

"What's not green?" my mother asked.

"My pop."

Eyes turned our direction. Mom didn't like the attention. She shifted awkwardly on her side of the booth.

"Shhh," she said. "Go ahead and enjoy your pop."

"It's supposed to be green," I protested.

"Shhh. Calm down."

Mom took my glass and sipped from the bubbling soda. "See?" she said. "It tastes good."

As I saw it, if it didn't look right, it couldn't taste right. I quit drinking 7-Up and switched to lime-flavored, genuinely green, Kool-Aid. I didn't want to do business with cheaters. That solution was simple. And if it worked with pop, why not with churches? Maybe I would have a better chance at everlasting life if I switched to a new church. St. Mary's was nearby, practically next door, and Father O'Sullivan, dressed in serious clothes, worked at his religion on his front porch every day. Our minister, Reverend McDonald, often stopped by at Dad's garage in casual slacks and a sports shirt to laugh and talk with Dad and his pals. Father O'Sullivan never visited McKibbin's Garage, never strayed from his house or church, and never ceased pacing and reading in the work of the Lord. I thought Father O'Sullivan had better connections with God than Reverend McDonald and might put in a good word for me concerning everlasting life.

"Mom," I asked. "Why don't we go to Father O'Sullivan's church?"

My mother stopped ironing and looked me in the eye. "We don't go to that church. Catholics are different."

"Do they have a different God?"

Mom set her iron in its upright position, draped the shirt she had finished on a hanger, and hung it over the top hinge of the kitchen door. "No, they don't have a different God, but they run their church differently."

"What do they do different?" The only difference I had noticed was Catholics drove to church and lined our block with cars. Methodists walked to church. Either the Catholics had more money or were lazier.

"Well, for one thing, they have to mind the Pope."

I thought ministers got their instructions straight from God. At church, while we remained still, Reverend McDonald talked directly to God, asking Him to forgive us for doing bad things and to help us whip the Nazis and Nips, what he called "the forces of evil."

"Who's the Pope?"

"He's the leader of all the Catholics in the world. He lives far away in Italy."

"*Italy!* That's where Hitler's friend Mussolini lives. Why doesn't the Pope move to America?"

"It's a nice day out. Don't you want to go play?"

Mom pulled one of Dad's blue work shirts from the wooden peach basket she lined with flour sack cloth and converted to laundry use.

"What else do Catholics do different?" My thoughts moved from concerns about everlasting life to the mysteries of the priest who lived next door and ran the church on the corner.

"They drink in church."

I understood what "drink" meant. It came from bottles marked "XXX," like those in drawings the WCTU ladies had us color at school. An image came to mind of Father O'Sullivan running a beer parlor, like the one Mr. Cornish owned on the corner next to Dad's garage. I could see Catholics passing bottles around in paper sacks like drunks in movies.

"Why do Catholics go to church to drink? Why don't they go to Mr. Cornish's place?"

"It's called communion. They drink wine and eat bread."

Our church believed smoking and drinking were sins. I had never tasted alcohol, but understood how disagreeable cigarette smoke could be. I walked through it every Sunday after church when men in our congregation gathered outside and lit up a Chesterfield or Lucky Strike.

"Isn't wine and bread what Jesus fed all those people that time?"

"It's going to get dark pretty soon. Don't you want to go play?"

"What else do people at St. Mary's do different?"

I smelled the scorch of a starched shirt as Mom worked her iron back and forth across a sleeve.

"They have to tell their sins to Father O'Sullivan, let him know everything they've done wrong. It's called confession."

Everything they've done wrong! Would I have to tell Father O'Sullivan, I wondered, that I spied on him? I didn't tell anyone all of my misdeeds – not Mom, not even Gab. My conscience knew everything and hounded me. That was enough. The case for remaining a Methodist grew stronger.

Referring to the lady who lived with Father O'Sullivan, I asked, "Why isn't Julia Anne called Mrs. O'Sullivan?"

"Oh, that's his sister, not his wife. Priests aren't allowed to get married."

"Is that why Father O'Sullivan doesn't have kids?"

"Yes, but they do believe in large families."

Both sets of twins in my kindy-garden class, Ronnie and Bobby Feilmeyer and Patrick and Mary Nolan, attended St. Mary's. If Catholics came two at a time, they would certainly multiply faster. Yet, Mom had nine brothers and sisters, and Reverend and Mrs. McDonald had seven children. It seemed to me that Methodists were also adding up pretty fast.

Mom's afternoon radio programs ended with "Front Page Farrell." Next up was "Jack Armstrong, the All-American Boy."

It was my turn to listen to the radio. I was more interested this day in the affairs of our stiff-collared neighbor.

"Bobby Feilmeyer told me he has to go to St. Mary's every weekend or will end up in Hell. Is that right?"

Mom flipped and ironed the back of a shirt while I awaited an answer. "Yes, they are required to go to church."

I had visions of Father O'Sullivan pulling my friends Ronnie and Bobby from their beds and dragging them to church by their heels.

"If they miss church, even once, they are punished at confession," Mom continued.

I wondered if Father O'Sullivan spanked Ronnie and Bobby or rapped their knuckles with a wooden ruler like Gab's teacher? Mom didn't give me a choice about going to Sunday school, but Reverend McDonald never spanked me.

Mom's arguments for not switching to Father O'Sullivan's church were convincing. I wouldn't need everlasting life for a while anyway, and telling on myself might have an immediate, perhaps painful, result. Besides, I liked the minced ham sandwiches served after our Sunday school. I would stick with Reverend McDonald for now, but be on the lookout for ways of improving my chances for everlasting life.

It occurred to me that more frequent church attendance might make a good impression on God. With Mom's blessing and encouragement, I decided to follow up the Methodist summer Bible school with similar sessions at the Christian and Baptist Churches.

All the churches in Guthrie Center were called "Christian," even St. Mary's. But the tan brick church across the alley from my dad's garage got to use "Christian" as its name. That seemed important, like God favored them. Thus, the Christian Church, with a ping-pong table the Methodist Church didn't have, seemed a good bet for another round of Bible school.

With two sessions of Bible school and an ever-increasing knowledge of biblical stories under my belt, I moved on to the Baptist Church for another two-week session. By now, I had learned about Jesus' friend, John the Baptist. Why, I wondered, didn't John attend the Methodist Church like Jesus? Then I learned John chased people around reminding them of their sins. I didn't need reminders. Just as well, I decided, that John went to the Baptist Church.

Three rounds of Bible school filled my head with biblical names and stories and a lot of questions. "Mom," I asked. "Is there more than one Jesus?"

"No, why do you ask?"

"At Bible school, sometimes we learned about Jesus of Nazareth and other times about Jesus Christ."

Mom turned from her sewing machine and smiled. "Nazareth is a town. That's where Jesus lived."

"Am I Carroll Ray of Guthrie Center?"

"Well, I guess so, but we don't use names of towns like that anymore. We use family names."

"What's our family name?"

"McKibbin. Your mother and father and brothers all have McKibbin as their family name."

"Is 'Christ' Jesus' family name?"

"I guess so."

"Then his parents were Mary and Joseph Christ?"

"No, you don't hear that."

I sat down on the linoleum floor next to where Mom was hemming a dress. "How 'bout Jesus' middle name. What was that?"

"He didn't have a middle name."

"Yes, he did. It started with an 'H.'"

"Where did you hear that?"

"Some of Dad's friends say 'Jesus H. Christ.'"

"You shouldn't listen to that, and you certainly shouldn't repeat it. That's swearing. That's taking the Lord's name in vain."

"Reverend McDonald says 'Jesus Christ' in church. Is he swearing?"

"No. He says it differently."

"Does the 'H' stand for a bad word?"

"I don't know what it stands for, but it's making fun of Jesus. Like I said, it's taking the Lord's name in vain and against the Third Commandment."

Now I caught on. Others made fun of my curls, glasses, gapped teeth, and things I couldn't figure out. I didn't like being made fun of and understood why Jesus had a rule against it. I just wished His rule applied to me.

***

The second coming of Christ and the end of the world were the two themes I heard most often at church and Bible school. It seemed clear to me that Jesus' arrival would have to come first, or He wouldn't have a place to land. Talk of the end of the world made me tremble. I worried too much to ask Mom, or even Gab, about our scary fate. I didn't want to hear or talk about it.

I learned Jesus died for our sins. I didn't think it fair to take the blame for something that happened long before my time. I felt the pain of Jesus on the cross and shuddered at the thought of someone driving one of Dad's big nails through my hands. Apparently, God thought we hadn't learned to get along together and was going to get rid of the whole lot of us. He had a point. Germans, Americans, Russians, and Japanese were blowing each other up left and right. I saw the bombs and guns in the newsreels every Saturday before the afternoon picture show at the Garden Theater.

The end of the world would come, so I gathered, when a

wall of flames fried us to a crisp. I had nightmares of fifty-foot flames coming down Tank Hill in one direction and down Fairgrounds Hill from the other, and meeting where we lived at 605 Main Street.

Fire had a real and harsh meaning to our family. My mother and brother were scarred for life and provided daily evidence of the awful consequences of fire. Now, walls of flames would come our direction again and, this time, get all of us.

The puzzles connected with this frightening prospect were several: Why would God go to all the trouble of creating the world and then destroy it? All those ball parks and dime stores and movie theaters – it must have taken a lot of work. And why would He lump us together with the Nazis and Nips? They were doing bad things we were trying to stop. It didn't seem right we should all face the same end. At church, I learned God was forgiving. Maybe we could be excused for telling an occasional fib and not cleaning up our plates every time.

The return of Jesus was mentioned so often I thought it was on the calendar. His arrival couldn't come too soon. I hoped we could talk Him out of doing away with us. I would do my part by promising to eat tomatoes, not sass, and share nice with my brothers.

No one explained the details of the return of Jesus, so I figured it out for myself. We would see a small dot in the sky surrounded by a huge glowing halo. The dot would get bigger and bigger until we saw a paratrooper in a white gown, His long brown hair flowing in the wind and His beard trimmed neatly like the one on a Van Dyke cigar box. When Jesus neared the ground, we would cheer and applaud and move back to clear a nice grassy spot for His landing.

Every story I heard at Sunday school, grade school, or home took place in the town of many hills, brick churches, and clapboard houses I shared with 2,000 people. Humpty Dumpty or

Jack and Jill or Little Jack Horner, it all happened in Guthrie Center. Thus, I was sure Jesus would land in our town. We had a vacant lot next to our house. He would be welcome to touch down there. But tall pine trees surrounded the grassy lawn. We would be embarrassed if His parachute snagged in one of our trees. Better He head for the courthouse lawn where there was more space. If He could steer clear of the Civil War statue, He would be home free.

Mr. Compton would be there directing the high school band playing the school fight song. Roy Stacy would move his popcorn machine from the corner next to Mr. Cornish's beer parlor to the courthouse lawn. And, I was sure, Mr. Bandholtz would be on hand to take photographs.

It seemed only right that Jesus would return to the city where He was born. In my mind, Joseph and Mary rode a donkey into town past Gillespie's apple orchard and stopped at the nearby Studio Hotel. Mr. Bandholtz told them he was now a full-time photographer and no longer rented rooms. He would be available, if they liked, to take baby pictures.

Joseph and Mary wandered further until they saw the Laughery Brothers' sale barn. Luckily, it wasn't their Thursday sale day when all the stalls were filled with bawling cattle and squealing pigs. Gerald and Lloyd said the couple was welcome to spend the evening in one of the empty stalls. Jesus was born there that night. Doc Thornberg would have helped out, but it was Christmas and he was out of town. The light on top of the water tower, high above Tank Hill, sparkled like a star the night Jesus was born in Guthrie Center.

The list of topics to discuss with Jesus was growing. We needed to persuade Him to convince His Dad not to destroy the world. We could also use some help with the Nazis and Nips. Reverend McDonald said Jesus and His Father were on our side. Instead of burning up the whole world, maybe God could just get rid of Hitler and Tojo. And, if I could get a quick moment alone with Jesus, I wanted to raise the issue of Santa Claus. Gab's comments were discouraging. I could use some reassurance about St. Nick.

***

My interest in church matters took a new turn when I discovered Reverend McDonald's youngest daughter, Joy, in my kindy-garden class. People asked constantly, "Do you have a girlfriend yet?" I took that to mean a girlfriend was a requirement for a full-fledged schoolboy. Otherwise, girls were of little value. They didn't roughhouse or climb trees, and tried to sucker me into playing dress-up or paper dolls. But if I had to have a girlfriend, the pixie Joy, with large blue eyes and blond hair, was a good candidate.

Joy paid no attention to me at school despite my efforts to catch her eye. In games of Billy Goat Gruff, when four little green chairs were set side-by-side to form a bridge, I volunteered to be the troll crouched below. Surely, she would notice me when I snorted and frightened classmates as they crossed the bridge. She didn't. Nor did she respond when I sidled up beside her at our classroom sandbox table, or when I discreetly placed my braided rug near hers at nap time. I needed a bolder move. But what?

I found the answer in a paper bracelet project in *Children's Activities* magazine. Big, black dashes showed where to cut the bracelet from the page. Triangles, squares, and circles, like the shapes we were learning in class, supplied the decoration. I colored each one with my Crayolas, being careful to stay inside the lines, and created a red circle, a green square, a blue triangle, and a beautiful piece of jewelry. I cut along the dashes with my snub-nosed scissors and removed the bracelet from the page. A generous brush of white paste from the classroom jar connected the ends of the bracelet and created a gift for my intended. In the cloakroom after school, I handed the bracelet to Joy. "I made this for you," I said with a toothy grin.

She accepted my gift, smiled, and placed it on her wrist. She said nothing. I took that as consent to a special relationship. Proud and impressed with my style, I scampered home to listen to the next episode of "Jack Armstrong, the All-American Boy." Jack's secret mission to Moscow was interrupted when the phone rang. My mother answered. I listened to the radio with one ear and to her phone conversation with the other.

"Hello, Mrs. McDonald. How are you?"

Mom didn't use last names much. The minister's wife was an exception. She was new in town and first lady of the church. Mom wanted to make a good impression.

"Yes, yes, it has turned cold lately. I'm hoping for a round of Indian summer before the real cold comes."

A Wheaties commercial broke into Jack's action and gave me an opportunity to watch Mom at the phone. She was smiling.

"A paper bracelet, you say. Isn't that sweet?"

The smile disappeared from Mom's face as she listened to the response of Mrs. McDonald. "I suppose it is a bit young. I'm sure he didn't mean anything by it."

I understood the drift of the conversation. The bracelet gift was getting me in trouble.

"I think that's an excellent idea," Mom continued. "He really is a good little boy. If you spend some time with him, I think you'll see that."

My mother's smile returned. "Okay, tomorrow after school. That'll be fine. It was nice talking to you. Bye now."

Mom returned the phone receiver to its hook and turned my direction. I had forgotten Jack Armstrong for the moment.

"Mrs. McDonald has invited you to come to the parsonage to play after school tomorrow. You can walk home with Joy and her friends."

The McDonalds lived in a large brick house next to the church. It looked like a regular house to me, but Mom called it a "parsonage." She also told me the McDonalds didn't own the house; it belonged to the church congregation. That bit of information had already gotten me into trouble with Mrs. McDonald. A few weeks before, classmates and I attended Joy's birthday party. Some of the boys, myself included, decided the sofa would make a good trampoline. Gab and I did a fair amount of jumping on furniture at home and Mom hadn't objected much. Besides, as I saw it, if the McDonalds didn't own their house, they probably didn't own the furniture we were bouncing on either. Mrs. McDonald didn't agree and gave us a scolding. What we saw as good fun, she branded as "bad manners." Our smiling faces and fun ended.

I was pleased with the prospect of spending time with Joy, but nervous about facing her mother again. I hoped she didn't remember me as part of the circus act that jumped up and down on her sofa.

After school the next day, I approached Joy in the cloakroom. "I'm going home with you," I said.

"I know," she replied.

She spoke to me! Two words wasn't much, but it was a start.

Billy Ferguson and I walked together and followed Joy and Joyce Brady down the Prairie Street hill to the Methodist parsonage. When we reached the McDonald home, Joy said "good-bye" to Joyce and I did likewise with Billy. Mrs. McDonald awaited us on the front porch. "Good afternoon, Carroll Ray," she said. "Welcome to our home."

Mrs. McDonald was very formal, "starchy" according to

Mom. At least Joy's mother didn't say anything about my bad behavior at the birthday party.

When we entered the parsonage, Mrs. McDonald took my coat and placed it in a closet. I sat down on the ill-famed sofa. Joy joined me, taking a seat at the opposite end. Her mother went into a nearby room, within easy listening and viewing distance. The silence of the large house with its tall ceilings weighed on me. Our house was never quiet. I waited for Joy to say something, anything. She remained silent.

"Wanna play cards?" I blurted.

Joy smiled and walked toward her mother.

"Mom, do we have any cards?"

Joy's question struck me as odd. I thought every family had playing cards. Mom kept several decks in a chest of drawers in our dining room.

Joy returned with cards of a sort I had never seen. Their fronts had only numbers and the backs a picture of a gawky bird with the word: "ROOK."

"Doncha have cards with pictures of kings and queens? Ya know, with hearts and clubs and that kinda thing?" I asked.

Joy returned to her mother. "Mom, do we have cards with kings and queens?"

I sat on the couch looking at the silly, no-fun Rook cards. Mrs. McDonald appeared. "I think that's enough play time for today," she said. She handed me my coat. "You better run on home."

My trip to the McDonald home had been a quick session. I was in and out as smoothly as a run through the revolving door at Younker's Department Store. One comment about cards with kings and queens and I was on my way home. Did I say something wrong? Cards were as much a part of our household as the radio that talked to us from wake-up to bedtime. Mom and her friends played bridge late into the night, laughing and talking and drinking coffee and deciding who won the first prize and who took the booby prize.

The crisp, fall air moved me along. Was I in trouble? I would find out soon enough. It only took five minutes to walk home, about the same time I spent with my first girlfriend. Mom was standing at the sink as I entered the kitchen door.

"You sure didn't stay long at the McDonald's. Didn't you have a good time?"

"I dunno. We never did nothin'."

The telephone rang. Mom walked the few steps to the wall phone opposite the sink and placed the receiver to her ear. "Hello, Mrs. McDonald. Yes, he just came in the door."

Mom loved to receive phone calls. Her eyes sparkled. A call from the minister's wife was always important.

"Rook? No, I don't know that game."

Mom shifted her feet and turned away from me.

"Gambling cards? Well, I suppose they could be used that way. I think we do have a deck like that around here somewhere. Seems . . . er . . . like Eldon's brother . . . ah . . . left them when he visited us."

Mom was fibbing! She played solitaire with aces and jacks and deuces all the time while at the hospital. I sat on her bed and helped arrange seven rows of cards on her silver dinner tray. And Mom loved to play bridge. She and her club talked and dealt, dealt and talked. And pitch. And hearts. Mom knew lots of card games and could shuffle and deal like a magician.

"I surely do not approve of gambling," Mom continued. "Carroll Ray has a birthday coming up. I'll look into getting him that Rook game. And thank you, Mrs. McDonald, for your helpful suggestion."

I had done something wrong. What could it be? Whatever

it was, it caused Mom to tell a fib. Was I in trouble again? I slipped away into the front room so my presence wouldn't invite punishment.

"Carroll Ray, come here," Mom called.

I dragged my feet to the kitchen to receive my sentence.

"Would you like to run an errand downtown with me? We could stop afterwards at Cronk's and have a root beer."

My image of Mom was slightly tarnished when I heard her fibbing, but I didn't understand what I had done wrong and saw no difference between cards with long-legged birds and those with kings and queens. I forgave her quickly and she did the same of me. We enjoyed a root beer together.

I did regret being on the bad side of Mrs. McDonald. Jumping up and down on her sofa wasn't nice and the baffling card problem made her unhappy. Mom said bad things came in threes. How might I again embarrass myself in the presence of the preacher's wife? I would soon find out.

Several weeks passed. Mom, Gab, and I sat together in church. Mrs. McDonald, with Joy and her two youngest sons, Merton and Earl, sat in front of us. The congregation sang, "It's me O Lord, standin' in the need of prayer." I wasn't standing, but I needed a quick favor from the Lord and was busy submitting a silent and urgent request.

Gases rumbled and tumbled in my belly, threatening an unwanted and unpredictable escape. Under the right circumstances, I welcomed one of Mother Nature's best jokes. On the playground or in the bedtime quiet of the room I shared with Gab, anywhere away from adults, we laughed over "letting one." In keeping with a nation at war, we honored each branch of the armed services. For the air force it was "bombs away," for the army "fire for effect," and for the submarine commander, "fire one." Those short of ammunition by normal means simulated the required noise by cupping a hand under their arm and pulling an elbow hard against their side or making imitative sounds with a fluttering tongue and loose lips.

Flatulence, a word I didn't learn until years later, was a private form of amusement for little boys and of little concern to men. Customers at Sanger's barber shop and the guys gathered around the pot-bellied stove in Dad's garage were nonchalant about their organ recitals. Gab and I eavesdropped on Mom's bridge club, listening to everything, but never heard a suspicious sound. Either women didn't function that way or we couldn't hear it above the constant chatter.

While seated on the dining room floor in the presence of adults, I noticed that seated men sometimes rocked to the side. I knew what they were up to. Women never did that.

"Gab," I asked after Mom had tucked us in our beds, "do girls fart?"

"Nah."

"Why not?"

"Hey, haven't ya noticed? They're built different."

I let it go at that. But if women didn't do such things, they were not ignorant of the subject. Mom occasionally referred to "breaking wind." I knew what she meant, but didn't understand what might be broken except, perhaps, silence. Mom also said there was a time and place for everything. At this moment, I was in the worst possible place for my problem. Churches were devoted to silence. Coughs were covered with a hand. Sneezes were muffled with a handkerchief. Talking was forbidden. The congregation didn't even clap for the choir. The Lord demanded quiet. I struggled in fearful silence of disobeying His rule.

Our song ended with: "Please, Lord. I said please, Lord. I'm standin' in the need of prayer." The words painfully echoed my urgency.

Mom told me the Lord helps those who help themselves.

He had not calmed my churning insides. I had to come up with another solution – and fast.

I grasped the rounded front edge of the oak pew and pulled down. A master stroke I thought. My maneuver drew no notice, and I had sealed off my enemy's escape route. The battle was over. I had won . . . or so I thought. The swirling foe within me fought back. I pulled harder. My arms grew tired.

"Please," I begged under my breath, "let 'em sing something loud like 'Onward, Christian Soldiers.' I can't hold out much longer."

My message didn't get through. "And now," Reverend McDonald directed, "let us pause for a minute of silent prayer for our fighting soldiers around the world."

Faced with holding out for another long minute, I pulled with all my remaining strength. Force met force. I lost.

Piiiiiiiiinnng! My futile efforts only succeeded in raising the pitch. The shrill sound interrupted the silent prayer for endless moments. A muffled snicker erupted from somewhere, another followed, and then another until the entire congregation was roaring with laughter. I shrank against the refuge of my mother who was biting a lip and jiggling with amusement.

Reverend McDonald put a hand to his mouth and kept his head bowed. His shoulders bounced. He finally raised his smiling face. "I see," he announced, "our air raid siren is working." Another wave of laughter swept through the congregation. I buried myself against my mother's side. Gab leaned toward my ear and whispered, "Good one."

***

After moving on to first grade, I again needed the Lord's help because of a gerbil named "Willy." Our tiny pet lived in a cage in the corner of our classroom. He played in a turning wheel and ate special food that our teacher, Miss Thomas, placed in his cage along with drinking water. We were told never to open Willy's cage.

"Gerbils are delicate. They don't like to be handled and a cat might get him," Miss Thomas said. "Just watch and enjoy him. Do not reach in the cage, do not open the door, and do not tease him."

We and our little pet lived under so many "do nots" it was hard to enjoy each other's company. Willy seemed so restricted, so confined, so cooped up. It didn't seem fair.

During a lunch hour when Miss Thomas was out of the room, several of us decided Willy had earned a short furlough from his jail. Besides, he was so cute and furry, it would be fun to hold him, to pull him near, and see what he looked like up close. I opened Willy's jail door and felt his fuzzy, warm body crawl onto my hand. His fur tickled my palm. I placed him on the chalky rail of the blackboard. Willy scampered along, paused, and scampered again. We howled with laughter watching our little friend wiggle his nose, flick his head about, and then continue his journey along the blackboard. Willy paused again. With a nudge of a thumb, I encouraged him to continue. He skittered on, ran blindly into an eraser, and plummeted to the wooden floor quicker than my outstretched, desperate hand could rescue him.

Willy lay motionless on the floor. I tapped him with a finger. He didn't move. A hush fogged the room. Although no one said anything, it was clear I was the villain. I picked up the motionless Willy, hoping he would show signs of life. He didn't. I placed him back in his cage. We all sat uncommonly quiet awaiting the return of Miss Thomas.

The afternoon passed quietly. The feeding time for Willy, normally a gleeful moment, approached. Miss Thomas had not noticed the inactive wheel in the gerbil cage, its lifeless occupant lying on paper shreds in a corner.

"It's time to feed our little friend, children," Miss Thomas announced with her usual smile. "Gather around. Let's see what his appetite is like today."

Thirty children, all in the know, gathered silently around Willy's cage. Miss Thomas joined us with a handful of grain for Willy's lunch. "My goodness, what do we have here?" she wondered aloud. "Our little friend doesn't look well."

She opened the cage and nudged Willy with a finger. He didn't respond. I was praying no one would speak. Colina was the class tattletale. I sent thought waves and a glance her direction hoping to still her tongue. "She and the others were in on it," I told my conscience. "No one said not to do it. Everyone laughed. I'm not in on this alone." But I felt alone – and responsible for the death of Willy.

"It's pretty drafty over here by the window," Miss Thomas said. "I guess it's my fault for putting him there."

Our teacher looked sad and on the brink of shedding a tear. I had already released several. I had enough of a burden on my conscience without Miss Thomas taking the blame. Sniffles erupted here and there. Collective guilt did little to release me from my shame.

"Let's take our seats now, children. We'll look after Willy in a bit."

Miss Thomas turned her back to us and began to write spelling words on the board. Her shoulders jiggled. Once before, I had seen our teacher cry. It was unbearable. A knock at the door had interrupted our reading about the adventures of "Dick and Jane." Miss Thomas went to the door, opened it, and spoke to a lady in a hushed voice. She turned toward the class.

"Allen," Miss Thomas said. "You are excused for the day to go home with your aunt."

Allen Gilson, who sat in front of me, put his crayons away

in his desk and shuffled toward the door. My first thought was of his good fortune in getting to go home early. But when I watched his reluctant legs move slowly toward the door, I realized he wasn't happy about leaving. Miss Thomas put her arm around Allen's shoulder. The door closed behind them as they disappeared into the cloak room.

The classroom normally burst into shouts and laughter when we were left alone. Not this time. A heavy silence hung over us. The door opened slowly and Miss Thomas reappeared. Her eyes were red, her head tilted downward. She seemed stunned into deep thought. Her lips trembled. She opened her mouth and forced words: "Allen has no mother. She passed away today."

No mother! What would life be without Mom? Would there be a life? My mother and I were joined in so many ways I couldn't imagine an existence without her. I snuggled beside her in bed listening to "Dr. I.Q." on the radio. We held hands at Hopalong Cassidy matinees. She assured me Nazi U-boats couldn't make their way up the Raccoon River to Guthrie Center.

My thoughts were jarred back to the moment when Miss Thomas called my name. "Carroll Ray, please come up here. I want you to take Willy to his final resting place."

I wondered why she was calling me. Did Miss Thomas know of my role in the death of Willy? Was this her way of punishing me? "It was an accident," I repeated to my doubtful conscience.

Her way or not, I felt punished. I would have preferred to have nothing more to do with Willy. I wanted desperately to forget that brief time when I coaxed Willy along the blackboard ledge until he fell to his death.

I walked to the teacher's desk. She opened a drawer and removed a White Owl cigar box. "We'll use the war bond stamp box for Willy's coffin," she said softly.

Miss Thomas poured the pink stamps with their Minuteman picture from the box into a compartment of her desk drawer. She placed a couple of fluffed Kleenex tissues in the bottom of the casket and gingerly placed the deceased Willy on the soft white bedding. She closed the lid, a merciful gesture I appreciated, and sealed it with a piece of Scotch tape. Miss Thomas handed me the box and leaned toward my ear. "Take this to the garbage dump behind the high school," she whispered.

A jumble of emotions swept through me. I was pleased Miss Thomas selected me for this important assignment, although I was not sure of her motives. Maybe she could read my mind like Mom and was punishing me.

The central hallway of the grade school was vacant and silent as I carried Willy in his White Owl coffin to his final rest. Away from others, I shed tears as I descended the grooved wooden stairs that led to the playground between the elementary and high schools. With every step, the rocking motion of Willy within his casket reminded me of my guilt.

A garbage dump didn't seem an appropriate burial spot for Willy. I looked for something better while crossing the gravel playground and approaching the back of the high school. A pile of ashes supplied the answer. Mom said the "Hands of Heaven" reached from the sky and delivered souls to the gates of Saint Peter. If I placed Willy atop the ash heap, the Hands of Heaven could reach him more easily and ensure a quick trip to the great beyond. I held the coffin aloft in my right hand and crawled up the ten-foot stack. The purple-black cinders clawed at the flesh of my left hand and ripped at my knees as I made my way to the peak. The climb was painful, physically and emotionally, but an effort my conscience appreciated. I placed the White Owl casket at the summit of the ash pile, flushed with the triumph of a good deed and certain that the Hands of Heaven would soon come for Willy.

I didn't rush back to the classroom. A sense of freedom emerged as I strolled across the vacant playground beyond the eyes and rules of grown-ups. I went to the basement boys' room, washed the charcoal cinder stains from my hands, and returned to class.

The next morning, during recess, I strayed behind the high school to see if the Hands of Heaven had taken Willy skyward. Mom was correct again. Willy was gone all right. But I had overdone it. The entire ash pile went with Willy!

Chapter 3

Bad Boxes

"Carroll Ray, come here. I have an errand for you to run." Mom called to me every month, usually from the bathroom, to go on a secret mission. She and I were in cahoots on something serious. Her confidence made me feel important. Outside the bathroom door, I awaited my orders.

The opening door released a fragrance of scented soap and shampoo from Mom's sanctuary, where she escaped from a male-dominated dwelling blackened by the grease of a mechanic husband and littered by the coats and caps and comic books of three sons. The bathroom was Mom's refuge, a place of privacy for enjoying her womanhood.

"Sweetheart, take this message to Frances Millhollin at the Square Deal store. Do not open the envelope. Do not dally along the way. Do not stop to play. Do not let anyone see the envelope. Frances will give you something and further instructions."

Mom's orders included, as always, a list of "do nots." The

longer the list, so I figured, the more important the mission. Four "do nots" qualified as top secret.

Mom folded the sealed envelope and pushed it to the bottom of my shirt pocket. "Make sure you look twice at the crossing," she cautioned. Soldiers had their written orders – so did I.

I was allowed to walk two paths on my own. One went down the Seventh Street hill, across State Street and, when Joe Hollar, the crossing guard, gave the go ahead, up the hill to the red brick grade school with its bell tower. The other, more exciting way, took me past Father O'Sullivan's house, St. Mary's Church, the Civil War statue on the courthouse lawn, and across Fifth Street. Ahead on my right, next to the town's four-way stop, a black and white sign painted on the outside wall of Sue's Lunch read: "5¢ Hamburgers 5¢: Buy 'em By the Sack." The ad had weathered the years. Hamburgers now cost two nickels.

Under the neon sign of the corner cafe, I stood at the gateway to the wonders of downtown Guthrie Center: three gently sloping blocks of opportunity to spend a nickel. A nickel would buy an ice cream cone at Ferguson's Bakery or a cherry coke at Cronk's Cafe or a Whiz candy bar at Fred Scott's grocery store. Two would buy a "Plastic Man" comic book at Dowd's Drug or admission to the Garden Theater to watch Tarzan or Abbot and Costello.

I was on a mission and under strict orders not to dally. The delights of the business district must wait another day. I passed up an opportunity to ogle Walnettoes, Tootsie Rolls, and Black Crows through the window of Sue's Lunch and walked next door to the Square Deal.

I glanced over my shoulder before entering Mom's favorite store to make sure I wasn't followed. In my imagination, I feared the pursuit of German spies. In reality, I worried that my pals, Pink or Bull or Zag, might see me enter a women's store with windows filled with pink petticoats and panties. No real man would be seen in such a place, and few were. Bill Sanger's barber shop across the street was a man's place. There, amid cigar smoke and naughty words, I listened to discussions on the comparative shortstop abilities of Marty Marion and Pee Wee Reese and watched men read *The Sporting News* and *Field and Stream.*

The interior of the Square Deal was familiar territory – too familiar. I spent hours trapped in Mrs. Millhollin's store while Mom gabbed, and I begged to go home. At least this time I wouldn't be held against my will.

Winding my way past counters of Gossard girdles, J.P. Coates thread, and Butterick dress patterns, I found Mrs. Millhollin at the sales counter. "What can I do for you today, Carroll Ray?" she asked.

I handed her the secret envelope. "Mom said to give you this."

The white-haired lady took the sealed envelope and slit it open with a silver-handled letter opener. She turned her back, removed the message, and read it with half-lens glasses extended at arm's length. Mrs. Millhollin never wore her glasses like others. She used hers like a magnifying glass, holding them next to whatever she was reading. A strange way to use glasses, I thought, but just one of many mysteries in her store.

"Wait here a minute," Mrs. Millhollin directed. "I'll be right back." She slipped the folded envelope down a secret pocket inside her blouse, walked into a room behind the sales counter, and closed the door.

I admired Mrs. Millhollin. The tall and stately woman had silvery hair pulled into a bun at the back of her head. A sharp-tipped yellow pencil pierced the ball of hair, like a bone in the nose of one of Tarzan's native friends. She would slip the pencil from her hair with a quick and graceful motion, add num-

bers on a scrap of brown wrapping paper, and, without looking, jab the pencil back into the bun. Her blind and daring aim
was impressive. I took pride in delivering important documents
to the owner of the Square Deal.

Mrs. Millhollin remained in the secret room for a long
time. I assumed she was consulting with someone important,
like an air raid warden. Finally, she reappeared with a parcel
wrapped in sleek, brown paper. Double strands of coarse white
string, tied in a hard knot, encircled the secret package.

Mrs. Millhollin handed me the neatly wrapped, fully-
secured parcel. As light as cotton candy and obviously a
box, I figured it must contain important papers.

The list of "do nots" began. "Do not let anyone touch this
but your mother. Do not unwrap the package. Do not stop to
play along the way. Now hurry along."

The light box promoted feelings of strength and manli-
ness as I walked home. I did not run, my preferred means of
transportation, because I couldn't see over the package. For
once, Mom's "do not run" rule made sense.

I felt my mother's eyes from the kitchen window when I
crossed the street at St. Mary's. She knew how long the trip
should take. I was on schedule. A block's worth of brisk
strides took me to 605 Main Street, where I entered and
handed over the secret parcel to Mom. With the mysterious
package in hand, she disappeared into the bathroom. I never
knew the content of Mom's monthly messages or what was
in the box. Good soldiers, as I understood, followed orders
and didn't ask questions.

***

Mom and I often went to the Square Deal together, but not by
my choice. I preferred to spend more time at Mr. Sanger's
Ideal Barber Shop and less, or none, at Mrs. Millhollin's store.
Unfortunately, my fifty-cent haircuts were as infrequent as

Dad could manage, and I couldn't think of another excuse, just yet, to go to my favorite man's place. My monthly solo trips to the Square Deal provided satisfactions that accompanying my mother did not. On those occasions, I felt trusted, responsible, important, and in control of my time. The mission took only as long as my legs needed to propel me to the Square Deal and back. With Mom, I was stuck with her schedule and marooned in a ladies' store, an aspiring man tangled in the web of woman things.

At an earlier age, I led the way to the Square Deal on a leash. I had disappeared into crowds a couple of times and made my mother cry for reasons I didn't understand. Her solution for my wandering was a tan, leather chest harness with a matching leash. En route to the Square Deal, I strained at the leash, like a sled dog, to show my displeasure. I felt a spectacle, especially when wandering dogs paused and seemed to smile.

I had been broken to use a potty, broken from picking my nose, and supposedly broken from sucking my thumb – broken more ways than Humpty Dumpty. Now satisfied I was also broken of running away, Mom unharnessed me, but insisted on holding my hand in public. A measure of my dignity was restored, but my freedom of movement still suffered.

I tugged at Mom's arm and begged, "Let's go home, Mommy," while she spent endless time visiting with lady friends at the Square Deal. They talked of purls not connected with the treasure of pirates, of tacking that did not require hammers, and of darts for dresses rather than game boards. But the favored topic of the assembled mothers, one that involved lengthy and boring and personally humiliating comparisons, concerned their children.

"Hazel, is Carroll Ray still a thumb-sucker?" a lady asked.

"No, I broke him of that a long time ago," my mother exaggerated.

The word "sucker" fell hard on my ears, an identity I did not want. A sucker was a fool, a worthless dog or horse, or a local man whose name set off jokes and laughter at the barber shop. I hated being identified with nitwits, egg-sucking mutts, wind-sucking nags, and social outcasts. I welcomed Mom's efforts to rid me of my bad habit. I tried to cooperate. But at night, when asleep, the Devil pushed my thumb into an eager mouth.

Mom first attempted to break my thumb-sucking habit by tucking me into homemade quilted pajamas with a draw string parka, attached mittens and footies, and a zipper down the front. Supposedly, my mouth and thumbs could not connect while locked up in my head-to-toe straight jacket. Stuffed inside and sealed for the night, I looked like a bloated ginger-bread man.

I called Mom's invention my "shopping bag," something to be dropped in for temporary storage. I was warm and comfortable lying on top of a soft quilt in an unheated bedroom. But while asleep, I chewed and gnawed at mittens that became damp and dirty health hazards. Worse, I could not attend to nature's business by myself, leading to several late night accidents. Mom gave up, let me have my hands back, and turned to the Jewel Tea man for a remedy.

The friendly salesman, who parked his brown truck at our curb to offer his foods and wares, gave Mom hope. "I've got just the thing, Mrs. McKibbin. Guaranteed to cure thumb-suckers." He opened a blue bottle and shoved it under Mom's nose. "Take a load of this stuff. It'll knock your socks off."

Mom winced and turned her head. I got a whiff from where I stood several feet away. The potion smelled like rotten eggs in an outhouse.

"Just dab some of this on the little fella's fingers, and I guarantee you he'll never again put his hands near his mouth."

"I'll take the small bottle and give it a try," Mom said.

Every morning and every night, my fingertips were dipped in the disgusting greenish-brown goo. It worked. I couldn't bear to put my smelly hands anywhere near my nose. At night, when the Devil pushed my thumbs nearer and nearer my mouth, the awful odor awakened me and fought off the determined demon.

Unfortunately, my hands also made me repulsive to others. I felt an outcast. And to Mom's chagrin, the sticky goo left indelible stains on towels and clothes. She gave up on the Jewel Tea tactic and confessed to her friends that she had a non-broken, addicted, thumb-sucking son.

I feasted for awhile on my liberated thumbs until Mother Nature shut down the suckling urge and I quit. Momentarily. And then Satan introduced me to nail-biting.

Bragging rights among Mom and her lady friends were based on how quickly their children learned good habits and were broken of bad ones. To be in good standing, a baby had to be walking at one year, talking soon thereafter, and potty-trained by two. No thumb-sucking or bed-wetting was allowed after three years of age, and by four a kid should know some colors and numbers. At five and the start of kindergarten, the child must be fully certified in good manners. Deviations from those standards met with poorly disguised ridicule that I overheard much too often.

"You mean Carroll Ray is now biting his nails? My goodness, I thought you would put a stop to that like you did his thumb-sucking. My Robert started on his nails when he was two and I broke him of that in a hurry. Does your little boy also wet the bed?"

Mom took liberties with the truth to keep me in the child-raising sweepstakes, but could not conceal my obvious nail-biting. To Mom's friends, nail-biting was considered as bad as thumb-sucking and a sure sign of retarded development. I met the standard on everything but that unforgivable habit and an occasional relapse on bed-wetting. I spouted numbers left and right, knew the basic colors by heart, and worked hard on good manners. But I was committed to nail-biting – a hopeless case who could not keep his fingers out of his mouth.

Mom tried to direct attention away from my gnawed nails by reminding her friends of my luxurious curls. I tilted my head forward as she spoke and kept my hands in my pockets. But the truth could not be concealed. Nail-biting did me in. I was an ashamed addict – hooked, beaten, whipped, and hopeless. Mom was embarrassed, and so was I. But I could not stop.

Eventually, Mom's conversation with her friends about the triumphs of their children and my shortcomings wound down to a blissful end. She drifted toward the pattern table. Sorting through rows of paper packets required both her hands. She released her grip on mine. I took a couple of side steps to test her reaction. When certain she was absorbed with the lure of Butterick and Simplicity, I slipped away.

I knew not to escape the Square Deal and risk being harnessed and leashed again. I wandered to the front window where I could watch the car traffic. Across the street, men laughed and smoked at Mr. Sanger's barber shop. An exit and a few steps would take me to the candy counter of Sue's Lunch. A few steps the other direction would lead me to the forbidden excitement of Andy Hansen's pool hall. And I stood marooned among brassieres.

Fearful of being spotted by my buddies in a ladies' store, I moved away from the window. Boredom pushed and curiosity pulled as I began my rounds of the Square Deal.

I examined the oiled wooden floors and smelled the sea green sweeping compound embedded in its seams and cracks. Counters and tables, piled high with bolts of cloth, sweaters, stockings, and other clothing items, towered over my head and created hidden walkways for exploration, like the maze in the fun house at the county fair. I had time on my hands and no destination in mind.

Drifting about below counter level and out of view of adults gave me a sense of freedom. I stopped to feel coarse burlap and sleek silk and soft velvet. I followed my nose to a counter of Jergen's lotion and Camay soap and Johnson's powder – smells so rich they left a taste in my mouth.

I discovered a white porcelain water fountain, but resisted the temptation to cover part of the opening and squirt water like Pink and I did with a similar fountain on State Street. I liked the power of turning the silver knob and watching the fountain respond to my control. I allowed the water to graze my lips as though I was at the fountain for serious purposes.

I opened doors and drawers wherever I found them. I wanted nothing more than something to do, anything to occupy my mind and absorb endless time.

My meandering led to the lingerie section. I understood gentlemen didn't look at ladies' underthings, but had given into curiosity with Mom's Sears and Roebuck catalog. I took advantage of this opportunity as well.

The girdles and corsets, with their straps, snaps, and stays, looked more like military gear than clothing. I had seen less fortified equipment in an army surplus store. Why, I wondered, would anyone wear such contraptions?

I noted the differences between the unfamiliar underwear of girls and the familiar ones of boys. Ours were white and plain and cotton with a gap in front. Theirs were pink and fancy and made of all kinds of material, even some I could see through, and gapless. Girl underthings had bows and ribbons and designs, including days of the week. Did that mean girls changed their underwear every day? I got clean shorts after my Saturday night bath. If I changed every day, I wouldn't get past Tuesday.

I heard the rip of material and the sound of voices at the fabric-cutting table. I moved to the corner of a nearby counter to watch. Mrs. Millhollin yanked at the end of an oval-shaped bolt of material and made it thump, thump, thump across the table top like a car with a flat tire. She made a quick measure against a yardstick attached to the edge of the table, and with a quick snip of scissors and a vigorous rip by hand, tore the fabric in two.

How did she get the edge so straight? When I cut out pictures in workbooks at school, I had a hard time keeping my snub-nosed scissors on the dotted line. When I tried to tear construction paper neatly, it never ended up the way I wanted. But that magician, Mrs. Millhollin, made a snip and a rip and produced an evenly cut piece of fabric. Amazing!

I made my way to the rolling ladder used to reach items high on the wall shelves. When Mrs. Millhollin wasn't busy, she sometimes treated me to a ride on the ladder. This time, I was by myself and in forbidden territory behind the cash register counter. Mrs. Millhollin's business affairs didn't interest me, but the room where she wrapped secret packages held my attention. The door was straight ahead and open. I took a quick look over my shoulder. No one was watching. I entered the mystery room.

I had expected to see war equipment. Instead, I found a clutter of boxes, dress racks, brooms, and wastebaskets. Not a single bazooka or Tommy gun was in sight. Disappointed but determined, I decided to continue my search.

Wandering and looking about, I bumped a box off a table.

I picked it up. The cardboard carton was about a foot square, a third as wide, and very light. More of the blue and black boxes with white letters were stored under the table and a variety of sizes stacked nearby. I lifted the largest one with ease. Wow! I had discovered huge building blocks.

I forgot about looking for hand grenades and began to construct a fort. My new blocks had five white letters on the sides. At school, our blocks had different colored letters and only one on each side. I knew all the letters and was learning words in my "Dick and Jane" reader, but I didn't know the word on the boxes: KOTEX.

Absorbed in my work and delighted with the light construction materials, my fortress quickly took form. I had completed four walls, a door, and a window when I heard the fast approach of my mother's feet.

"What are you doing?" she shrieked. I recognized the sound of trouble. Mom yanked me to my feet and scolded, "Those are bad boxes. You must stay away from them. I never want you to touch them again. Those are bad boxes. Do you understand?"

"I'm sorry, Mommy," I said. But I didn't know what I was sorry for, and didn't ask. I had never seen Mom so upset and concluded quickly that something awful was hidden in the mysterious cartons.

Mom's scolding erased all thoughts of again using the blue and black building blocks, but sparked my curiosity about the evil contents. I wondered why a nice lady like Mrs. Millhollin would have bad boxes in her store. Wartime included a lot of secrets. Perhaps, so I hoped, the bad boxes somehow connected with our battle against the Nazis and Nips.

***

When Christmas approached and my thoughts turned to the joys of the holiday season, my curiosity over the cardboard containers with the large white letters subsided. Tinker Toys occupied my mind. Mom had found a used set of the wooden playthings at a rummage sale and gave it to me for a birthday gift. Although the dowels were splintered and grayed by the use of many hands, I adored the precious Tinker Toys. I took them to bed at night and went by the nickname of "Tinker" for a short time.

I dreamed of receiving a new set of Tinker Toys for Christmas. After opening the standard gifts of clothing items, I realized my dream wouldn't come true that day. I shed no tears. Sacrifice was required for the war effort. I would have to wait.

After all the packages were opened and I was stuffing wrapping paper into sacks for Paper Trooper collection, Mom interrupted my work. "Why don't you go look in my closet and see if I forgot to wrap something."

The closet in the folks' bedroom was off limits. I knew its location in the corner beyond Mom's dresser with the floral decals on the drawers, but was instructed not to enter the secret chamber. Many things connected with the war were hush-hush and off limits. Perhaps, so I figured, some of them were located in Mom and Dad's closet.

In a moment of Christmas joy, Mom had dropped her guard and granted me permission to enter her private room. The prospect of viewing the interior of the forbidden chamber excited me almost as much as the present I expected to find.

I raced up the stairs, rushed into the folks' bedroom, and swung open the large closet door for the first time. I saw nothing connected with the war. Disappointment replaced enthusiasm as I viewed a normal closet with clothes on hangers, hat boxes on a shelf, and shoes on the floor.

Turning my head toward a far corner, I saw the glint of a round tin lid. *Tinker Toys!* I fell to my knees, grabbed the cardboard canister, and pressed it to the side of my face. I removed the lid and inspected the contents: clean and smooth dowels and disks that smelled of fresh wood.

Absorbed in my good fortune, I turned to leave the closet and rejoin the family celebration. I brushed one of mom's long dresses and bumped a hard object behind it. Pulling the dress aside, I discovered a long-barreled gun leaning against the back wall of the closet. The gun, I thought to myself, must be the reason for placing the closet off limits. Maybe Dad is a secret soldier and plans to trade his bib overalls for a uniform.

I kneeled to get a closer look at the gun and saw, behind a wastebasket, the corner of a box. The carton was blue and black, just like the bad boxes at the Square Deal. I pulled the wastebasket aside for a better look. The container had the same letters on the side: KOTEX. Mom had a bad box in her closet! The joy of the Tinker Toy discovery gave way to the dismay of learning of Mom's awful secret. My tears of happiness turned to tears of distress.

I returned to the party downstairs, did my best to put on a happy face, and began to play with my new Tinker Toys.

"Do you like them? Mom asked.

I tried to match the enthusiasm of my mother's voice, but my thoughts were elsewhere. "Uh-huh. They're nice," I replied.

Thoughts and concerns about my mother's goodness troubled me all day as I tried to enjoy the Christmas celebration. In the evening, Mom tucked me in bed, saying the usual, "Close the eyes and lips," while running soft fingertips across my eyelids and mouth and kissing my cheek.

As soon as Mom closed our bedroom door, I sprung the question that had worried me since my trip to her closet. "Gab, do you know about bad boxes?"

"Sure, what d'ya wanna know," came a reply from the dark.

"Well, I was playing with some blue and black boxes at the Square Deal and Mom yanked me away and said they are bad and I was not to play with 'em. D'ya know what's inside?"

"Sure."

I raised up on an elbow and leaned Gab's direction. "Well, what? Is it something pretty bad?"

"Yeah, it's pretty bad, all right. Why d'ya ask?"

"You know the folks' closet, the one you said Mom lets you go in all the time?"

"Yeah, what about it?"

"You know the new set of Tinker Toys I got today? Mom told me to go up to her closet and look for something that wasn't under the Christmas tree. I had never been in her closet before."

"What'd ya see in there?"

"I thought ya said Mom lets you go in her closet."

"She does, but it's been a few days and I wondered if she added some new stuff."

I lowered my voice and leaned across the edge of my bed. "If I tell you what else I saw, will you tell me what's in the bad boxes?"

"Sure, what'd ya see?"

"I saw a long gun leaned up against the wall. D'ya know what it's for?"

"Yeah, it's for shooting Germans."

"Is Dad gonna join the army?"

"No, you dope. Doncha know about those Nazis in the prisoner of war camp in Audubon?"

"Sure, I know 'bout that. I heard Dad and Uncle Ernie talking about it when we visited in Audubon last week. Uncle Ernie said they keep German prisoners behind barbed wire in the middle of the horse track at the fairgrounds."

"Have ya ever thought about those Nazis breaking out and coming to Guthrie Center? It's not very far, ya know."

Gab had a way of worrying me and exposing my ignorance in one blow. I had enough to think about with the bad boxes, an issue he seemed to be avoiding, and now my brother raised another scary possibility. I watched "Mrs. Miniver" at the Garden Theater and worried about finding a German soldier, like the British lady in the movie, in our backyard.

"If the Nazis come to Guthrie Center . . ." Gab paused for effect and caught my full attention. "Dad is gonna stand out on the front porch and shoot 'em, one-by-one."

Gab seemed more intent on talking about Dad's gun and a battle with Nazis than the contents of the mysterious boxes. As always, I followed his lead.

"Does Father O'Sullivan have a gun?" I asked.

The thought of the saintly priest picking off Nazis with a Tommy gun as they passed St. Mary's Church was unbelievable, but intriguing. I had never seen Father O'Sullivan hold anything but the book he read while pacing back and forth on his front porch.

"You bet," Gab responded. "Emerson Ely has a gun, too, and so does Ivan Hasbrouck and Earl Vinson. They'll all be on their front porches mowing down Germans."

Gab's use of the first names of adult neighbors, an informality Mom did not allow, made his statement more believable, like he was more their equal than a kid.

I returned to my original question about the blue and black boxes. "Gab, I saw one of those bad boxes in Mom's closet, just like the ones I got in trouble over at the Square Deal."

"Yeah, so what?"

"Well, I was thinkin', if those are boxes with bad things in 'em and Mom has one in her closet, does that mean she's bad, too?"

"Hey, when are ya gonna grow up? If Mom's got a bad box, she's up to no good. No one's perfect. Now go to sleep."

I couldn't. Until then, I thought Mom was perfect.

***

The black and blue colors of the terrible cartons matched my bruised image of Mom. I wondered if I had convicted her unfairly. I wanted to declare my mother innocent and restore her goodness. I needed to see what was inside the bad boxes.

With Dad at work and Mom busy in the kitchen, I entered their off limits closet and located the mystery box. Guilt and intrigue competed for my attention as I reached inside the open flap of the blue and black carton. I felt netting, like the veil of Mom's church hat, wrapped around a soft pad. I lifted the mysterious item from the box.

The burden of Mom's guilt vanished and her purity returned when I discovered the forbidden item was nothing more than a cotton and gauze dressing. Obviously designed for head wounds, I gave the white bandage a try by stretching it across my forehead and looking in Mom's dresser mirror. The image reminded me of a wounded soldier in "Gone With the Wind."

"So Mom's part of the war effort after all," I murmured to myself. "She's a nurse!"

I admired my mother's skill in pulling the little orange thread to open a Band-Aid, something I couldn't get the hang of, but I didn't know she was a nurse. That meant my missions to the Square Deal were truly part of the war effort. Mrs. Millhollin had enough bandages for the whole town. Maybe Gab wasn't exaggerating about a possible Nazi attack.

I put the innocent bandage back in its carton, brimming with pride over my mother's unending talents and patriotic service, and feeling guilty for thinking she could do anything wrong.

I raced downstairs to the kitchen where Mom was peeling potatoes. I gave her a hug from behind, my cheek crushed against her bottom as I tried to reach around her hips. "I love you, Mommy."

My mother turned from the sink, caught off-guard by the unexpected arrival of affection. She dried her hands on a dish towel and lifted me onto a chair. Face-to-face, she hugged and kissed me. "I love you too," she said.

"Mom," I asked. "How did you learn to be a nurse?"

Chapter 4

Peter Principles

"**C**arroll Ray, let's go to the Square Deal," Mom called. For once, I was enthusiastic about visiting the ladies' store. I had confirmed Mom and Mrs. Millhollin were working together, with my assistance, on a war project. Their supplies were stored in the secret room behind the counter with the brass cash register. I had discovered the secret stockpile of bandages and figured the war room of the Square Deal also contained other hidden supplies, like guns and bullets.

Mom and I were both happy that day. She loved thumbing through patterns, inspecting fabrics, and visiting with lady friends at her favorite store. I was thrilled over my new Tinker Toys and a Christmas card I received from S/Sgt. Howard Ely. Inside, I found a war souvenir – a silk identity document written in English, French, and Chinese – that I displayed at school during "show and tell." But most of all, I was relieved and happy to learn that Mom as a nurse and Mrs. Millhollin as a supplier of important materials were quietly and heroically supporting the war effort.

On a bright and crisp January day, I held Mom's hand and skipped along, trying to whistle, as we walked past the courthouse on our way to the Square Deal. I had in mind sneaking into Mrs. Millhollin's secret room and learning more of what went on inside. If she stored bandages there, she must have other important things. I intended to find out.

My scheme for investigating Mrs. Millhollin's war room was thoroughly planned. Mom told me to stay away from the bandage boxes, but she didn't tell me I was forbidden to enter the secret chamber. I understood her intentions included staying out of the room, but she did not say that word-for-word, and playing dumb was always good for one free round. If caught in the war room, I could easily predict the dialogue. I even rehearsed it.

"What are you doing? I told you to stay out of here."

"Mommy," I reply innocently, "you told me not to touch the blue and black boxes, and I haven't. You didn't say anything about not going in there."

"Well, I'm saying it now. You are never to come in this room alone. Do you understand?"

"Yes, mother."

I used "mother" to add respect while practicing my scheme. I was certain this tactic would allow one trip to the forbidden storage area without getting into trouble. If I got in and out without being discovered, I could go again and again until found out. With one free pass to investigate the mystery chamber, I was punishment-proof this day, or so I thought.

Plotting against my mother bothered me, but did not alter my plan. She was easy to read and predict, and unlikely to punish me in any case. I could out-maneuver her easily, and with no great harm intended.

The warmth of the Square Deal provided instant relief to the nippy winter air. I hoped Mom would move quickly to the pattern table, my best opportunity for a getaway. I went into my good behavior mode to avoid undue attention. I didn't yank on her arm and chant "Let's go home, Mommy." Indeed, I didn't want to go home, even with Tinker Toys waiting, until I could explore the war room. I waited patiently and obediently until I could make my break.

Mom stopped at the fabric section and began to pull out bolts of cloth from wall shelves. She freed enough material to finger the edges, pulling the cloth backward to inspect both sides. Some bolts slid with difficulty, causing Mom to lift and push and pull to reveal enough cloth to satisfy her curiosity. She momentarily released my hand, but I didn't try to slip away just yet. She was not as absorbed in feeling the fabrics as she would be later when making calculations at the pattern table.

I figured out Mom's routine with dress patterns. She reviewed the fat packets for ideas and required materials, scribbled notes on a small spiral note pad, and then went home and cut her own patterns out of newspapers. Note-taking and arithmetic required her full attention, while inspecting yard goods provided cover for the real purpose of her visit. I knew Mom's thoughts and plots. I hoped she didn't know mine.

My mother's working supply of cloth came from wherever she found fabric at cut-rate prices, like the white nylon parachute she bought at a war surplus store and converted to blouses for several nieces. Mom's shopping at the Square Deal was mostly a game. She did buy thread and a few other small items, but most of the material she used for family sewing came from rummage sales. She got down to business in that setting, examining clothing for moth holes, wear, stains, and other damage. She then made purchases for a few coins and took the clothing home to convert to family apparel. With seam cutting, washing, and pressing, the rummage sale items became raw materials for Mom's handiwork. Buttons and zippers were salvaged and stored, the buttons in a row of jars on a high shelf in the family closet across from Mom's sewing machine.

My "good clothes" came from rummage sale materials. Mom made me a pair of gray wool Sunday school trousers from a man's pants. I looked good in her fitting mirror, but the out-of-view unaltered front pockets extended clear to my knees. A penny in my pocket took an effort to retrieve as I leaned far to the side to send a hand fishing to the bottom for the copper coin. The back pockets, also unaltered, met at the center seam, giving the appearance of one huge pocket across the seat. Since I had nothing to put in a back pocket, certainly not a billfold, I never worried about the rear of my pants. I was bothered more by the multi-brown interior waistband, stained with the sweat of the previous owner. Try as she might, Mom could not return the waistband to the original color, whatever that might have been. Wearing the enduring sweat of an unknown person was almost as uncomfortable as the prickly wool scratching my legs.

Mom moved from the yard goods to the button drawers. If she didn't find the right set in her dozen jars of used buttons, she matched swatches of fabric and strands of thread against Mrs. Millhollin's endless variety of buttons attached to cardboard squares. Behind the button drawers, a display of girls' underwear caught my eye. With Mom at my side, this wasn't the time to look.

A rumor was circulating among my pals that girls didn't have peters. How, I wondered, could anyone get along without that essential item, especially on picnics? With all the frills and bows, it was clear girl underthings were different. Mom

called underwear for boys and girls the same thing: under-
pants. If they were called the same thing, so I figured, they
must be concealing the same thing.

Mom left the button drawers and moved on to the pattern
table. "Good morning, Hazel," Mrs. Millhollin greeted. "And
good morning to you, Carroll Ray. Was Santa good to you?"

Gab had confused the Santa Claus issue. "Ya don't believe
in that Santa Claus shit, do ya?" he challenged. I did, and I
wanted to. Gab made true believers sound like dopes. Believe
or not, I played the game for what it was worth.

"I got a set of Tinker Toys," I responded.

"That's nice. I'm sure you're having a good time playing
with them."

"Mrs. Millhollin," I asked. "Are you a nurse, too?"

The kind lady with the pencil through the bun of her hair
didn't respond to my question. Instead, she turned toward my
mother, a puzzled look on her face. Mom was already busy
thumbing through rows of Butterick and Simplicity patterns.

Mrs. Millhollin selected a packet with a picture of a sleeve-
less dress and tapped Mom's shoulder. "Here, Hazel. This is a
cute jumper."

I felt Mom's leash hand relax and disconnect from mine. I
hesitated, and then took a half step away, not too far to recover
if Mom reached for me. When she didn't, I strolled toward the
front counter. My plan was going perfectly. Both people I
needed out of the way were busy talking to each other. No one
else was in the store. The time had come to search the secret
chamber.

I stepped carefully on the nailed ends of the wooden floor
planks where they didn't squeak, slipped behind the front
counter, and sneaked toward my destination. Luck served me
well. I found the door open enough to slither through sideways. On my first visit to the secret room, I thought Mrs.

Millhollin didn't pick up her things. Now, I understood the messy room helped camouflage guns and ammo.

As the messenger in the secret activities of Mom and Mrs. Millhollin, I wanted to know more about our operation. I recognized the blue and black boxes, but did not touch the medical supplies. I moved other items carefully and put them back in place, making sure not to leave any evidence. As long as my work went undiscovered, I could return another time.

I found pink things with buckles and straps and snaps, similar to items in the front of the store. Soldiers didn't wear pink. That was a girl's color. Next to some brassieres, items I recognized from helping Mom hang washing on the backyard clothes line, I found soft rubber items shaped like a half grapefruit with small bumps on the rounded side. I squeezed the spongy rubber of what I figured were helmet liners.

A rack of terry cloth robes obstructed my view of the far corner. I moved around the rack and bumped into a half-naked plastic woman with long hair and two large bumps on her chest. I knew about mannequins. Mom made one at home from chicken wire and paper tape for fitting clothes. Her mannequin had no head, no legs, and only a rough idea of a chest and shoulders.

Mrs. Millhollin's naked lady, wearing only a half slip, seemed complete, almost real, and as pretty as Betty Grable. Golden hair flowed to her shoulders. Red lips smiled, and dimples dented her rouged cheeks. A graceful arm extended to a hand on her hip, the other arm reaching outward with slender fingers tipped with pink nail polish. Her large blue eyes, highlighted with long and curled lashes, watched my every move, but not as closely as mine inspected her every detail. My interest in war equipment disappeared.

Fate had presented me with an opportunity to settle the long-debated issue about girls. I lifted the half-slip and peeked.

Girls, as I could see, were not equipped the same as boys.

I searched up and down, back and forth, front and back. Mom told me not to stare, but I did, and with full force. Nothing. Dismayed to be proved wrong in the ongoing debate with my chums, I at least had foolproof evidence. Girls did not have peters.

I decided to leave the room before Mom found me and I lost out on a return trip. When I moved around a tall stack of empty boxes, I discovered another naked mannequin. This one had short hair and no bumps on the chest, obviously a man. He had no more equipment where necessary than the plastic woman. I didn't claim to know about women, but I knew about men. He was missing something important. And if he was missing something he should have, maybe the female mannequin was too. The mystery, solved moments before, returned. I still did not know the truth about women. I was more determined than ever to find out.

I peeked through the slightly open door. Mom was not in sight. A few steps ahead, high on her rolling ladder, Mrs. Millhollin was dusting an upper shelf. Fully occupied with her work, she didn't notice my presence. Her full skirt beckoned. Better evidence than the storeroom dummies was straight ahead. I positioned myself below her for the best possible view, almost falling over backwards as I tilted my head and gawked.

I didn't see much beyond a little leg skin and some straps holding up Mrs. Millhollin's stockings. The higher I looked up her legs, the dimmer the view. I couldn't see what I was searching for or much of anything else.

My focused attention disconnected me from my surroundings until I felt the rushing approach of my mother. "Never mind," she whispered in my ear with emphasis, trying to avoid the attention of Mrs. Millhollin. Mom's leash hand snapped on mine like handcuffs and pulled me out the front door of the Square Deal. I expected a scolding, but Mom said nothing. She quickened her pace, as though the greater the distance from the Square Deal, the less likely Frances Millhollin would realize Mom had a pervert for a son. My perfect plot had failed. I didn't discover more military supplies in the war room. I didn't resolve the burning issue of the female anatomy. And I got in trouble with Mom. My feelings suffered, but my curiosity about the female form remained intact.

My options for discovering the truth about girls were nearly exhausted. I looked through the lingerie sections of the Sears and Roebuck and Montgomery Ward catalogs without success. I inspected pictures in *National Geographic*, but those were of black women and the photos only showed their tops. Some of the native women had saucers under their lips and piles of ringlets around their necks. I couldn't connect anything in the magazine with what I saw in Guthrie Center. I watched girls on swings. I tried to steal a peek at a cousin my age while she changed into a bathing suit, but a quick turn interrupted my view, leaving only the news that little girls' behinds looked the same as little boys. The lady mannequin at the Square Deal had given promise of an answer, but left frustration instead. And my efforts to find the ultimate answer with the unknowing assistance of Mrs. Millhollin produced no evidence and got me in trouble.

Dad probably knew. His friends at the garage used a lot of words for peters. But Dad was only a few words short of being a mute, and I didn't talk to him about anything. I never considered asking Mom. I didn't think of her as a woman. She was a Mom. Darrell's explanations were always scientifically correct and beyond understanding. "Darrell," I once asked. "Are there man-eating plants? You know, like the giant dandelion in the Tarzan movie that ate the Nazi."

"There are carnivorous plants, like the Venus Fly Trap," he explained. "But they only ingest microscopic insects."

Darrell, quite unintentionally, made me feel stupid. Gab intended that result and succeeded. He only spent time with me when he had no other options, like when we went to bed. Such was the case when he discovered a book, *Perfect Boyhood*, lying on Darrell's pillow. Apparently, Mom could not bring herself to discuss birds and bees with her teenage son and hoped *Perfect Boyhood* would supply the necessary information. By the time she worked up the courage to explain the facts of life with her drop-and-run approach, Darrell was well informed. Gab and I were not. We turned the pages of *Perfect Boyhood* in search of forbidden information. Gab did the reading. I asked the questions.

"What's self abuse?"

"Oh, that's somethin' you're not supposed to do to yourself."

"What does abuse mean?"

"It's like being bad."

"Why would anyone want to be bad to himself?"

"Some people ain't that smart. That's why they have to be reminded."

We turned pages with pictures of caterpillars and butterflies, a fat sow with baby pigs, and a boy brushing his teeth. Gab continued to read, the topic turning to the perils of petting.

"What's wrong with petting?" I asked. "I pet Barry's cat and Uncle Arch's dog all the time."

"It's not like that. They mean girls."

"Who would wanna pet a girl?"

"They mean like holding hands and kissin' and stuff like that. Ya know, like in the movies."

"Don't girls wash their hands? I hold hands with Mom all the time."

"Moms are okay, but be careful of girls."

Listening to Gab read *Perfect Boyhood* led to more questions than answers. The biggest question, the one about the anatomy of girls, went unanswered. I was stuck with Gab's earlier taunt: "That's for me to know and you to find out."

Maybe if I joined Gab's secret club, he and his friends would share what they knew. "Gab," I asked. "Can I join your club?"

"Sure. But ya gotta be initiated."

Filled with excitement, I went to the next club meeting of Gab's friends, held in a small, nearly-hidden space in the corner of our backyard and next to Father O'Sullivan's garage.

"This here's my kid brother, Ked," Gab announced. "He wants to be initiated into our club." My moment had arrived. I was about to become a member of Gab's club and learn the secrets of older boys.

"What do I hafta do?" I asked.

"Tell us the three dirtiest words you know," a voice demanded.

"Peter, pee pee, and poop," I replied proudly.

"The kid doesn't know shit," said an unimpressed voice.

"Am I a member now?" I asked.

"Not yet," Gab replied. "Next ya gotta kiss the Blarney stone." My brother wrapped one of Dad's blue bandanas around my eyes and tied it behind my head. "Get down on your knees," he instructed.

I did as told, hoping my initiation was about over and we could start talking about grown-up things. "Pucker up and kiss," Gab commanded. A hand pushed my head forward. My face met a fleshy crease. Gab yanked the bandana from my head while his friends laughed. A pal of his was pulling up his pants. I ran bawling and spitting to the porch swing, my dreams of joining Gab's club shattered.

Gab and his chums were not the answer. I needed someone who knew for certain, someone with the evidence, someone willing to share: Ruby!

Ruby Rosenthal was my age, my size, and a classmate at grade school and Sunday school. The Rosenthals lived on the north end of Twelfth Street, as far as one could get from our house and still be in town – perfect for my intentions. If my plan backfired, it wouldn't become a neighborhood incident.

Ruby wore jeans, boots, and a cowboy shirt with flaps on the pockets. She tucked two tightly braided pigtails under a blue Chicago Cubs' baseball cap. She rode horses, shinnied up trees, and threw snowballs at boys. Mom called her a tomboy. I called Ruby my best bet.

Mom and Mrs. Rosenthal were friends and visited back and forth for coffee and conversation. During those times, Ruby and I were left on our own to play. We got along fine. She didn't insist on playing dolls or house or dress-up. She enjoyed running and climbing as much as I did. She didn't talk much, but when she did was bold, blunt, and capable of naughty words. I began to plot.

Gab told me about a game called "show me yours and I'll show you mine," but I thought that approach too risky. I needed a plan most likely to provide the answer with the least possibility of punishment. A simple question would do the trick. I could make the meaning clear but the words fuzzy enough that I could deny them or say they were misunderstood if Ruby went running to her mother. My opportunity came several days later.

***

"Carroll Ray, would you like to play with Ruby while I have coffee with her mother?" Mom asked.

"Sure, Mom," I replied eagerly.

That afternoon Mom and I climbed the Main Street hill to Twelfth Street and walked north to the Rosenthal home. The

Victorian structure with its wrap-around porch occupied a large lot with tall trees and a barn in the back. There was much to explore at the Rosenthal residence, and that was exactly what I had in mind. Today, I would ask Ruby the ultimate question.

"You kids run and play," suggested Ruby's mother as she set a coffee pot on the kitchen table. Ruby and I moved into the parlor.

"Wanna play house?" I asked. My suggestion was not sincere. I needed to lock Ruby in place for my question. She went along with my offer and arranged a dinner on the coffee table with toy dishes and silverware. I sat on the sofa and smoked an imaginary pipe and read an imaginary newspaper.

"Will you kids be all right while Hazel and I run an errand to Masters' Grocery Store," Ruby's mother called from the kitchen.

"Okay, Mom," Ruby replied.

Our mothers would be gone long enough for me to get an answer, if I had enough gumption to ask the question. I watched the Rosenthal Oldsmobile pull out of the driveway and head south.

"Ruby, let's play like we've finished dinner and are reading a book together on the davenport."

"Okay."

"Here, we can use your 'Archie' comic book."

"Okay."

We sat beside each other on a brown, worn sofa with its arms falling away from the base. Small yellow cushions embroidered with pink flowers helped fill the gaps.

"I'll read first," I suggested.

"Okay."

Neither of us could read much. We made up the dialogue as we viewed pictures of Archie, Jughead, Betty, and Veronica. I finished a page and turned to Ruby.

"Ruby . . . uh . . . I was . . . I was wondering . . . if . . . er .
. . maybe . . . uh . . . could I ask you a question?"

"Like what?"

"Well . . . you know . . . uh . . . down there . . ."

"Down where?"

I directed my eyes and nodded toward her lap. "You know."

"Yeah. So?"

"I was . . . uh . . . wondering. Do girls have weenies?" I
had asked the question. A shudder of relief rippled through
me. Ruby giggled. I took her response to mean I had asked a
dumb question.

Ruby leaned back against the sofa and unzipped her Levis.
"Why doncha find out for yourself?"

Why, I wondered, didn't she just say "yes" or "no?" I had
no follow-up plan for her answer.

"How?" I asked lamely.

"Ya gotta hand doncha?"

I had two, but neither was inclined to stray into such for-
bidding territory. My plot had not included this challenge to
my courage. Reaching might mean trouble. Not reaching meant
I was a sissy. My original question no longer seemed important.

"Hello, anyone home?"

Ruby's dad entered the front door at the far end of a hallway that looked toward the sofa. He had a clear view of us,
but from thirty feet away. Ruby grabbed the "Archie" comic
book and placed it across her gapping fly. I slid away from her
and clasped my hands behind my head, half in surrender and
half in an effort to remove any hint that my hands might be
connected with Ruby's open zipper.

Mr. Rosenthal slumped into an overstuffed chair across
the room from us. He was relaxed, comfortable, and in a mood
to talk. He wore a suit and tie, a sure sign to me of importance.

"Where's your mothers?" he asked.

"Oh . . . they went to the grocery store," Ruby replied.

I was impressed with her composure. I had lost mine. My heart was pounding so hard I could hear it. My teeth threatened to chatter. I needed to give Ruby a chance to zip up without drawing the attention of her dad. I was thinking as hard as panic would allow.

"So what've you kids been up to?"

"Nothin' much, Dad, just playin'."

As long as Mr. Rosenthal remained seated across the room and Ruby held the comic book across her lap, we were not likely to be found out. But if he moved toward us and saw what we were up to, I would be in big trouble.

"They didn't have comic books when I was a kid," Mr. Rosenthal continued.

I was thinking hard, trying to work my way out of trouble.

"Yes, sir, we sure didn't have things like that to read when I was growing up. Here, let me have a look at Archie and Jughead." Mr. Rosenthal rose from his chair and took a step toward the sofa.

"Sir, I think the mailman's at your door," I blurted.

"Oh, I better see what he wants." Ruby's dad turned and walked toward the front door. She arched her back, zipped up, and placed the comic book back in her lap.

"There's no one there," Mr. Rosenthal said when he returned to the parlor.

I moved my hands from behind my head and silently exhaled with relief. "I'm sorry, sir, I thought I saw Ivyl Moraine through the window in your front door."

Politeness led grown-ups away from the misdoings of kids. I couldn't be pinned with anything now. Sometimes I was naughty and knew it, but didn't get in trouble. Other times I came to grief for unknown reasons. Trouble and I seemed to be more connected by luck than by deed.

I didn't uncover the dark secret that day and almost had a nervous breakdown. It seemed that God, or whoever controls such issues, did not want me to know about girls. "Patience has its own reward," Mom reminded me many times. I decided to let patience have a try rather than risk my neck.

Mother's wisdom again proved correct. Patience and fate presented another opportunity soon after the failure of the Ruby scheme. A friend and I went to his bathroom to play Navy with a gray plastic PT boat he received for his birthday. When I opened the door, his mother shrieked as she stepped from the tub. I hesitated an instant before closing the door to get one solid gawk at her fully exposed nudity. I was awed by the beauty and grace of her form. She was as fancy as I was plain. Still, I didn't let the wonder of the moment interfere with the unexpected opportunity. I saw what was there. More importantly, I saw what wasn't. I knew for sure and certain, once and for all.

At bedtime, I passed along my discovery to Gab. "You know what? Girls don't have peters."

"Well, la dee da, the kid finally figured it out."

"You knew?"

"Yeah, who didn't?"

Gab had a way of adding a word or two to make me feel even dumber. At least I solved one item of ignorance and was free to move on to another issue I debated with my pals: Can Superman see your underwear?

"Gab, why didn't you tell me?" I asked.

"You ask a dumb question; you get a dumb answer. Sometimes dopey kids just have to figure things out for themselves."

Gab leaned over the edge of his bed. "How'd ya find out?" His voice was filled with curiosity. I could tell I had his attention. For once, I was in control. I made him wait.

"Well?" he asked.

"I saw Dick's mom getting out of the bathtub."

"Were you spying on her?"

"Nah, we were going to play navy in the tub and just walked in on her."

"Does she have big boobs?"

"What are boobs?"

"You know, tits . . . knockers."

Gab's vocabulary was impressive. He knew several words for naughty parts of the body, while I was learning them one at a time and afraid to say any.

"Yeah, I guess so. Now go to sleep."

Chapter 5

Wives and Knives

"**M**om, what does covet mean?"

"That means you want something with all your heart and soul. Why do you ask?"

"We're learning the Ten Commandments at Sunday school. Covet's something you're not supposed to do with your neighbor's wife. That's rule number ten."

"Well, that's not for a seven-year-old to worry about. It's something you deal with when you're a man."

"Does Dad covet Mrs. Riaski?"

"I certainly hope not . . . why don't you run and play."

I didn't ask more. "Run and play" and "never mind" and "that'll do" meant additional questions were unwanted. At least I learned a new word. I coveted a pocket knife. I wanted one with all my heart, with all my soul – and then some.

The place to go for a pocket knife in Guthrie Center was Rowley Hardware. No secret about that. Above the entrance, a huge wooden pocket knife with an orange handle and opened silver blades spanned half the width of the store front. A glass case inside displayed an eye-popping collection that drew my full attention.

A stop at Rowley's meant an encounter with an owner intent on making a sale to anyone who crossed his threshold. The jingling entrance bell betrayed my arrival and set the trap. Before I took a second breath of the metallic smell of nails and screws, Mr. Rowley sprang forth to meet his latest customer.

A large man, dressed in tan work pants and matching shirt with rolled-up sleeves, huddled over me so close I could smell his morning coffee. "What are you buying today, Dockie? Whatcha need is what I got. What say we do a little business?" Mr. Rowley's lips popped as he talked and sprayed my glasses. I took a step backward.

The non-stop chatter of Paul Rowley, so unlike my dad, amused me. Withstanding his forceful manner, like facing a northwest gale, took courage. What captured my attention, however, was an unusual physical feature. Mr. Rowley had no hair. None. Not a single strand. I had seen bald men, but never one without whiskers, without eyelashes, without eyebrows. Some said he lost his hair during a mustard gas attack in World War I. Others said it disappeared after his brother died in an elevator accident at the store. Still others said it was the result of an unknown disease. Whatever the reason, he was hairless and huge and hovering over me like a Boris Karloff character. I was scared. But he was the source of pocket knives, and I coveted a pocket knife more than I feared Mr. Rowley.

Few left Rowley Hardware without buying something. A small item perhaps, but something. Mr. Rowley spoke of his merchandise as mandatory, not optional, purchases. Most shopkeepers greeted customers with a "good day," or "How may I help you?" Mr. Rowley asked, "What are you buying today, Dockie?" He called everyone "Dockie"; young or old, male or female, we were all "Dockie."

My only salvation when bombarded by Mr. Rowley's relentless sales pitch was lack of money. But on this day, with a nickel grasped in a sweaty palm and held tightly in the depths of a trouser pocket, I prepared to meet Mr. Rowley's challenge and "do a little business." I edged around him and made my way to the knife display.

"Lookin' for a pocket knife, huh? Better get it now while it's still there, Dockie. When it's gone, there won't be no more. There's a war on ya know. Better buy it while ya can. I'll give ya a good American deal."

Sometimes, perhaps in a patriotic mood, Mr. Rowley offered "a good American deal." At other times, he proposed "a good Christian deal." The difference between an American deal and a Christian deal wasn't clear. Either way, Mr. Rowley apparently hoped Uncle Sam or the Lord would help close a sale.

A small mother-of-pearl knife shaped like a bowling pin captured my attention. Solid glass and seventy cents separated us. I needed that knife. I wanted it with all my heart and all my soul, just like in the Tenth Commandment.

Mr. Rowley's endless patter hammered away. "I can send that bowling pin beauty home with ya, Dockie. Only seventy cents and that treasure is yours. What's a dime or two among friends? A few silver coins you'll never miss anyhow. Every boy should have a knife like that, Dockie. How much money ya got?"

"I only got a nickel, Mr. Rowley."

"That's fine, my young man. I can fix you up with a knife for a buffalo head."

I couldn't believe my good fortune. The bowling pin knife would soon be mine, and for only five cents. Mr. Rowley reached under the counter where a shiny brass cash register stood at attention. I assumed he was reaching for the key to open the knife case.

"I got something here for you, Dockie, that's better than that pip-squeak of a knife. Why, that thing's only for kids. What I got here is for a real man. Heck, that pantywaist thing's only good for cleaning your finger nails. Got something that'll take caps off bottles, open cans, and do a whole bunch of stuff. It's the best doggone thing a nickel can buy."

Mr. Rowley snatched the sweaty nickel from my hand and popped it into the cash register in one uninterrupted motion ending with a "clink." He handed me a knife unlike any I had ever seen. Made of flat silver metal, it was almost as long as my six-inch ruler at school. One end of my new knife was shaped into a hook; the other was pointed and bent. It wasn't what I expected, but Mr. Rowley said it was a man's knife. I took his word for it. He knew about knives and was a man.

I scurried home to share my good fortune with Mom, pausing on the courthouse lawn to admire my knife. The silvery surface glittered in the sun. I turned the knife over. A long line of letters was stamped in the metal: B-U-D-W-E-I-S-E-R. I didn't know about knife companies, but figured this one must be important to have such a long name. I hopped and skipped past St. Mary's and on home.

Mom was standing at the kitchen sink humming and peeling potatoes. Potato peels flipped and fluttered as she spoke without interrupting her work. "Where did you go? I thought you were playing outside."

Mom spoke without turning. How could she tell who had entered the house? She said she had eyes in the back of her head. I believed her.

"I went downtown and bought a knife."

Mom whirled toward me, her left eyebrow raised in a question mark.

"A knife? Where'd you get the money for that?"

"It only cost a nickel."

"Where on earth did you buy a knife for five cents?"

"Rowley's. Wanna see it?"

"I *certainly* do."

My satisfaction of a moment before turned to concern. I handed Mom my BUDWEISER knife. When she saw the name of the knife company, her face turned as red as her checkered apron. She whipped off the apron, hit the latch of the screen door with the heel of her hand, and bolted out of the house. I ran to the front porch to see where Mom was going in such a hurry. She had already passed St. Mary's, taking strides longer than Simon Sez giant steps.

I awaited her return. It didn't take long.

Mom entered the kitchen panting, paused a moment to catch her breath, and then reached high on a kitchen cabinet and placed something out of my reach. "I think we better just set this nickel up here until you learn to use better judgment. A fool and his money are soon parted."

I didn't understand fully the meaning of Mom's words, but I knew too well the identity of the fool. I felt like one. I had neither the knife nor the nickel.

***

The mother-of-pearl treasure remained locked in the glass knife case at Rowley Hardware. I still hungered for it, but where would I get seventy cents? Mom said I lacked good judgment. Asking for her advice would eliminate that problem.

"Mom, d'ya know how I could earn seventy cents to buy Mr. Rowley's knife?"

"Hmmm . . . let me see. Maybe you could wash the windows at your dad's shop. They certainly need it."

Need it? Dad had occupied the building for twenty years and never touched the windows. Twenty years of soot and smoke from his pot-belly stove, twenty years of grease and grime, twenty years of spiders spinning dust-covered webs over clouded windows that denied all but the brightest sunshine. A professional window washer would have joined the army to avoid tackling Dad's dreadful windows. And yet, I wanted the pretty little knife.

Mom didn't allow tension at the dinner table, saying it was bad for digestion, and nothing caused more strain in the family than a money request of Dad. A window of opportunity occurred after dinner when he got up from his chair, scratched his back by rubbing against the nearby door frame, and dropped into his rocker for a catnap. Once he reached his snooze position, time ran short. Sleep struck the instant Dad's head touched the worn spot on the back of his chair. Ten minutes of raspy snoring and snorts and sighs followed while the rest of the family covered mouths to keep from laughing. At the sound of the one o'clock whistle, he stood, took five steps, grabbed his greasy work jacket and engineer's cap from the kitchen door knob, and returned to work.

I approached Dad the instant he slumped into his rocker. I dreaded asking him for money, and even more so after a recent experience. He had returned from a run in his sideline taxi business with a smile on his face and two quarters in his hand.

"Can I have fifty cents to get my hair cut?" I asked.

"There, just take it," he snorted, and threw the two quarters on the kitchen floor.

Prying fifty cents out of Dad for a mother-mandated haircut was hard enough. Now, I was about to ask for a seventy-cent job. I reached for my courage. Only a consuming interest in Mr. Rowley's knife kept me from running. Dad nestled into his nap position. I stood before him with my head bowed.

"Mom says you might hire me to wash the shop windows."

"Whadda ya wanna do *that* for?"

"I need seventy cents to buy a knife."

"Why d'ya want *that*?"

Dad reduced the wants of those pressuring his change purse to insignificance. To him, the mother-of-pearl knife I longed for was nothing more than a meaningless, pointless, non-essential "that."

"I dunno," I replied in little more than a whimper.

"Didn't have no knife at your age. Didn't get one 'til near twelve. Worked damned hard for it. Picked corn with my bare hands in ice and snow to buy the blamed thing. Still got it, too."

Dad pulled a faded yellow-handled knife from his pocket and displayed it proudly in his bear's paw of a hand.

"I'll work for my knife . . . just like you did."

Dad pocketed his keepsake and leaned his head back. Satisfied in silence, he closed his eyes. I felt the slap of being ignored. My lower lip quivered. Dreams of a knife trickled down my cheeks.

Mom approached from behind and placed her hands on my trembling shoulders. "Eldon, don't you think he could earn the seventy cents?" she asked gently.

Mom often said, "I have a method in my madness," which meant in this case allowing me to probe Dad's defenses. By tactics of delay, deafness, and indifference, he assumed I would grow weary, lose my courage, and accept defeat. Without Mom in reserve, he was right – I would have surrendered every time. But with her support, words, timing, and tactics, I had a chance at success.

"You always say the boys should work for what they get," Mom continued.

Dad said that all right, but he didn't expect to get stuck with the payroll. Mom and I awaited Dad's verdict. His mute deliberations, his showdown of silence, took an aggravating length of time. If we walked away in frustration, we lost. Mom and I stood together, stood our ground, testing her rule that "patience has its own reward."

At an earlier time, and quite by chance, I beat Dad's dummy routine. "Can I have a nickel?" I asked. I waited and waited. Nothing. Frustration cranked my courage. With nothing to lose, I blurted, "Can I have a dime?"

"Heard ya the first time," Dad replied, and handed me a nickel.

"Aha," I thought. Good approach. Make Dad feel he's getting off cheap by raising the ante. But I couldn't do that with a request for seventy cents, nearly a quarter more than the cost of a haircut. This was big money. I was in unfamiliar territory. Dad remained silent, his eyes closed. I feared snores would come before a response.

"Whadda ya think, Dad?"

I became amazingly brave with Mom beside me, braver than I thought possible. The wait continued.

Dad's eyes opened to a slit. "S'pose it wouldn't hurt nothin'." He had spoken – at last. Was that a "yes?" His last ditch defense on money questions was to leave the issue hanging. Maybe the matter, he seemed to think, would be forgotten, and he could hold onto his change.

Dad leaned his head back and began his delayed nap. Mom hugged me and smiled.

An immediate follow-up was required when Dad gave in. His memory was short and self-serving. Mom waited a strategic thirty minutes after his departure for work before calling me.

"OK, my little man, time to get on the job. Go get your work clothes on while I organize your window cleaning supplies."

"What are my work clothes?"

"Same as your play clothes, your overalls and a T-shirt. I'll fix a cap for you from one of your dad's."

I hated bib overalls. Those formless, faded, eyesores were an insult to the human shape. Bibs were for babies. But now, on the threshold of being a wage earner and a junior partner at McKibbin's Garage, my attitude changed. I donned the patched overalls gladly and selected a blue T-shirt of a color similar to Dad's work shirts.

"You look terrific," Mom exclaimed as I returned to the kitchen in my work clothes. "All you need is a cap. Here, try this."

She handed me one of Dad's denim engineer caps, folded in the back and secured with a large safety pin. The adjusted circumference fit nicely, but the top soared high above. I looked more like a chef than a window washer. No matter. I was a working man and a bread – spelled k-n-i-f-e – winner.

"Here are all the supplies you'll need. Just go to the shop and go to work. Don't say anything to your father."

Mom and I had become co-conspirators, plotting on how to wedge seventy cents out of Dad. Her involvement bolstered my confidence and raised my hopes that one day the little knife would be mine. I could almost feel the mother-of-pearl in my hand. But what I felt first was a bar of Bon Ami soap Mom handed me, along with a fistful of gray grease rags. Dad's grease rags were found everywhere and used for everything. He blew his nose on the coarse gray handkerchief-size cloth. He dried his hands and cleaned his ears with grease rags. If Mom had allowed, he would have used them for table napkins. And now the multi-purpose grease rags were about to become window cleaners.

"Here, put your rags and soap in this bucket, and go to your father's shop and get busy."

The bucket was a converted five-quart Pennzoil can with a

wire handle Mom fashioned from baling wire. "Nothing works without baling wire," the local saying went, and the handle on the yellow Pennzoil can gave proof to the proverb.

"How do I wash windows?" I asked.

"It's just like washing your face, except you scrub the window instead. Put some wet Bon Ami on your rag, spread it on the window pane, and then wash the soap and dirt off with another rag soaked with clean water. That's all there is to it."

Grown-ups often said, "That's all there is to it." When I heard those words, I knew there would be more "to it" – there always was.

I was determined and ready. I left the house with a sense of importance and purpose. Within minutes, I would be working at McKibbin's Garage and earning money – a grown-up, happy prospect.

I swung my work bucket to and fro playing "making candy" as I skipped past St. Mary's Church. Mom invented the game to move me along when I dawdled on the way to the Square Deal. Grasping my hand, she swung my arm back and forth in exaggerated motions while we chanted, "Making candy, making candy." Then, with a few quick steps and a lot of laughter, she shouted, "Throw it all out," and hoisted me into the air in a large forward arc. Several rounds of the game delivered us to our destination.

My arrival at McKibbin's Garage sobered my mood. Without Mom, I felt alone, very alone. I said nothing to Dad. A window in the opposite corner from where he worked, concealed from his view by a raised car hood, seemed a good place to start. A nearby upside-down water faucet that washed hands, relieved thirst, and flushed the drain Dad and his friends used as a urinal, would supply water for my work. I wanted to get underway as quickly as possible before someone came my way for a drink or a call of nature and drew attention to my presence. Once I began washing Dad's windows, so I figured, he couldn't back out on our deal.

I knew Dad's shop windows were filthy and covered with spider webs. But now, faced with cleaning them, I looked more carefully. Grimy drippings of yellowy-green goo and purplish-black smudges of grease gripped the glass. A chipped crack crossed the pane. Dead June bugs lay on the sill, their needle-thin legs gnarled and twisted. Equally dead orange and black box-elder bugs shared the window sill cemetery, along with deceased flies and gnats and moths and other nameless bugs. Big black scary spiders, very much alive, waited for a careless insect to get trapped in their thick webs.

I was sickened by the dead bugs and filth of the window and petrified by the large, menacing spiders that patrolled their domain. My recent failure to clear a ditch in a game of follow-the-leader left my legs dangling into a spider-infested pit. I screamed at the prospect of black, furry legs crawling up my jeans until my laughing cousin, Dwayne Gene, pulled me free. With that scare fresh in my mind, the allure of the mother-of-pearl knife reached its full test.

Mom said washing windows was like washing my face. Peanut butter, taffy, jam, and other sticky, greasy substances scrubbed off my skin with a thorough application of Lifebuoy soap. Surely, the tougher Bon Ami could do the same to the muck that covered the window pane. Mom also said the scary spiders did not bite and were more afraid of me than I was of them, something I found hard to believe. I took Mom's word for it and began my preparations.

I moved the can of Dad's hand-cleaning soap paste from the window sill to the rust-stained concrete floor beneath the water faucet. An Exide battery, shoved into place under the window, served as a step stool.

The dreadful task of clearing the window of spider webs

and dead insects came next. With a whisk broom as my weapon, I gulped hard and swept away a bevy of bugs. A swipe at the thick spider tangle didn't go as well. Filmy filaments grasped the broom and wrapped around my wrist. I shook my hand frantically, trying to free it of webs and bugs and spiders. I shuddered, whirled to the faucet, and rinsed the creepy lot of dead and crawling creatures from my shaking hand. After pausing to catch my breath and recover my courage, I switched to a long-handled broom and got rid of the remaining spiders.

I ran water into the Pennzoil bucket, dipped a rag, and prepared to clean the window like I washed my face – just as Mom instructed. I swirled the bar of Bon Ami against the glass, this way and that, up and down, back and forth, making circles and figure eights. I was getting nowhere, even losing ground. The mixture of pinkish suds and twenty years of muck and grime formed a thick goo that robbed the window of its last trace of transparency.

"Hey, sonny, that's quite a job you're doin' there," one of Dad's cronies teased. "Are you washin' that thing or finger painting?"

I had attracted the unwanted attention of Dad's daily audience of loafers. Seated on a bench at the front of the shop or standing around the nearby pot-belly stove, this assortment of 4-F draft rejects, retirees, the infirm of mind or body, and farmers in town for the day gathered to observe the excitement of auto repairs and discuss the progress of the war. The amused eyes of Dad's pals followed my futile efforts as the greasy glass gave no hint of surrender. Trying to ignore my smiling, unwanted audience and inspired more by pride than progress, I continued my fruitless task.

I smelled Dad's approach from behind. An odor of oil, grease, and sweat revealed his presence. I knew it well. His rocking chair, his work coat hanging on the kitchen door, and his overalls on a hook in the bathroom all carried his trade-mark aroma. His attention added anxiety to my problems. Would he find fault with my efforts? Would he send me home and terminate my opportunity to buy the prized knife?

"Did ya put my hand cleaner on the floor where people piss?"

I had never heard Dad say such a naughty word. Mom did not allow cussing, and I wouldn't have known the term except for Gab's tutoring. I had progressed from "do-do," Mom's preferred term, to "pee-pee," to just plain "pee." Gab knew alternatives, like "take a leak" or "water the lilies," and occasionally used the daring and manly, "take a piss." Dad's use of Gab's word shocked me.

"I'm sorry," I murmured.

Dad moved the hand cleaner can aside with his foot, gulped a slug of water from the faucet, and returned to his work. Having survived that confrontation, my only success of the day, I resumed my futile efforts.

More designs with the moist bar of soap did little to clean the window. The snickers of Dad's friends mounted. My efforts had succeeded only in making me the object of amusement. The dream of a knife withered as the wound in my ego deepened. Summoning one last bit of composure, I strolled away from my first job and out the door as though taking a break. Up the alley and out of sight of McKibbin's Garage, I wiped sniffles with a grease rag and plodded on home.

"Are you done already?" Mom asked from her sewing machine.

"No, not really. I don't want no knife."

"Where's your bucket and soap?"

"I left 'em at Dad's shop. I don't ever wanna see 'em again."

"So you just laid down on the job. You quit. Is that right?"

"Sorta."

"*Can't* never did anything."

I felt my mother's disappointment, but didn't respond.

"Come here, sweetheart, and tell me what happened." When Mom wrapped her arms around me, I lost my self-control and began to sob.

"Tell me about it," Mom asked while drying my tears with a lacy handkerchief.

"I couldn't get the window clean and Dad's friends were laughing at me and I made Dad say a naughty word."

"Maybe it would help if I went with you and got you started. We could play a game of 'making candy' on the way to the shop. What do you think of that?"

I nodded my agreement.

"Good. We'll just call this a lunch break. I'll fix you a peanut butter sandwich. You can eat while I get ready."

Mom's offer of assistance delighted me. Whenever she came to my rescue the outcome was certain and positive. She set the standard of performance, supplied the encouragement, and determined the ultimate reward. Her magical impact on Dad's stubborn behavior produced results worthy of Houdini.

I was bringing the cavalry, and a fashionable one at that, as Mom and I swung hands on our way to McKibbin's Garage. Her white dress with red piping around the collar, a matching red tie around the waist, and lacy white anklets and sandals would lend needed elegance to Dad's shop. Mom's clothes, like her personality, were colorful and confident, and in marked contrast to the dull and functional blue denim of my dad.

Male settings made Mom uncomfortable. Beer parlors and pool halls were unacceptable and off limits. She occasionally stuck her head in the door of the barber shop to see if my haircut was finished. She seemed awkward and out of place in Dad's auto repair shop, like a queen in a coal mine, and did

APRON STRINGS

not go there frequently. I knew we were on a special mission as we entered McKibbin's Garage.

One of Dad's buddies, a cigar held by his side, rose from his position on the loafers' bench and doffed his hat. "Good morning, Hazel," he greeted.

The behavior and language of the assembled men changed with Mom's arrival. They seemed uneasy in her presence. Their naughty words and spitting stopped.

Mom smiled at the man but did not approach him, turning instead to the object of her mission. She pulled her dress tightly against her leg to keep it from touching the greasy surroundings. "Hand me the Bon Ami and let's get to work," she said. Mom took the bar of soap, dipped it in the bucket of water, and rubbed tiny circles of lather on the pane. She then rinsed the glass with a wet grease rag and dried the window with another.

"There," she said while handing the soap and rag to me. "Just do a little bit at a time and pretty soon you'll have the whole window done. It's not going to look like new. Just do the best you can."

Mom planted a kiss on my cheek and left for home. Her presence had quieted Dad's chuckling friends and renewed my confidence. The window looked smaller and a new knife more likely as I returned to my work.

***

Three windows and as many days later, I finished my first wage-earning effort. I had converted the dim, shadowy interior of Dad's shop into a sunshine-flooded solarium – at least in my imagination. The reality was considerably less than that, but I had done my best and achieved a sort of hazy improvement.

"I'm done!" I announced.

Mom turned from her task at the sink and saw me standing, Pennzoil bucket in hand, at the kitchen door. She swiped her wet hands across her apron and leaned over to hug me. "I knew you could do it!" she exclaimed. I was giddy with pride and relieved when she did not ask to review the results, an inspection I feared would reveal a substandard performance. I didn't worry about Dad's response over windows he had ignored for twenty years, and I was dead certain he wouldn't object to the removal of my spying presence from the Fraternal Order of the McKibbin Garage.

"Wait here. I have something for you," Mom said. She disappeared into the family closet, where she went to retrieve "sewing money," and returned a few moments later with three quarters in her palm.

"Here. Your father said to give you these when you were finished. He said you did such a good job he wanted you to have a little extra."

Three quarters! From my usual allotment of a few pennies and a nickel or two I had moved into the big time of quarters.

"Can I go get my knife now?"

"Well, I think we better get you cleaned up first. It wouldn't do to go shopping with potato patches in your ears. And I think for this special occasion you should wear school clothes. Go get into clean jeans and your plaid, short-sleeve shirt."

I was going shopping, just like grown-ups. I had chiseled pennies and nickels for peanuts and candy bars and been trusted with ten cents for Sunday school, movies, and war bond stamps. Now, I owned quarters and was about to buy my own knife.

I quickly dressed and reported to Mom for inspection and the required finger curling of my hair. When she finally said, "Okay," I bolted out the door. Skipping and prancing past St. Mary's, I came to a skidding halt at the nearby intersection, crossed the street carefully, and sailed across the courthouse lawn. According to my calculations, I had enough money to buy the knife and have a nickel left for a Whiz candy bar. I could already feel the knife and taste the chocolate.

I swaggered into Rowley Hardware. "What can I sell you today, Dockie," Mr. Rowley asked. "I'll bet you came for the knife."

"Uh-huh."

Mr. Rowley removed the mother-of-pearl knife from the glass display case with one hand while holding the other open for my quarters. The three precious coins had belonged to me only a matter of minutes, perhaps fifteen or so. I liked the feel of wealth in my grasp. Now, I would have to give it up. After a couple seconds of agony and hesitation, I dropped the fleeting treasure, my reward for three miserable days of fighting goo and grime and grisly spiders, into Mr. Rowley's outstretched palm.

The cash register swallowed my quarters with a drawer-closing "clank" of finality. I awaited my nickel change. Instead, Mr. Rowley launched another sales talk.

"With that little gem, you'll need a leather case. Wouldn't do to lose it now, would it? I got just what ya need."

"Mr. Rowley, don't I get a nickel back?" I asked.

"Why, no, my little man. That goes to Mr. Hickenlooper, the governor. They call it a sales tax. Don't you know 'bout taxes?"

I didn't, and felt ignorant. Who was this man Mr. Rowley called the governor? And why would he want to eat my Whiz candy bar?

Chapter 6

Fly Bye

"Mom, wanna see my new knife?" My mother's Singer stopped whirring when she released the knee lever and swiveled toward me. I ran to her side, my new knife in an outstretched palm. She cradled my hand in hers and inspected my treasure.

"Here, let me see. My, that's a beauty."

"Do you like it? Mr. Rowley said the pretty stuff is mother-of-pearl."

"Yes, I do like it, but you must be careful. I wouldn't want you to cut a finger."

"I'll be careful. I promise."

"You see the value of a little work? Now run along and enjoy your knife, and don't lose it."

I liked the sense of ownership that came with the knife in my hand. I liked the feel of it in my pocket, rubbing against my leg as I ran to the front porch. I forgot about spying on

Father O'Sullivan and turned my attention to my new pearl-handled prize.

I sat in the swing and admired the knife in my hand. Thoughts of whittling wood and slicing apples ran through my mind. My small fingers tried to grip the blade and pull it open. The back of the blade, only slightly exposed, had a tiny slit for a fingernail, something my fully pruned finger-tips did not possess. Again and again, from every angle and with increasing frustration, my small, nail-less fingers tried to grip the blade. No luck. Nails chewed to the quick left nothing to insert in the tiny slit. I began to wonder if I had invested three days of hard labor and seventy-five cents in a pocket knife that might be useless.

My teeth didn't work any better on the smooth metal. Several attempts to bite and grip the blade only succeeded in clacking my teeth together and threatening a trip to the dentist. The blade remained closed and smug while I became aggravated.

Dad used his yellow-handled knife for opening letters, cleaning his finger nails, sharpening pencils, and clearing his ears – all accomplished with an open blade. A knife without a blade was only an ornament, as useless as a cone without ice cream.

Mom said I would one day pay a price for chewing my nails. That time had seemed far away. Now, that one day became today. I could not ask Mom for help and stir the nail-biting issue.

Dad had tools for everything, including, I was sure, opening knives. His tools, however, were as guarded as his money and hidden away in an off limits cabinet.

Gab had answers for everything, and probably for dealing with stubborn knives. But his solutions usually benefited him more than me. I already feared my knife would end up in his pocket.

Alone, I faced the problem of a useless knife with a blade sealed in its handle. My lips were also sealed, but I was thinking and searching for a way to solve my predicament.

***

Richard Beane and I sat beside each other at Sunday school. A fly on his collar captured my attention. It didn't act like the flies that flitted about during steamy Iowa summers. This one remained motionless, like a dog taught to sit. I wondered if Richard had a pet fly.

I was an experienced fly watcher. I watched the tiny insects pestering horses, making them swish their tails and shake their heads in frustration. I watched flies plummet to earth like downed Jap Zeros when Uncle Arch popped them between his hands. I watched them struggle in the spiral strip of Tanglefoot flypaper hanging from our kitchen light, as doomed as a man in overshoes caught in quicksand. I felt sorry for the little black creatures glued to eternity and futilely fanning their wings.

The fly on Richard's collar was behaving strangely. Flies didn't stay in one place very long. When they did, they wiggled their bottoms like hula dancers and rubbed their legs together. Richard's fly was neither dancing nor rubbing. It just sat on his white collar.

I kept an eye on the fly through a chorus of "Jesus Loves Me." It didn't move.

"Richard," I whispered. "There's a fly on your collar."

"I know," he murmured.

We moved on to "Jesus Loves the Little Children." I tried to lip sync forbidden whispers with the well-known lyrics. "Is it a pet?"

"Nah, it's a fake. It ain't real."

I looked closer at the little bug with transparent wings of purple tint, six thread-thin legs, and reddish eyes. It looked real to me. "Where'd ya get it? Is it stuffed?"

"Later," Richard muttered while singing "red and yellow, black and white . . ."

I was spellbound by the fly. After Sunday school, I asked again. "Where'd ya get the fly?"

"Pinky's."

Pinky's Novelty Shop in Des Moines was my dream store. Stocked with clever items like plastic dog poop, exploding cigarettes, pepper gum, and Frankenstein masks, the tiny store was filled with amusing things.

"How much d'ya pay for it?"

"A buck."

That's big money, I thought, and far beyond my pennies and nickels. Richard's dad, the ag teacher at the high school, included his son in a livestock business. My friend was definitely in the big time. He had a billfold, dollars, and a fly. I had no wallet, no money, and no fly – only a pocket knife with a buried blade.

"Wanna see my new knife?"

I pulled the useless item from my pocket and handed it to Richard. A strong finger nail opened the blade with ease. I went into a Paul Rowley sales pitch.

"Ain't that a beauty. Hard to come by these days. Bet you'd like to have one like that."

"Yeah, but Mom don't want me to have no knife. She says they're dangerous."

"Heck, she'd never know about this little one. How 'bout swappin' your fly for my knife?"

Unloading a useless seventy-cent knife for an exciting one-dollar fly seemed to give me the better end of the trade. I waited for Richard's response.

"Deal!" he replied.

My friend pocketed the pearl-handled knife and pulled the fly from his collar. The life-like creature was attached to a straight pin that disappeared from sight when inserted in cloth. I pinned the fly to the outside of my jacket pocket where I could keep an admiring eye on it.

After Sunday school, I walked briskly toward home with the intent of inflicting envy on Gab. I stopped at the Fifth Street intersection, took a proud glimpse at the fly, and continued my journey across the thick grass of the courthouse lawn. At the next intersection, I looked down again. The fly was gone. Nowhere in sight. My heart sank. My prized possession had fallen off during my block-long walk across the courthouse square.

I retraced my steps. Looking for a fly in the deep green grass was fruitless. Tears blurred my eyes as I walked slowly across the turf, my head bowed as much by grief as by my search for the tiny fly. It was lost. So was I.

I sat on a bench near the Civil War monument, trying to clear my eyes and my thoughts. The past few days had moved from spiders to knives to flies to nothingness. My original nickel bought a Budweiser knife that, according to Mom, wasn't a knife. She held my nickel while I washed windows to earn seventy cents to buy the mother-of-pearl treasure. My three quarters disappeared as quickly as I could walk to Rowley Hardware, and the governor took my candy bar nickel. That left me with no money, but with a knife whose blade I couldn't open without fingernails. I swapped the seventy-cent knife for a dollar fly and more than recovered my fortune. Then, when the fly disappeared into the courthouse lawn, I was back to nothing. Dad's shop windows were a little cleaner, Mr. Rowley was richer, Richard Beane had my knife, and Governor Hickenlooper ate my candy bar. I had no money, no knife, no fly. How could I explain all that to Mom?

Dad still had the knife he bought as a kid. Mine didn't last two days. Mom didn't like flies and battled them with swatters, sprays, and sticky paper. She would never understand why I traded the pretty little knife for an ugly insect.

Only Richard and I knew about our deal. Mom thought I owned a knife. If I no longer had one, it was because I sold, traded, or lost it. If I said I sold the knife, I needed money to show for it. I had none. I could say I traded for something, which indeed I had. That option required admitting I traded for a dumb fly, or coming up with something else. I didn't have something else. I was down to my last option – I could tell Mom I lost the knife. That was kinda true and would save me telling the story about the fly. Besides, we were in this together because she convinced Dad to let me clean his windows. Yes, I would tell Mom I lost my knife – but only if she asked. In the meantime, I had caught the bug for earning money. Intentionally or not, Dad taught me working was better than begging. I began thinking about ways to earn money. One thing was sure – I didn't do windows.

***

Several days passed. The confession I feared faded from my mind. I watched Father O'Sullivan from our porch swing. At the end of the block, I saw Richard Beane's mother approaching. The Beanes lived on the edge of town on Twelfth Street. It was unusual to see any of their family in our neighborhood. I hoped the dark-eyed, pretty Mrs. Beane would walk past our house. Instead, she mounted the three concrete steps from the front sidewalk and the three splintered wooden ones leading to our front door. She noticed me in the swing and turned.

"Is your mother home, Carroll Ray?"

I wanted to say, "No," but the whirring sewing machine in the background said otherwise.

"I guess so," I responded.

Mom opened the front door as Mrs. Beane cocked her arm to knock. "Good morning, Maxine. Won't you come in?"

"I really can't, Hazel. I just stopped by for a moment."

I sat quietly at the end of the porch and listened for the words I feared.

"It seems my Richard and your youngest boy have been conducting a little business. I suppose Carroll Ray told you about it."

I hadn't said a word and had no idea what Richard told his mother.

"Yes, of course, Maxine. Carroll Ray tells me everything."

I couldn't believe my ears. Why was Mom covering for me?

"Then you understand why I'm here to return your son's knife." Mrs. Beane offered the mother-of-pearl knife in her palm. "I don't allow Richard to have a knife. I think he's much too young. Don't you?"

What could Mom say? Richard was a year ahead of me in school. "Children do vary in their maturity," she replied without hesitation.

Mom was sticking up for me. But why?

"Richard would like to have his dollar back. I'm sure you understand."

I wondered what Richard told his mother. It seemed he didn't tell the truth either.

"Yes, of course. Carroll Ray always gives me his dollar bills for safekeeping."

Wow! Mom was into whoppers now. I had no dollar bills – not one. What was she talking about?

"If you'll wait a minute, I'll get one of his dollars from his bank." Mom returned moments later with a dollar bill and handed it to Mrs. Beane. She took the money and left.

My sad tale seemed to have no ending. The knife was back, but in Mom's hands, and she was minus a dollar she took from a bank I didn't have. I worried about the next episode in the knife story.

***

When Dad worked on Monday nights, Mom let me crawl into bed with her and listen to "Dr. I.Q." on the radio. It was dark and cozy warm as we listened.

"I have a lady in the balcony," a roving announcer called to Dr. I.Q. The doctor asked the lady a question that she answered correctly.

"And a box of Mars bars to the kind lady," said the announcer.

When Dr. I.Q.'s questions ended, Mom's began. "Why did you sell your knife to Richard for a dollar? You know you didn't pay that much for it."

Mom had stuck up for me with Mrs. Beane. I would return the favor by telling her the truth, at least most of it, about the deal with Richard. "There wasn't no dollar. Richard traded me a fly."

"A fly?"

"Uh-huh. It was a fake. But it was really neat – looked real and everything. It was on a pin he got at Pinky's in Des Moines.

"So where's the fly?"

"It fell off the pin in my jacket when I was walking past the courthouse after Sunday school. Couldn't find it in all that grass."

"Let me see if I got this straight. You traded the knife you worked so hard for to Richard for a phony fly you lost on the courthouse lawn. Richard's mother didn't know about the fly, and he told her he paid you a dollar for the knife. Is that right?"

"I guess so."

Several moments of silence followed while I awaited Mom's verdict. I felt the bed jiggle, then heard Mom laughing. She continued until she pulled a Kleenex from a box and dabbed at her eyes.

I loved to hear Mom laugh, especially when I knew a pardon would follow. Perhaps I gained an advantage because Richard fibbed to his mother, while I, for all she knew, told the whole story.

That ended my confession. I didn't have to raise the most awkward issue of all – my nail-less fingers that couldn't open a knife blade. Mom wouldn't laugh at that.

When Mom finished wiping her eyes, she turned to me. "Well, my boy, it looks like I got a knife until you pay me a dollar."

How many times, I wondered, would I have to buy that thing? I parted with three quarters the first round, and now I needed another dollar. Everyone but me gained from my efforts. Mom, the current owner of the knife, joined a growing list of beneficiaries that included Dad, Mr. Rowley, Governor Hickenlooper, and Richard Beane. I was supporting everyone, and with nothing to show for it but a debt and a growing list of bad memories that started with creepy spiders and wash-proof windows and was headed for who knew where.

"How am I gonna earn a dollar?"

"Run along to bed. We can talk about that tomorrow."

I did go to bed, but I couldn't wait to talk about earning a dollar. Big money matters weighed on me.

"Gab, Mom says I owe her a dollar and I ain't got no money."

"Now what'd you do?"

"Ya know the knife I bought with the money I got for cleaning Dad's windows?"

"Yeah, what about it?"

"I traded it for a fake fly Richard Beane got at Pinky's."

Gab sat up in bed. I had his attention.

"Hey, neat. Lemme see it."

"I can't. The fly fell off in the courthouse grass and I couldn't find it and Richard said he paid a dollar for it and Mom gave Mrs. Beane a dollar and now she says I gotta pay her back and . . ."

"Slow down, little brother. Are ya gonna beat Mom out of a buck?"

"I don't wanna. But I ain't got no money. Got any ideas?"

A pause followed. Gab had ideas for everything. "Jack Lee sold some salve and earned some money. There's an ad for it on the back of my 'Plastic Man' comic book."

"Who'd buy salve?"

"Relatives and neighbors. They're suckers for kids sellin' stuff."

"Why don't you sell salve, Gab, if you know all about it?"

"That's for kids. Not enough in it for me."

Maybe Gab didn't find "enough in it," but I did. A dollar would get me out of debt with Mom. Getting the knife back was only a reminder of a bad habit, but being on good terms with Mom was important.

The next morning, I took Gab's comic book to Mom and showed her an ad for UCA-Mentho salve.

"What does this say, Mommy? Gab says Jack Lee earned a dollar selling this stuff."

"Let's see. Well, you send four dollars to their company in Chicago. They send you twenty tins of salve that you sell for a quarter apiece. You keep the dollar that's left over."

Mom's arithmetic was too fast for me. I did understand the part about earning a dollar.

"Where would I get four dollars? I already owe you one."

"What if I loaned you the money? When you sell the twenty cans, you can give me the five dollars, we'll be even, and you can have your knife back."

Mom made it sound easy.

"Who would buy the salve?"

"Oh, I imagine your grandmothers, the Elys, the Vincents, maybe Father O'Sullivan. We could use a couple of cans. It says it's good for chigger and mosquito bites."

Mom filled out the coupon on the comic book and cut it out neatly with her sewing scissors. She addressed an envelope to the UCA-Mentho Laboratories in Chicago, Illinois, and let me lick the three cent stamp.

"That's done," she said. "Now all we need is a money order. We can get that at the post office and send the letter at the same time."

Mom disappeared into the family closet. She always closed the door behind her when withdrawing cash from her sewing money account. I never knew what went on inside, except she returned with a smile and her pocketbook.

Three games of "making candy" and a lot of skipping on my part took us to the post office. Mom filled out a light blue form she called a "money order" and handed Mr. Houk some dollars. She placed the form in the envelope, let me lick the flap, sealed the letter, and dropped it into the mail slot.

"There," she said. "You're in business."

I liked the sound of her words. I would soon be working for the UCA-Mentho Company.

Two weeks later, a small box addressed to Carroll Ray McKibbin, 605 Main Street, Guthrie Center, Iowa, was delivered to our front door. I filled with pride at the sight of my name on an address. Mom opened the carton with a paring knife. Inside, four stacks of five cans each greeted my eyes. The tins were the size of Mom's oatmeal cookies, the thickness of a deck of cards, and decorated on the side with blue and yellow checkers. A lengthy list of ailments the salve would "aid in the treatment of" was written on the back. Some, like cuts and sores and colds, I recognized. Others, like erysipelas and catarrh, I didn't, but they sounded important and menacing. I knew the word "piles," but wondered, "piles of what?"

I was ready to start my career as a salesman. "Can I go now, Mommy?" I asked.

"It's a little late in the day. What say we get you cleaned up and underway after breakfast tomorrow?"

The next morning I gulped down the last spoonful of Pep cereal and asked again, "Can I go now, Mommy?"

"Okay, okay. Go get into your Sunday school clothes."

I raced up the stairs. No bib overalls this time. I dressed in my good clothes that hung together in my bedroom closet: a white shirt, tan sports coat, gray wool trousers, and Buster Brown shoes. The coat was warm, the pants itchy, and the shoes stiff, but all discomfort disappeared in the enthusiasm of going door-to-door as spiffed up as the Electrolux man.

I zipped downstairs for inspection. Mom checked my ears, inspected my neck, combed my hair, and pronounced me fit for duty. "Looks like you're ready to go," she said. "When people come to the door, tell them you're a representative of the UCA salve company and have a product good for their health for only twenty-five cents. Whether they buy or not, be sure to tell them 'thank you.' And don't forget to say 'please.' You can't say 'please' too often."

"What do I call people, Mom?"

"Misses or miss or mister or ma'am or sir. Do not use first names. Put these nickels and dimes in your right pocket for change, and put the money people give you in your left pocket. Your customers should give you a quarter, two dimes and a nickel, or a dime and three nickels. If it gets more complicated than that, just let them make their own change with your extra dimes and nickels. Okay? Now, here's an old purse of mine that'll hold ten cans. If you sell all those, you can come back for more. Are you ready?"

Was I ready! I was dressed up, fired up, and ready to join the ranks of the salesmen who came to our door. They sold Electrolux vacuum sweepers, Fuller brushes, and Jewel Tea products. I sold UCA salve. I skipped straight to Grandma McKibbin's little brown house a block away and knocked at her door.

"Grandma, ma'am, please would ya like to buy some salve please. Only twenty-five cents. It cures a whole bunch of stuff," I spouted as soon as the door opened.

My grandmother invited me to come in for a visit and refreshments. With a quarter in my cash pocket and a glass of lemonade in my tummy, I told grandma good-bye and moved on to my next customer, Aunt Edri. Again, I was invited inside, this time for finger sandwiches with the crust removed and a glass of milk. Next, I climbed the hill to Grandma Phippen's house. I closed that deal and stayed to listen to "Boston Blackie" and eat a couple of chocolate chip cookies.

Additional stops at friends and neighbors emptied my satchel of UCA salve and filled my cash pocket and stomach. I returned home with money, but no appetite.

I sold out the next day to other friends and relatives, repaid my debt to Mom, and regained possession of a knife I no longer wanted. I dropped the bad memory into a drawer in my little rolltop desk, where it remained beside a "Clean House with Dewey" button for years.

My first sales effort was an outstanding success. I had a good time, made money, and paid off my debt to Mom. I was still broke, but had the feel for easy money. Why not a second round to earn a dollar for myself?

"Mom," I asked. "Could you loan me four dollars for another box of UCA salve?"

"Don't you think you saturated the market?"

"What does that mean?"

"It means you have sold salve to all the customers that are interested in buying."

"You bought two cans. And UCA salve is good for you. It cures a whole bunch of stuff."

Like the salesman I had become, I rattled off my line as though I believed it. I was ready for another round of hugs and cookies and a pocket filled with coins.

"Are you sure you want to go again? People who don't know you may not be so willing to buy. You'll owe me another four dollars, you know."

Mom was enthusiastic the first time. Why, I wondered, did she turn into a spoilsport? She dropped her questioning, however, and agreed to the loan. Two weeks later, a second box of UCA salve arrived. I was charged up and ready for another round of fun, food, and fast money.

Unlike my first effort, when each stop registered a sale, my second round to non-friends, non-neighbors, and non-relatives didn't go as well. The itch of my Sunday school pants, the pinch of my shoes, and the sweat from my wool jacket returned. Tank Hill and Main Street Hill became steeper. I strayed farther and farther from home. I was getting more "no thank yous" and "come back tomorrows" than sales. A scary, barking German shepherd raced at me until a long leash, unseen by me, stretched tight and yanked the dog off its feet. I bypassed that house. At the next one, a lady was sleeping on a sofa. I could see her through the screen door. She wasn't wearing much. I didn't want to disturb her. I waited at the door, watching and waiting, but mostly watching. When she didn't wake up after ten minutes, I decided to call it a day and go home.

"How did it go?" Mom asked.

"Only sold two cans. A dog ran at me, no one invited me in for lemonade, and a lot of people said to come back another time."

"You can get a fresh start tomorrow. Maybe some of the merchants downtown would be interested."

Mom was full of good ideas. I hadn't thought of the people downtown. They had cash registers full of money.

The next day, fresh and clean, I headed for the business district and quickly racked up a sale with Mrs. Millhollin at the Square Deal. My next stop was Dowd's Drug, operated by the father of my friend, Pink. Dressed in a white smock and a bow tie, Mr. Dowd stood behind a counter that smelled like my salve.

"Would ya like to buy some UCA salve, Mr. Dowd? It cures a whole bunch of stuff."

The tall man with a ready smile looked down at me. I held a can of UCA salve in my palm. "Carroll Ray, are you trying to cut into my business?"

Mr. Dowd made no move toward the cash register. I didn't understand his words, but assumed it meant no sale. I did make a few more sales downtown, but didn't go near Rowley Hardware, where I feared I was more likely to buy than sell, and I didn't go to McKibbin's Garage where Dad's friends might make fun of me.

On my way home, I stopped at the jail. I occasionally ran errands for the inmates that Mom called jailbirds. If they had money for cigarettes and candy bars, so I figured, they must also have money for salve. My friends at the jail were always in a good mood and ready to talk. One stood at the window facing the courthouse, a cigarette pinched between his nicotine-stained fingers and a hand grasping a rusty bar.

"You wanna buy some UCA salve? It cures about everything and only costs a quarter."

The pock-faced man pulled the cigarette to his lips, puffed smoke through the bars, and turned his head to the inside. "Hey, you cons," he shouted. "Wanna buy some salve from this kid?"

"Does it cure crabs?" a voice responded amid laughter.

"Sure," I said, with no notion of the meaning of the comment.

"You're sure gussied up today, kiddo. It ain't Sunday, ya know."

"Yeah, I know. Mom makes me wear my good clothes to sell stuff."

"Hey, you guys, what say we take up a collection and buy this little fella's salve. We could all use some help with you-know-what." More laughter followed. Two brownish fingers dropped a quarter in my hand.

Mom told me not to go near the jail. But I did, and more and more with the passage of time. The men inside were nice. They laughed and talked and sent me on nickel-earning errands. Tramps passing through town stopped at the jail and added to the fun. Hair Breath Harry traded me poems he wrote on scraps of paper for a peanut butter sandwich I fetched from home. Sack Shoe Sam wore gunny sacks wrapped about his feet for shoes, securing them around his ankles with jar rubbers. During one of my mid-winter visits to the jail, Sack Shoe showed up with a dead rabbit he peeled off Fifth Street. The animal he slung over his shoulder by its ears was a mangled mess of fur and blood, and rolled as flat as Mom's pie crusts. Sack Shoe leaned the board-solid remains against the wall of the jail and said he was having rabbit stew for supper.

"Are you really gonna eat that squashed rabbit, Mr. Sack Shoe," I asked.

"Sure, kid. Wanna join me?"

"Uh-uh. Why would you eat something like *that*?

"Look, sonny, life's nothing more than something to eat and a place to sleep."

The never-forgotten dismal words of Sack Shoe Sam spurred my efforts to sell more UCA salve. Money would buy a Whiz candy bar that was a lot more appetizing than a flat rabbit with tire tracks across the back.

Two weeks of climbing hills, knocking on doors, and hearing "no thanks" left four tins of UCA salve in my pocketbook satchel. I was tired of selling, tired of climbing, and tired of wearing Sunday school clothes. I had the four dollars to pay off my debt to Mom and four leftover tins, enough salve to combat a lifetime of mosquito and chigger bites.

"Mom, I can't sell no more of this stuff. I've been to every house and store in town." I held out a palm full of change. "Here's the four dollars I owe you."

"You know, sweetie, Christmas is coming. What if I bought the last four cans for presents?"

Mom's offer sounded good to me, but I wondered who she might surprise with a gift of UCA salve. Anyone on her gift list already had a tin or two of my miracle product. The family supply in our bathroom cabinet, plentiful at two cans, increased to six. Christmas came and went, and many more thereafter. The six UCA cans remained on the top shelf, neatly stacked, unopened, and rusting.

Mom's dollar bill felt weightless and strange in a pocket accustomed to a few pennies. No matter. The dollar wouldn't be in my pocket long. I ran downtown with a shopping list running through my mind. I would buy gifts for Mom and my grandmothers, my best salve customers; a toy for myself; and a haircut.

Beach's Five and Ten was my first stop. I hesitated, and then walked past the glass candy case with bins of red hots, spice drops, and orange slices. I moved on to counters of treasures separated into squares with glass dividers. At the back of each square, a red price tag in a metal holder told me how much money I would have to sacrifice.

Searching for the right gift for Mom, I sorted through unfamiliar woman things: long-handled combs, barrettes, and lipsticks. Thirty minutes of looking produced nothing until I found a round, plastic lapel pin with a gold edge, a purple background, and a gold star in the middle. "Gold Star Mother" read the attached card. I knew gold stars on window service banners were special and those at Sunday school meant perfect attendance. Mom was special and perfect. Easy decision. She deserved the pin and credit for being a "Gold Star Mother," although that title, unknown to me, was reserved for mothers who had lost a son in the war.

After my initial purchase had converted my dollar to ninety cents in change, I placed two quarters in my left pants pocket for haircut money and moved on to look at toys. I discovered a red top the size of a coffee can and shaped like a Buck Rogers space ship. A yellow thunderbolt, like the one on Captain Marvel's chest, was painted on the side. A handle on top, when pumped, energized the toy and sent it spinning. The irregular wooden floors of Mr. Beach's store didn't provide the best surface for the top, but I saw the potential. I parted with another thirty cents and began my search for gifts, two nickels in hand, for my salve-buying grandmothers. Clear plastic salt and pepper shakers caught my eye. Two grandmothers, two shakers, two nickels – perfect. Grandma Phippen would get the shaker with the black cap and Grandmother McKibbin the one with the white cap. With a sack of gifts and two quarters remaining for a haircut, I skipped to Mr. Sanger's barber shop.

The decision to buy a haircut was easy. Mom saw my luxurious curls as a shrine requiring regular and careful maintenance. To Dad, my hair was a mop that drained his change purse of fifty cents every six weeks. Haircut days caused tension between Mom and Dad, with me in the role of a pawn and beggar. I was happy to pay the price of freedom. Besides, Mr. Sanger's large expanse of linoleum offered a wonderful arena for my new toy.

While waiting my turn for a haircut, I prepared my top for its debut. I pumped the handle furiously and turned it loose. *Whireeee* it screeched across the flat floor, flashing red and yellow as it glided about like Sonja Henie. When the top ran out of energy, slowed to a wobble, and finally tipped over, I ran after my toy, pumped it up again, and set it free. *Whireeee* it shrieked.

I loved the high-pitched sound, the whirling colors, and the spinning haphazard path of my new toy. I pumped it up again and again, scurrying after it, and setting it free over and over. *Whireeee.* The top bumped against Mr. Sanger's foot and stopped. In my excitement, I had forgotten the presence of others.

Mr. Sanger looked down at me with his hands on his hips. "Kibbie, why don't you put that thing away and play with your peter." The several waiting customers laughed. I understood it was time to quit playing with my top, but didn't understand Mr. Sanger's suggestion.

Grandma Phippen slapped my hand when I was in the bathtub playing a solo game of doctor. "Don't play with yourself," she scolded.

Later, when I complained to my mother that I had no one to play with, she said, "Play by yourself."

"I can't," I replied. "Grandma told me not to." Now Mr. Sanger also talked of something that made Grandma scold, Mom frown, and men laugh.

My beggar-free haircut took my remaining money, but I

was happy. I ran home with my sack of gifts, thrilled at the prospect of giving Mom the special brooch.

"Look, Mom, I got a really neat pin for you."

My mother set down her rolling pin and wiped hands dusty with flour on her apron. "That's awfully nice of you. Let's see what you've got."

My open palm held the lapel pin with the gold star. Mom's reaction didn't match my enthusiasm.

"Aren't you gonna put it on?"

"Yes, of course. Here, help me attach it to my apron . . . doesn't that look nice?" It did. I smiled with great satisfaction.

Someone knocked at the front door. Mom removed the pin from her apron and slipped it into her pocket before responding. I wondered why. I thought she would wear my gift with pride. When Sunday came and we prepared for church, I was sure Mom would display the new pin on her best clothes. She didn't.

"Mom, doncha like your gold star pin?" I asked.

My mother drew me close and gave me a big hug. "Of course I like it. It is so precious I only wear it around the house. I wouldn't want to lose it like your fly."

Mom had a point. Case closed.

Chapter 7

Money Matters

I lost a fake fly but gained an appetite for what money could buy. I felt the joy of giving when Mom wore her gold star pin and my grandmothers displayed their, one each, salt and pepper shakers. I felt the delight of adding a toy top to my few possessions. But most importantly, I felt liberated from begging for haircut money.

Dad wasn't on my gift list. He didn't hug me, hold me, or hand me cookies. His contributions to the household, the roof over our heads and the groceries he lugged home, went unnoticed when compared to a warm oatmeal cookie accompanied with a smile and a kiss. Besides, he had a wallet in his chest pocket that was warmed by his heart and lined with enough green bills to supply everyone in town with popcorn. My conscience gave me a full pardon for tricking, fooling, or bamboozling my dad. He didn't share nice.

"Gab," I asked. "Why doesn't Dad like us?"

"Because we're on his shit list."

"What'd we do wrong?"

"We asked for money."

I understood Gab's point. I wanted to get along with Dad, and learn about cars and guns and fishing. Money was the roadblock. He seemed to think children should be no trouble and no expense. I worked at staying out of mischief, but with the town loaded with UCA-Mentho salve, my income was reduced to an occasional nickel errand for my jailbird friends and a weekly five pennies from Mom's sewing money.

I felt some sympathy for Dad when I handed over two hard-earned quarters – enough for five movies or ten candy bars – to Mr. Sanger for a haircut. Picture shows, however, were different. I considered the Garden Theater's Saturday matinee a God-given right, a necessity for which Dad was the custodian of a dime. Mom gave me a dime to buy a war bond stamp at school and another to drop in the collection plate at church. All three dimes went for a worthy cause: one for Uncle Sam to buy bullets, one for Jesus to make us good, and one for Ted Allen to bring us Tarzan movies.

Dad coughed up ten cents for a trip to the Garden Theater with less grief than a half dollar for a haircut. I figured the rate of return at a penny per minute while Dad puttered and fiddled around his shop before finally unshackling a dime from his Fig Newton-shaped change purse. With thoughts of spending an afternoon with Bugs Bunny and Roy Rogers, I didn't mind a ten-minute wait. Haircut days were another matter.

When my hair reached the length of a curly-headed sheep dog, my mother called to me: "Carroll Ray, go to your father and get money for a hair cut."

Mom made it sound easy. It wasn't. Dad's bag of tricks for avoiding money requests included temporary deafness. I repeated three or more times, with courage-building intervals: "Mom says I need a haircut."

I didn't mention the amount. He knew. Dad thought barbers and picture show operators were getting rich by gouging unsuspecting customers. Eventually, he spit out his usual response: "Ya don't need no haircut."

I returned home, knowing Mom would be miffed, and said my lines: "Dad says I don't need no haircut."

A phone call followed. "Eldon, I sent that boy to get a haircut . . . I know business has been slow . . . I'll give up something else. I'm sending him back."

Mom hung up the phone, turned to me, and smiled. "Your father is waiting for you." Her manner and words gave the impression he was throwing a party in my honor. I knew better. Her good humor and persistence were impressive, but she wasn't the one sent trudging back to McKibbin's Garage for round number two.

Just once, I hoped my dad would smile and greet me with: "Hi, kiddo. Looks like you need a haircut. Here's fifty cents for that and a nickel for an ice cream cone." It never happened. Instead, I stood at the garage door quietly waiting, and waiting some more.

"Mac, isn't that one of your boys?" a man asked from the loafers' bench at the front of the shop. Dad turned my direction as though surprised by my presence. Resigned and unhappy, he walked toward me and slapped two quarters against my palm. I fled for the barber shop.

Mom claimed boasting rights on a physical feature of each of her sons. Darrell was tall, several inches taller than Dad, and over six feet when he entered high school. Gab had long and slender fingers suitable for piano playing. I was the shortest in the family and had chewed stubs for fingers, but on top of my head grew waves and curls as thick as sheep wool.

Darrell grew taller and Gab's fingers grew longer, but neither as quickly and costly as the care and clipping of my curls.

Mom's treasure was Dad's curse and caused friction. They negotiated a truce and instructed Bill Sanger to clip the sides of my head just short of scalping and let the mop on top grow like a tropical forest. I looked like a hedge, but didn't care much so long as family unity followed.

The peace of mind I had purchased with a fifty-cent haircut was threatened when my curls, as usual, sprouted quickly and reached for my ears and beyond. I had no money for another haircut and dreaded the prospect of again shuttling back and forth between 605 Main Street and McKibbin's Garage.

Cutting hair didn't seem difficult. Mr. Sanger snipped and jabbered and laughed all day. Why not do it myself? When Mom went on an errand, I seized the moment and her do-not-touch scissors from atop the sewing machine. I stood in front of her tall fitting mirror and grabbed a strand of curls. Snip. I grabbed another. Snip. And then another. Snip-snip.

Sure enough, the scissors cut hair easily. Clumps of curls fell to the linoleum floor, some catching on my neck and arms and making me itch. I didn't care. I had discovered a cheap and easy solution to the hair problem. Snip. Snip-snip-snip.

Cutting hair was a cinch. Making it look right wasn't. The more I cut, the less I liked what I saw in the mirror. My hair was longer on the right side than the left. A round of scissor-work took care of that, but now the top was too long. A clip and a snip fixed that. Now my head looked like a deflated basketball. More clipping made matters worse. Less and less hair remained and I couldn't start over. I looked like a half-sheared sheep. I turned away from the mirror. Tears flowed.

I was still standing with my back to the mirror and hands

dangling at my side when Mom returned a few moments later. Her precious sewing scissors hung from a hand. Piles of curls lay on the floor. Her sorry sight of a son with a scalp of swatches of hair and whiskered bald spots awaited the words of punishment. Instead, I heard laughter I did not share. Mom capped her amusement with a hand over her mouth.

"Can you fix it, Mommy?" I wailed.

She paused to catch her breath. "I'm afraid it's too late for that. What got into you?"

I hung my head and sputtered words between sobs. "I didn't want . . . Dad . . . to pay for no more haircuts . . . and I don't have no money."

Hands on my shoulders drew me to the warmth of my mother. A gentle hug and love rubs on my back followed. I looked up at smiling, glistening eyes.

"You won't have to bother with that anymore. And don't worry about your hair, it will grow back more beautiful than ever. Now, put my scissors back where they belong and let's see if Bill Sanger can improve your hair style."

Muffled laughter rumbled at the Ideal Barber Shop that afternoon while customers in bib overalls and baseball caps watched Bill Sanger's barbering skills fully tested by the scraggy turf on my head. Mom endured it all, sitting uncomfortably in a print dress and white sandals amid cigar smoke and spittoons. She had whispered word of my hair-cutting venture to Mr. Sanger when we arrived. He played it straight. "So you wanna be a barber, Kibbie," he said. "Got plenty of work 'round here. Come by anytime."

Bill Sanger did his best to cover up my handiwork, but my hair was still patchy and uneven, looking like a tooth brush in one spot and a bald tire in another. Mom brought along a red corduroy cap for me to wear home, one with ear flaps I seldom used. This time, I pulled the flaps over my ears and tied them snuggly under my chin, hiding as much of my nearly hairless head as possible.

The supper table was quiet that evening. Dad hardly looked up from his plate. Darrell, with much of his head covered with scars, seemed sympathetic, but said nothing. Mom tried to jump-start a conversation without luck. Gab stared and grinned. I could feel his about-to-burst curiosity. I would be at his mercy as soon as we were alone.

At bedtime, Mom tucked us in and closed the bedroom door with a "good night and sleep tight" to her two youngest sons.

"Good night, mother," Gab said.

I heard the folks' bedroom door open and close. Gab began to chuckle. He chortled. He hooted. He laughed at tear-spilling levels at my expense. I nearly glowed in the dark with embarrassment. A question would come, I was sure, when he regained control.

"Hey, Ked, who fucked up your hair?"

"Me, I guess."

"What the hell for? You're a sorry looking little shit, I can tell you that."

Gab didn't need to remind me. I already worried about how long my hair would take to grow back.

"I didn't want to ask Dad for haircut money no more and make the folks fuss."

"Yeah, I know whatcha mean. Ya gotta wise up."

Gab seemed surprisingly sympathetic. I didn't understand "wise up," but had noted that everyone in the family had money but me. Dad kept his dollars and coins snapped tightly in the chest pockets of his bib overalls. Mom hid her sewing money in some mysterious location in the family closet. Darrell earned money working at the Garden Theater, and Gab, who seem-ingly had no income, always had money for popcorn and pool and an occasional chocolate sundae. He and his buddies slipped each other into the picture show through the back door. Beyond that, I wasn't sure what he meant by "wising up." I hoped to find out.

I went to sleep that night worried about my scruffy scalp, but content with Mom's promise to rescue me from haircut money trips to Dad's garage. My hair grew quickly and Mom kept her word. With her money on the line and now in full control of my locks, she instructed Mr. Sanger on sculpturing my curls. I was relieved to get rid of the hedge look but would have accepted anything, including a Toni Home Permanent, to avoid facing Dad on haircut day.

Bill Sanger's invitation to visit his barber shop, haircut or not, was a side benefit to my haircutting venture. I stopped by the Ideal Barber Shop at every opportunity, sometimes several times a day, to listen to baseball and fishing chatter and words Mom didn't want me to hear. And I didn't forget Gab's advice to "wise up." A new gum machine attached to the front of Dowd's Drug gave me an opportunity to follow-up on his tip.

The gum dispenser, the size and shape of an upright shoe box with a window, contained two stacks of chewing gum, one with red wrappers and the taste of Dentyne and the other with green wrappers and the taste of Spearmint. A penny in the slot and a push on a green or red button would drop a like-colored stick of gum into a tray at the bottom.

Chewing gum was important because it lasted longer than candy – clear through a movie and into the next day with proper overnight storage on a bedpost. Before the new machine, I either did without gum or bought a package that cost a whole nickel. I no longer faced that problem, until the afternoon I was on my way to the Garden Theater without gum and without a penny. I needed to wise up or sit through a movie minus a treat.

I had noticed trays of washers across the back of Dad's workbench. Some seemed about the size of a penny. McKibbin's Garage wasn't far away. I wondered . . .

Two greasy work shoes sticking out from under a car told me Dad was busy and could not see what I was up to. Nimbly making my way to his workbench, I selected several penny-sized washers and returned to the gum machine. I dropped a washer into the coin slot and heard the "clink" of metal on metal. A push on the green button sent a spearmint-flavored stick sliding into the tray. It worked! I had wised up with washers and gone from penniless to rich. It occurred to me I could "buy" more gum, perhaps even sell it for real pennies, but dismissed that possibility as dishonest. I watched the Hopalong Cassidy movie that afternoon feeling plush with the prospect of unlimited gum.

I developed a gum and movie routine on Saturday after-noons that started with sitting on the floor in front of Dowd's comic book rack and reading the adventures of Archie and other favorites while keeping an eye on the clock. As show time neared, I moved to the soda fountain and turned slow circles on a stool while keeping an eye on the gum dispenser. When the machine was alone and waiting, I traded a washer for gum and went to the matinee.

My conscience didn't bother me over doing business with the gum machine. I didn't know who owned the faceless, name-less device, although its attachment to Dowd's drug store was a good clue. Besides, as I figured, a washer was probably worth a penny or more anyway, and Dad had more than he needed.

My gum scheme continued without a hitch for several weeks until one day the machine didn't want my "money." I pushed and forced the washer until it disappeared from sight. The familiar "clink" didn't follow. No gum dropped into the tray when I pushed first the red and then the green button. I went to the picture show that day feeling cheated and minus the taste of spearmint. A week later, the machine vanished, along with my good fortune of free gum.

***

The removal of the golden goose of a gum machine was a blow, but I had a good run and saved three nickels along the way for my next move into the big time: a three-dipper ice cream cone at Ferguson's Bakery. I had never eaten a two-dip cone, let alone a three-dipper, but watched enviously as friends took their turns with the high-topped treat.

On a roasting hot Saturday afternoon, I marched into Ferguson's Bakery and palmed three nickels onto the counter with a "clank," like the bad guy in a western ordering a shot of red-eye. "A three-dipper cone of black walnut," I commanded in my deepest voice.

A girl in a white dress flipped open one of the metal lids that covered ice cream containers below. She reached elbow-deep inside with her scoop and emerged with a ball of off-white ice cream that she tucked, rounding here and there, into a pointed cone. Overhead, a fan turned slowly, adding little relief to the sweltering heat. The young lady added a second round dip to one that was losing its shape. Creamy liquid oozed down the cone and across her fingers. She added a third dip and handed me a cone topped with a melting mound of black walnut wonder.

The ice cream was heavy, the cone moist and dripping. I moved outside to avoid making a mess on the bakery floor and, more importantly, to have an audience on State Street for my debut as a three-dipper man.

The July sun attacked the ice cream and sent the gooey runoff down my fingers, down my arms, and dripping from my elbows. I licked here and there trying to contain the flow and clean my hands and arms. The cone softened under my grasp. The pointed bottom sprung a leak and dribbled down the front of my jeans. I licked frantically at my melting fortune. The three-dipper teetered. The cone collapsed. Falling ice cream slithered through the desperate grab of my left hand and fell to the sidewalk.

I stood stunned in disappointment. My hands were sticky and dripping, the ice cream on the warm concrete thawing quickly. An impulse to drop to my knees and lick up what I could shot through my mind. It worked for dogs, but flies with the same idea were already at work. My second thought, more appropriate for my mature seven years, was to walk away and act like I was not connected with the fly-ridden mess on the sidewalk. I took one last look at my melting fifteen cents. My splash into the big time had ended with a splash on the sidewalk. I walked the few steps to the corner water fountain and washed away the remains of a momentary triumph turned to a bad memory.

***

While recovering from the nightmare of fifteen cents worth of ice cream expiring before my eyes, the Izaak Walton League's annual children's fishing contest provided another opportunity for wising up and gaining riches. I had reached the minimum age for the event to be held at Uncle Arch's farm pond and had high hopes of catching a fish and claiming a prize.

When Uncle Arch and Aunt Mildred came to town on their regular Saturday trip to sell eggs, Gab and I caught a ride home with them to be on hand for the Sunday contest. The next morning, Uncle Arch prepared cane poles for us with twine lines and red and white striped bobbers. Gab and I skipped the short distance to the pond and joined other contestants circling the prize table and ogling rods, reels, lures, and other rewards. The fishing equipment looked interesting, but what caught my attention was a small roll of rose-colored movie tickets donated by Ted Allen, owner of the Garden Theater. Mr. Allen considered his picture show tickets legal tender and used them to pay his paper boy, laundry lady, and anyone else who would accept his cardboard money. I knew nothing of rods and reels, but I did know how to use a movie ticket. I was already thinking how I might convert Mr. Allen's prize into popcorn money.

Dozens of kids, standing shoulder-to-shoulder, lined the edge of the pond. I squirmed with the worm while stabbing the slimy brown bait on my hook. But with the prospect of winning movie tickets, I shuddered and added worm after worm until I had enough bait to feed a shark.

"Drop your hooks," the contest judge shouted. I splashed my bundle of worms into the murky green water. The red and white bobber wobbled and tipped this way and that, ready to alert me to a hungry fish on my hook.

A short time passed. The bobber jerked and dipped below the rippling surface. I yanked on my pole and watched a small fish with blue fins sail over my head and land in the grass behind. Holding the flipping fish with a foot, I ripped the hook from the poor creature's mouth and ran to the judge's table with the cold, squirming catch in hand.

"Looks like you caught yourself a blue gill," Sam Robinson announced. "Do you see a prize you'd like?"

Did I! I snatched up the small roll of tickets secured with a rubber band and jammed it into my pocket. I tossed the fidgeting blue gill back in the water and returned to my pole. My mind whirred as fast as Mom's sewing machine. According to my developing plan, I didn't dare catch another fish. I swung a baitless hook into the water and waited for the end of the contest, plotting and thinking of the popcorn ahead if my scheme played out as intended.

I would have to keep Mom and Dad in the dark, but my

conscience demanded that I tell someone. Gab was an easy choice. He was more interested in plots than virtue and had recently helped me through a conscience crisis involving a long overdue library book. I could see nickel fines spinning past my eyes like a whirling gas pump meter.

"Gab," I asked. "D'ya remember that book I showed you with the lion pictures?"

"Ya mean that silly one for kids?"

"Well, yeah, I guess so."

"What about it?"

"I kinda forgot to take it back and Mrs. Miller said I had to pay five cents for every day it was late."

Gab looked serious for once. "How long d'ya have it?"

"I dunno. A long time. There was still snow on the ground when I got it. How much d'ya think I owe?"

"A bundle. Did ya tell Mom?"

"Uh-uh. I kinda took care of it myself."

Gab leaned forward. "Where'd ya get that kinda money?"

"I didn't. I threw it in that brick thing behind Thomas Hardware where they burn trash. Was that a bad thing to do?"

"Yeah, but who'll know the difference. You're smarter than I thought."

My attention returned to the fishing contest when Mr. Robinson approached and shouted, "Pull your hooks, kids. The contest is over. Hope you had a good time."

I wound the line around my fishing pole, hoisted it to my shoulder, and walked up the hill to Uncle Arch's house. Gab soon followed. He proudly showed me an Ocean City reel he had won. "Did ya win anything?" he asked.

"I'll tell ya 'bout it later."

Cousin Eugene, his ever-present cigarette dangling from the corner of his mouth, interrupted: "If you boys want a ride back to Guthrie, let's get goin'. I've got a date tonight."

Fifteen minutes later, Gab and I were home. "Catch any fish today?" Dad asked from his rocker.

"No, not really," I replied. Since I threw the blue gill back, I didn't consider it a "catch," at least for the sake of my conscience. Dad leaned his head back and resumed his nap.

Mom, thankfully, was not home. I went upstairs to avoid her return and questions. Gab was lying on his bed reading a comic book.

"Gab, I caught a fish today, but didn't tell anyone."

"Yeah, so what?"

"Dad asked, and I said I didn't win nothin'. Should I tell?"

"What d'ya win?"

"Ten movie tickets. Ya know how Dad never gives us popcorn money? I was thinkin' I could use one of my tickets to get in and the money he gives me for popcorn."

Gab sat up in his bed. "Hey, that's good. You're comin' along. Don't tell Dad you won those tickets or he'll make you use 'em and we won't have popcorn money."

"I know, I know. That's why I told him a fib." My response rolled out of my mouth before Gab's use of "we" sank in. What did he have in mind?

"What d'ya say we go fifty-fifty on the deal. Then, if anything goes wrong, we're in it together."

"What does fifty-fifty mean?"

"It means you give me five tickets, we both get popcorn, and if Dad finds out, we get in trouble together."

Gab had a lot of experience getting in trouble and often talked his way out with awe-inspiring imagination. If Dad found out we were snitching popcorn money from him, I'd rather Gab did the talking, like a "mouthpiece" in a gangster movie. I pulled the roll of tickets from my pocket, tore off five, and handed them to my brother.

"One, two, three, four, five," he counted in verifying his take. "Okay," he announced. "We're in this together."

I didn't know if I had reinforced my scheme or been bilked, but there was no turning back. Gab and I were partners in crime.

The first few weeks of the popcorn plan went well. Dad didn't suspect anything, and I sat in the Garden Theater on Saturday afternoons watching Bugs Bunny and munching hot buttered popcorn. I figured on many weeks of matinees with goodies. Gab would be eating popcorn longer because he continued to sneak in the back door of the theater under the "Exit Only" sign, taking turns with one of his pals opening the door from the inside after using one of my fishing contest tickets for admission. "Mr. District Attorney" warned us every week on the radio that crime doesn't pay. Watching Gab made me wonder.

A ticket fee increase from a dime to twelve cents brought the popcorn scheme and picture shows to a halt. When Mr. Allen raised his price, Dad raised the roof. "Not payin' that kinda money," he snorted. It seemed like two pennies to me, but to Dad it was an outrageous twenty-percent increase. Either way, Gab and I were caught up in Dad's boycott of the Garden Theater. My brother could continue to sneak into the darkened theater, but would be minus Dad's dime for popcorn. I faced going without popcorn *and* the movie. I could get along without popcorn; I had done that for a long time. Going without a movie, however, was a near-death crisis. I never missed a Saturday matinee at the Garden Theater. I agonized over having tickets I couldn't use without getting in trouble over the popcorn plot.

Mom felt Dad's decision was harsh, but didn't want to challenge his verdict – at least not entirely. She told Gab and me to seat ourselves on the davenport after inducing her sewing money genie to hand over twelve cents. "You boys will have to alternate going to the Saturday movie. Gary, you're the older." She handed Gab a dime and two pennies. "When you get home, you will have to tell your younger brother about the movie. Understand?"

I couldn't be a tattletale, the ultimate sin of a little brother, and tell Mom that Gab would go to the movie with the help of his friends, use her money for popcorn, and pocket a profit. My disappointment showed. I had accepted hand-me-down everything, but never second-hand movies. Mom noticed my moistened eyes.

"Your turn will come," she said. I wondered when. The family pecking order always placed me at the bottom, penalizing me for being born last. I got end-of-the-line pickings on everything: my brothers' used clothes in their third cycle, fruit pies so cleaned out of goodie before I got my piece that I ate little more than collapsed crusts, and now waving a tearful good-bye to Gab on his way to a Gene Autry western.

I waited on the front porch for Gab's return, keeping an eye on the pacing Father O'Sullivan and listening to a Chicago Cubs' baseball game from Emerson Ely's booming radio across the street. When I saw my brother walking past St. Mary's Church, I ran to meet him. He had popcorn on his breath. "Was it any good, Gab?"

"Hold your horses, I'll tell you 'bout it when we get to the porch."

Gab told me about the movie all right. His version lasted as long as the film and was more fun than any western I had seen. He cut out the kissing, leaving just the good parts. "Reach for the sky, hombre, or I'll blow your fuckin' head off," Gene Autry shouted at the bad guy in Gab's account. No one talked like that in movies, but I laughed and urged my brother on. He changed the lyrics of Gene's song from "ki-yi-yippie-yippieyea" to "I'm gonna tie my pecker to a tree, to a tree. . . ." I laughed until my eyes spilled.

The next week, I attended the matinee and returned home to tell Gab about it. He yawned through my five-minute description. I didn't blame him. His version of a movie was better than what I had seen.

I saw an opportunity. "Mom, I think Gary should go to the movies all the time. He's older. My turn'll come."

Mom looked surprised and pleased. "Why, that's so generous. I'm proud of you." I beamed in response.

While Gab attended the matinee the following Saturday, Mom, as a reward for my generosity, took me to Cronk's Cafe for my first chocolate sundae. I got a double treat when Gab returned from a pirate movie and passed along his adult-rated version, mixing in pool hall poetry. "For forty days and forty nights," he began in a hushed voice, "they sailed the broad Atlantic; until upon the shore, they spied a whore, and the whole damned crew went frantic. . . ."

After Gab finished his lengthy account of the pirate movie, I raced up the hill to the home of my friend, Barry. My pal was a year ahead of me in school, smart beyond his years, and owned a green-covered Winston dictionary. We had already discovered that "nude" meant naked and "lewd" meant nasty. We now turned our detective skills to learning about Gab's word: "whore." For a frustrating hour, we turned pages and ran our fingers down columns of words beginning with "H."

Dad's boycott of the Garden Theater ended on a Sunday afternoon when birds were chirping and bees buzzing. "Your mother and me are gonna take a nap," he said. He held out a grease-lined palm with a dime and two pennies. "Doncha wanna go to the picture show?"

Dad's words and manner seemed more of a plea than an

offer. I wasn't much interested in the dull musicals or duller love stories offered on Sundays. I wanted to see Tarzan swinging on jungle vines, not Ginger Rogers swinging on the arm of Fred Astaire. Even worse was the replacement of cartoons with "Travel Talks." Instead of laughing at Bugs Bunny and hearing Porky Pig sign off a Looney Tunes comedy with: "That's all Folks," we were stuck with the dull voice of James A. Fitzpatrick droning on about the wonders of some tropical island.

Dad's unexpected offer caught me off guard. "Your mother and me need a little rest," he repeated. "Thought ya might wanna see a show."

Dad's voice seemed urgent, hinting at begging. I knew the feeling. I felt smug making him wait.

"Thanks, Dad, but I think I'll just stay home and listen to the radio," I finally responded.

"Here's a nickel for popcorn."

Dad's outstretched leathery palm now held a dime, a nickel, and two pennies. I took the bait and skipped out the door with four coins squeezed in my hand. My mind turned as quickly as my feet as I raced across the courthouse lawn. I had no intention of wasting money to watch Carmen Miranda dance with fruit on her head and sing goofy songs in another language. I could buy candy with my pennies and still have three weeks of popcorn money. Mom and Dad wouldn't know if I went to the movie or not. They would be taking a nap while I ate Tootsie Rolls and read comic books at Dowd's Drug. When the show was over and the crowd walked past, I would ask someone about the movie.

Two hours later, after reading about the adventures of Archie, Superman, and Captain Marvel, the after-show crowd filed past the large front windows of the drug store. A friend, Jack Applegate, was among them. I ran after him. "Hey, Gator,"

I hollered. "Hold up. What was the movie about?"

"Nothin' much. Just a bunch of mush and music."

"Who all was in it?"

"The woman with the banana hat and that guy with the same first name that plays the piano real good."

"Carmen Cavallaro?"

"Yeah, I think so."

With the necessary movie information committed to memory, I returned home. I hoped Mom and Dad were still napping and I could slip into the house unnoticed and unquestioned. I didn't want to get caught up in a fib. Mom, however, stood at the kitchen sink preparing supper. "Was the movie good?" she asked.

"Yeah."

"Who was in it?"

"Carmen Miranda and Carmen Cavallaro," I responded as practiced.

"Oh, yes, I love the way he plays the piano," Mom replied while still facing her work. I hadn't made up anything yet, just passed along second-hand information. I moved out of the kitchen before my mother could ask another question.

Dad sat in his rocker, relaxed and satisfied, looking at a dog-eared, grease-smudged road atlas. He took make-believe trips on Sunday afternoons, a thick finger tracing routes across the country as he murmured names of cities, highways, and directions. "Let's see . . . could take 40 into Salina . . . turn south on 81. . . go to Wichita."

In 1920, Dad drove a Model T from Guthrie Center to Los Angeles, a real adventure at the time. Cross-country roads had not been completed, motels were non-existent, and gasoline was mostly purchased at hardware stores in jerry cans that Dad strapped to the running boards of the Ford. Now, saddled with war rationing and a family, Dad traveled by road atlas, covering thousands of miles in his rocker.

I slipped past my preoccupied father and upstairs, hoping interest in my movie attendance would fade in my absence. I dropped a few coins into the toe of my Sunday school shoe hiding place and awaited the call for supper.

***

Dad's boycott came to an end that day. He could hardly complain about movie prices after pleading with me to go to the Sunday matinee. I returned to the Garden Theater the next Saturday, bought a ticket, and waited in line to hand it to the theater owner.

The chattering Ted Allen provided a warm-up act for his movies. With a glint in his eye and a mischievous grin, the jolly, pillow-soft man in rimless glasses teased and taunted his customers. He had nicknames for everyone. Rosa Hubbard, a matronly clerk at the Iowa Electric office, was "queen of the kilowatts," and Lew Messner, a man who drove a purple, slope-backed Buick, "Luther and the purple dragon." Mr. Allen, like Mr. Sanger, called me "Kibbie."

"Where ya been, Kibbie?" Ted Allen asked when I handed him my ticket. "You've missed some good shows."

"I know. Dad wonders how you can raise prices."

"Nothin' to it, Kibbie. I just changed the zero to a two. How 'bout some popcorn today?"

I had thought about movie popcorn. Down to my last fishing contest ticket, and saving money for the approaching county fair, I only had two pennies to spend. Mr. Allen, flipping a quarter between taking tickets, offered customers "double or nothing" for admission and popcorn. I couldn't risk missing a movie, but would gamble on the popcorn if necessary.

"Could I buy a penny's worth of popcorn, Mr. Allen?" I asked.

The theater owner's grin widened. "All at once? You sure

you can afford it, Kibbie? The sack costs me that much."

I felt a need to defend my offer and my ego. "I'll go double or nothing."

"Yeah, I'm sure you will. Tell you what, Kibbie. Why don't you save your pennies until you have five. Then I can sell you a whole bag of popcorn."

I went without a treat that day. A short time later, however, penny candy showed up at the Garden Theater in the form of a new jelly bean machine with a shiny red base and a glass globe chock-full of colorful candies. I felt a connection between my failed penny popcorn offer and the arrival of the new dispenser. Ted Allen had the reputation for being as tight-fisted as Scrooge McDuck. Perhaps, so I gathered, the loss of a penny sale persuaded him to go into the jelly bean business. The thought made me feel grown-up and important, like Ted Allen and I were kind of in business together. To Mr. Allen I had a name; I wasn't "you" or "one of you kids." I was Kibbie and I helped bring a new penny-a-pop jelly bean machine to the Garden Theater.

***

The summer of 1945 ended with V-J Day and a delirious celebration. The town whistle shrilled for fifteen minutes. Bottle-waving men started an impromptu parade, riding down State Street on the back bumpers of cars like Ben Hur. A spontaneous crowd gathered at the city bandstand and sang "It's a Grand Old Flag" and other patriotic songs until late into the evening. Two days of free movies, free ice cream, flags, speeches, street dances, and marching bands followed.

While Uncle Sam stood undefeated, I closed out the summer with a record of six wins and two losses. On the win side was Bill Sanger's standing invitation to visit his barber shop. I was again sitting in the front row at Saturday matinees and had tasted a chocolate sundae. My popcorn plot with fishing contest movie tickets, interrupted by Dad's boycott of Ted Allen's theater, was an overall success and went undetected by my parents. I helped bring a new jelly bean machine to the lobby of the Garden Theater, and Mom's sewing money rescued me from doing battle with Dad on haircut day.

In the defeat column, I suffered the loss of the generous gum machine and was still haunted by the sight of a three-dipper ice cream cone, all fifteen cents worth, turning to soup on a warm sidewalk.

I had wised up, in Gab's terms, and could have gone undefeated that summer with a better grasp of Mom's oft-repeated story: "The Fortune and the Beggar." How, I wondered, could the beggar be so greedy, so foolish, and keep repeating his mistake? Another opportunity to learn from Mom's story would soon arise.

Chapter 8

The Fortune and the Beggar

I loved stories. "Hansel and Gretel" at school, "Bring 'em Back Alive" at the library story hour, "Mr. District Attorney" on the radio, or "David and Goliath" at Sunday school – I listened eagerly to all of them. But my favorite, the one I asked Mom to repeat over and over, was "The Fortune and the Beggar."

Teachers, the radio, and Mom supplied the words to stories. My imagination added the pictures. As I saw it, Hansel and Gretel were lost on the trail around the lake at the nearby Springbrook State Park and Frank Buck hunted tigers and gorillas in the woods at Uncle Gilford's farm. Mr. District Attorney and his right-hand man, Harrington, operated out of the Guthrie County Courthouse at the end of our block, and David and Goliath were Glen Spillers, a slight-built man who ran the Jack Sprat grocery store, and Lawrence Reed, a 400-pound giant who sold John Deere tractors.

Mom's "Fortune and the Beggar," as with all stories I heard, took place in or near Guthrie Center. The beggar was a local man. The fairy godmother came from Exira, twenty miles to the west. The story began with Mom telling how a lonely and hungry man in tattered clothes shuffled down a dusty road. I saw the beggar making his way into Guthrie Center, trudging along the gravel road that separates the old and new sections of the cemetery. When he reached the tall concrete wall on the south side of the road, the wall that doomed Humpty Dumpty, the beggar's fairy godmother, my aunt Annie, descended from the heavens and landed in front of the poor man. My stocky aunt seemed a little heavy to float about in the sky, but had the soft-spoken saintliness of a fairy godmother.

The beggar was "Sleepy" Leib, an unfortunate man of slurred speech who dragged his feet about town. Originally, I thought of Raymond Leib as "Sleepy" in "Snow White and the Seven Dwarfs," but Mom said he was a victim of sleeping sickness and not a dwarf. I then recast him as the beggar in her tale.

As the story goes, the fairy godmother gives the beggar a paper sack and says, "I will fill your bag with as much gold as you like, but whatever touches the ground will turn to dust." The fairy godmother began dropping gold pieces into the paper sack. The beggar watched with glowing and eager eyes as his fortune piled higher and higher. When the golden mound neared the top of the bag, the fairy godmother paused and asked, "Is that enough?"

"No," said the beggar. "Keep going."

The fairy godmother added a few more pieces to the stuffed bag and paused again. "Is that enough?" she asked.

"No," said the beggar. "You can cram a little more down the sides."

The fairy godmother did as requested and asked once more, "Is that enough?"

"No," said the beggar. "There's room for a couple more on top."

The bag stretched a little more with each added piece of gold. I pleaded under my breath for the beggar to stop while he was ahead.

The fairy godmother did as the beggar asked and dropped two more nuggets on the loaded sack, bursting the paper bag and dumping all the contents on the ground. The beggar watched helplessly as all his gold turned to dust.

The moral of the story was obvious to me – as it applied to the beggar. Just once, so I hoped, he would wise up and save his fortune. I was slower to see a connection with my own bad judgment, such as loading an ice cream cone with three dippers or stuffing a gum machine with washers. Another opportunity to learn the message of "The Fortune and the Beggar" came a few months later.

On a cold November afternoon while counting the days to my eighth birthday, I played imaginary basketball in the house. I ran and jumped and tried to touch the "basket," the top of the door frame separating the kitchen from the dining room where Mom worked at her sewing machine. I tried again and again, landing each time on the hard linoleum floor with a *boom* that raised Mom out of her chair.

"Honey, please don't run in the house," she asked, as she had many times before.

Mom's pleas, "hang up your coat" or "wash your hands" or "don't run in the house," had the regularity of a clock and the impact of wall paper. I paid no attention. My running and jumping continued. Thump, thump, thump – *boom!* Thump, thump, thump – *boom!*

"Sweetheart," Mom said. "Here's a couple of pennies. Why don't you skip down to Sue's Lunch and get yourself a treat?" Mom's offer ended my game. I took the two coins and dropped them into the pocket of my jeans.

"Bundle up good," Mom said. Another oft-repeated instruction, "bundle up" meant donning a green corduroy jacket that in a prior life served as a long skirt Mom found at a rummage sale. She added a lining from the unworn edges of a frayed flannel sheet and secured wool mittens with yarn running through the sleeves. I loved the warm jacket in my favorite color, but hated the mittens. Gab had been promoted to gloves, while I was stuck with kiddie mittens. Mom's light-hearted repetition of the "Three Little Kittens Who Lost Their Mittens" didn't help.

I hated my overshoes even more than my mittens. The four-buckle hand-me-downs were too big, too heavy, and had a large red tire patch where a previous owner had met misfortune. The unsightly patch contrasted with the solid black of the overshoes and attracted unwanted attention. "Hey, tire patch, show us your clods," playmates taunted.

Sometimes I fussed about wearing overshoes. Not this time. No overshoes, no pennies, no goodies. Mom helped me with the buckles, tied the ear flaps of my red corduroy cap under my chin, and sent me on my way with a "take your time."

Three blocks of plodding in overshoes provided an opportunity to review the possibilities for spending two pennies. A penny would buy a Tootsie Roll or a cellophane-wrapped package of Walnettoes or a jaw breaker. A penny would also buy several peanuts from a vending machine near Sue's front door. The peanut machine, atop a tall chrome stand, had two glass cylinders filled with peanuts, each resting on a round metal base with a chute covered by a small metal door. One glass container was filled with small, husk-covered Spanish peanuts and the other with burnt orange candy-coated peanuts. A slot in each machine welcomed a copper coin, and a lever pushed horizontally to the side allowed a few peanuts to drop into the chute. I preferred the candy-coated peanuts, but seldom ate them because a penny only bought four or five, half the number I could get of Spanish peanuts. Quantity counted heavily in my penny-based budget. I had plenty of time to make up my mind. I was in no hurry.

I pushed open the heavy, sagging door to Sue's Lunch and stood in the black arc it had scraped through the linoleum surface. Warm swirling air smelling of coffee and frying grease swept over me from an overhead furnace fan. I warmed and relaxed. I felt free. Free to look about, free to take my time, and free to decide how to spend my two pennies.

Old Man Hansen, the one-legged owner with rumpled hair and a stubble of white whiskers, reminded me of Barry Fitzgerald. He stood on his good leg behind the far end of his unoccupied eight-stool counter, balancing with a single crutch. The stump of his missing leg, covered by a folded pant leg and pinned to the hip with a large safety pin, rested on the countertop. The elderly man worked his way back and forth along the counter as the wishes of an occasional customer required, never complaining and always standing. He said nothing to me on my candy trips, communicating instead with a look in his eye or a nod of his head while I craned over the countertop and inspected every goodie.

I removed my jacket, cap, and mittens and hung them on a coat hook. Since two pennies would buy as many candy-covered peanuts as one penny would of Spanish peanuts, I decided to go first class. I slipped a coin into the appropriate slot and slid the release lever to the right. I gave it an extra tug, as always, to make sure I received every possible peanut. Normally, the lever clicked and re-set, requiring an additional penny before releasing another round of goodies. This time, however, there was no click and no resistance when I pushed the lever. Did I receive, I wondered, a free round of the burnt orange peanuts? I placed my hand under the chute and lifted the lid. Five extra candy-covered peanuts slid into my palm. I dropped the booty into a side pocket of my jacket and pushed the lever without inserting a penny. Another round of goodies slid down the chute and into my hand.

I wondered if Mr. Hansen was watching. With no other customers, he had little to do. I looked innocently about the restaurant, keeping the old man in the corner of my eye. Sue's Lunch had seen better times. Three splintered plywood booths survived in eerie emptiness. A row of stools seated no one. A Dr. Pepper wall clock stood idle, its hands locked in time like the rest of the cafe.

The door swung open. Dutch Laude, Sue's other regular customer, entered and took his usual perch on stool number five. He wore, as Mom called it, "bachelor gray" everything: work pants, work shirt, and a short-billed cap. I felt a bond with Dutch Laude, although he never said a word to me. Together, we were the last loyal customers of Sue's Lunch.

Dutch worked as a radio repairmen through the night and spent much of the day drinking coffee on his favorite stool. Some locals considered Dutch Laude a genius, while others found him only strange. He disappeared for weeks at a time. I knew when he was gone. If he wasn't at Sue's, he wasn't in town. A tale spread after V-J Day that Dutch's absences were due to his work on the Atomic Bomb. The story was unfounded, but rumor-connected the town with the big news of the time.

Dutch Laude's gray form blocked Mr. Hansen's view of the peanut machine and put me back in business. I waited until the two were busy with their usual routine. Old Man Hansen hovered over his customer, coffee pot at the ready, while Dutch alternated sips of coffee with puffs on his cigarette. He stared straight ahead, his thin lips drawn tight in a perpetual semi-smile, never saying a word, only raising his cup when he needed a refill.

I went back to work harvesting peanuts. While stuffing

my pockets, my conscience showed up. Each push on the lever produced a twinge of guilt not experienced when dropping a washer into Dowd's gum machine. Was it because I was contributing nothing to the machine? Was it because others were present? I didn't know the source of my concern, but was beginning to feel the impact.

I also felt an urgent need to report to the bathroom. I was not allowed to leave the house without "doing my chores." In the rush to get to Sue's, however, I overlooked Mom's rule and she didn't notice. I could hold off my conscience awhile, but Mother Nature might not be as patient. I had to go bad, but wasn't yet ready to give up my good fortune.

Shifting foot to foot and clamping my legs together did little to relieve the painful pressure "down there," as Mom called that location. She also said: "Mind over matter works miracles." I was praying for one. Mother Nature was becoming more and more insistent. She had won out before, and I didn't want to face that humiliation again.

As the quantity of peanuts in the machine became smaller, my bladder and conscience problems stretched larger. My jacket pockets were full. I wouldn't be like the beggar in Mom's story. I would quit while I was ahead. Besides, I had run out of space for more candy-covered peanuts. I slipped out of Sue's Lunch without a backward glance at Old Man Hansen.

I emerged from the cafe into the gray shadows of the late afternoon and slogged my tire-patched overshoes toward home. My hands grew cold from the lack of mittens that, in my haste, were left dangling from my jacket sleeves. I struggled to walk faster, but the jumbo overshoes refused. I needed to get home before declared AWOL by Mom, before Mr. Hansen discovered his missing peanuts, and before I wet my pants.

I tried unsuccessfully to leave my conscience at Sue's

Lunch. Did I hear footsteps behind me? Had I been discovered? Surely it wasn't Old Man Hansen; he couldn't move very fast on one leg. I couldn't walk any faster and running was out of the question. I pushed past the courthouse and across Sixth Street toward St. Mary's Church. Clop, clop, clop. I was in the home stretch. Clop, clop, clop. The last rays of the afternoon sun reflected off the white clapboard siding of our house. I would be home in a minute with a fortune in candy-covered peanuts.

Ker-plop! Something tripped me in front of the church. I broke my fall with bare hands that skidded along the pigeon-spattered sidewalk. Skidding knees ground holes in my jeans, and the jolt of the fall spilled peanuts and Mother Nature's contents.

I lay dazed on the sidewalk, wet and defeated and covered with peanuts. St. Mary's pigeons, showing no regard for my plight, arrived in hordes and gorged themselves in their own version of "The Fortune and the Beggar."

I rose to my feet among fluttering birds and assessed the damage. My hands and knees hurt, but not as much as my pride. I couldn't tell Mom the truth about stealing peanuts and wetting my pants. I needed a dignity-saving story.

The pigeons were delighted when I cleared my pockets and conscience of the pilfered peanuts. I stretched out on my stomach on Father O'Sullivan's snow-covered lawn and played a round of face-down snow angel, trying to mix the moisture from internal sources with that of the outdoors.

My story was developing. I would confess to unintentionally getting my jeans wet while playing in the snow, a small offense. I once hid the evidence of a wet bed by making it before Mom found out. She changed the bedding that day and didn't say anything, so I figured my scheme worked. I could fool her again. As for the torn jeans, I would say the holes were caused by a fall. My scraped knees and hands would prove that.

I looked at the sidewalk to see what caused my fall. The concrete was level and clear in front of St. Mary's. What made me tumble? Mom said a church was God's house and He lived there. The conclusion was obvious: God tripped me for being bad. I was humbled at the thought as I staggered home and opened the kitchen door with an invented moan: "Mommy, I was playin' in the snow and got my jeans all wet and tripped and fell when I was trying to get home before I caught cold."

My mother stepped away from her dishwashing, wrapped an arm around me, and wiped my crocodile tears with the hem of her apron. "Let's get you out of those wet clothes and see where you hurt. Some Epsom Salts will fix you up."

I knew what Mom would say before she said it. She had two remedies for medical problems: stinging Epsom Salts for healing everything on the outside and an enema, a word she avoided in favor of the more discreet "physic," for all internal problems. I was relieved to remain upright this time without my nose pressed against the braided rug on the bathroom floor and Mom's notion of internal medicine plugged into my backside.

After my knees and hands received Mom's Epson Salts treatment, I dressed in clean flannel pajamas and went to the kitchen table where my mother sat. A cup of hot chocolate topped with tiny, floating marshmallows awaited my arrival. Mom patted my hand and smiled. I seized the opportunity. "I'm sorry, Mommy, for tearing my jeans and getting them wet."

"Don't worry, I'll give them a good wash. They smell a little musty anyway. When they dry, I'll patch them up as good as new." I sensed Mom knew more than she was letting on. She always did.

***

My dignity survived the peanut plot and my skin healed, but my conscience took a beating. I owed Mom one, and I knew exactly how to make it up to her. I would redouble my efforts to become a musician.

Mom loved music. In 1928, she purchased a Monarch piano and had it shipped from Chicago. She had no formal music training, no piano lessons. Nonetheless, she mastered "The Missouri Waltz" and "Beautiful Ohio" by placing a cardboard chart behind the keyboard and following the indicated finger placements. Numerous repetitions followed until an untrained ear could not tell the limits of Mom's training and would never know her repertoire was limited to two songs.

My mother hoped her three sons would share her interest in music. She started Darrell on piano lessons at an early age, but with little luck. Her first-born was more interested in using his hands to construct model airplanes. Mom saw Gab's long fingers as particularly suited for piano playing, but he preferred to use them to hold a pool cue.

Her last hope for a musician son had anything but piano hands. Short, stubby fingers with nails chewed to the nub were not a good match for the beautiful ivory keys of her prized piano. Mom never mentioned playing the piano to me, but she wanted a musician in the family, one way or another. Before I could refuse, before I could read, Mom took her third-time-is-a-charm son to the local bandmaster, J.R. Compton, and presented me as a budding musician. "This is my son, Carroll Ray," she said. "He would like to learn to play a musical instrument. What would you recommend?"

Mr. Compton, who played a violin with a handkerchief under his chin when not directing the high school band, looked the part of a musician. He had long and silvery hair, round rimless glasses, and resembled Tommy Dorsey.

"Mrs. McKibbin, I think we better start your son on a tonette and teach him to read music."

"What's a tonette?" Mom asked.

"Here, let me show you." Mr. Compton pulled a black plastic fife of sorts from a cardboard carton the size and shape of a toothpaste box. The instrument had a slotted mouthpiece and, at the opposite end, a small opening for the music to exit. In between, a row of holes allowed fingertip placements to produce different notes. I listened while the bandmaster ran through his rendition of "Twinkle, Twinkle, Little Star."

The maestro handed me the tonette. "Here, Carroll Ray, give it a try." I didn't like the taste of tobacco and whatever else had passed Mr. Compton's lips that day, but surprised myself and delighted my mother when something resembling music came out of the eight-inch instrument. Soon thereafter, I became a member of J.R. Compton's Tonette Band.

I learned quarter notes get one count, half notes two, and led a Fourth of July parade down State Street as part of the "Spirit of '76." With a bandage stained with tomato juice around my head and my tonette sticking out the side of my mouth like a real fife, I played "Yankee Doodle" and marched before a cheering crowd with two boy drummers who pounded away on oatmeal box "drums".

Mom was pleased with my interest in music and impatient for me to move on to a real instrument. A year later, we returned to the high school band room with its wooden floor and overhead steam pipes. "Don't you think, Mr. Compton, that Carroll Ray is ready for a real musical instrument?" Mom's voice reflected more insistence than inquiry.

"Well, perhaps he is. He is doing fine in the Tonette Band."

Mr. Compton drew me toward him. "Let's see your embouchure."

I wondered what the fancy word meant and what he planned to look at. He pulled my lips this way and that and looked at my teeth, like a horse trader in a western. He continued to search my mouth for several seconds before pronouncing, "I think he has an embouchure suitable for a clarinet. Would you like to try one?"

"Yes, he would," Mom answered before I could respond.

Mr. Compton opened a narrow case, fit the pieces of a black instrument with silver keys together, tightened the reed against the mouthpiece, and handed me the clarinet. "Here, place your fingers like this, lick the reed, and blow into the mouthpiece."

I was Artie Shaw. I was Bennie Goodman. I was ready for action, but nothing happened. Not a sound. I blew harder. Still nothing.

"Breathe from the diaphragm," the bandmaster instructed.

Mr. Compton was filled with fancy words, and I didn't know there was more than one way to breathe. It was just a habit to me, almost as natural as chewing my fingernails. He placed his hands on my shoulders. "Try it again and breathe without raising your shoulders. I'll hold them down for you."

The clarinet and I were not getting along. I didn't understand how I could breathe the way Mr. Compton required. Besides, the instrument had more gadgets than I could manage.

"How 'bout a cornet?" I blurted.

I had already lost interest in the complicated clarinet. A cornet, with only three things to push, seemed simpler. I had watched and listened with interest when James Dixon stood and played cornet solos with the high school band. With a nod of the head from J.R. Compton and a smile from my mother, I became an aspiring cornet player. All I needed was the three-valve instrument to get underway.

Mom found a used silver cornet with no case, a bell dented like a tin can, and a bent third valve with a tired spring. Thankfully, the third valve was not needed as much as numbers one and two. I learned to wedge number three back into position with a thumb, providing a hint, in my imagination, of Charlie Spivak's lip-slurring theme song.

I sat on Mom's piano bench and used the piano music holder for my practice sessions, while she worked at her sewing machine on the other side of a large arch that separated the dining and living rooms. Within easy ear range of my early honking efforts, she never interrupted, never said anything, but did keep track of the required thirty minutes of practice. I occasionally complained in the beginning about the required time, especially when I saw friends playing outside, but stopped after Mom rescued me from the peanut disaster.

I played in the Junior Band and was on my way to becoming another Harry James, my newest idol, until Mr. Compton introduced sharps and flats. New fingerings of valves and more complicated music reading were required. The third valve, now used more frequently, became a bigger problem. I had mastered "Twinkle, Twinkle Little Star" and "Jingle Bells," but the assigned song of the week, "Sweet and Low," was cluttered with so many sharps and flats that I thought about ending my music career.

I took my problem to Mom. "My third valve don't work right, Mommy, and Mr. Compton is making us play sharps and flats and . . ."

"Let's not worry about it now. I'll work with you on the music later and your father can repair the valve when he comes home for supper."

Problems seemingly beyond fixing didn't faze Mom. She met Dad at the door that evening, applied her usual kiss, and asked, "Can you fix a valve on Carroll Ray's cornet so it will go up and down correctly?"

Dad drew his pliers from a leg pocket in his overalls like a gunslinger in a western. He used his pliers to repair cars, open jar lids, and most anything else, including minor surgery on a screaming Gab when he jammed a shingle nail into his bare foot. Dad straightened the third valve stem slightly, tried it out a couple of times and, without a word, handed the cornet to me.

With Mom's help on sharps and flats and a third valve that worked better, I got the hang of "Sweet and Low" and resumed thoughts of becoming another Harry James. I could see myself with a trumpet in one hand playing "Ciribiribin" and the other wrapped around a movie star wife, like his Betty Grable. Meanwhile, I worked on "Pop Goes the Weasel."

Sitting at the piano playing my cornet became a point of pride. I was the end of the chain on other family matters: the last link in hand-me-down clothes, the last served at the table, and always the last to be mentioned. But I was the only one in the family who could read music and played in a band.

I used Mom's framed photos atop her upright piano as an audience for my daily practice sessions. The front row for my concert included Aunt Edri in a beauty contest gown with "McKibbin's Garage" across a sash; Mom and Dad in their 1924 wedding picture; Miss Thomas, Mom's favorite nurse at the Methodist Hospital in Des Moines; Gab in a winning pose at the county fair baby contest; and Darrell in a boy scout uniform.

Two other faces in the audience, both photographs of me, stirred mixed emotions. I was proud to wear an army uniform, the only khaki in the family, that Mom cut down to my size.

The other picture, that of a four-year-old boy with gapped teeth and a pile of curls, recalled a day I wanted to forget.

On a hot July afternoon, Mom and I joined a swarm of sweating mothers and crying kids for a photo-taking session in the darkened sitting room of the Cottage Hotel. The line was long and tempers short as Mr. Bandholtz, the local photographer, took pictures of children seated on a sea trunk covered with a red table cloth.

I was soaked with sweat and suffering in the heat when my turn came to pose on the trunk. Wool pants clawed my damp legs, Sunday school shoes pinched my feet, a tie strangled my neck, and my wool sports coat heated like a furnace. Bright, hot lights shined in my face. Mr. Bandholtz, under a hood like a condemned man at the stake, pointed his one-eyed camera on stilts at my nose. The crowd glared at me like owls in the woods. Sweat ran in my eyes and burned. "Smile," the photographer said.

"Hurry up!" a woman called from the crowd. I wanted to hurry up, to have something to smile about, and to escape the heat of Hell. I was so miserable that I just sat on my perch with the look of doom.

"Let's try something else," Mr. Bandholtz suggested. "Just say Sister Suzie sat at the seashore."

Nerves and gapped teeth combined to produce a half-lisped, half-whistled, "Thister Thuzie that at the theethore."

The crowd roared. I squirmed in embarrassment and fell off the back of the trunk. Mom scooped me up with a "let's get out of here," a move I welcomed, and raced us down the stairs and out the door. On a cooler, calmer day, Mom and I went to the studio of Mr. Bandholtz and produced the photo I looked at while finishing my latest tune.

Mom appeared beside the piano bench. "I really like the way you play 'You Are My Sunshine.' Keep up the good work and maybe Santa will bring you something special for Christmas."

***

The approach of another Christmas was signaled silently when Dad hauled home a fir tree from the Jack Sprat grocery store and Mom pulled down a box of decorations from a high shelf in the family closet. Marked "Xmas" in green crayon, the box was filled with joyful reminders: tinfoil icicles in rolled newspapers, gleaming globe ornaments of red and silver, tangled green wires with tiny lights, and the tree-topping angel of Mom's making with its golden hair and white paper gown.

While I carefully looped silvery icicles over sharp needles, Mom assembled her home-made fireplace, a box covered with red crepe paper and an opening cut in front. A crinkled mass of orange tissue paper placed before a tiny light bulb created the "flame."

Christmas time was underway. I knew by heart the events leading to the grand moment of opening presents. At church, after a session of singing carols, each child received a little brown sack of hard ribbon candy and unshelled peanuts. Mom served oyster stew for Christmas Eve supper and on Christmas morning I gulped down hot chocolate and home-made cinnamon rolls before racing to the front room and taking a place near the presents clustered at the foot of our Christmas tree.

"I'll pass out the presents," I volunteered. Dad dropped into his rocker, Mom and Darrell sat on the piano bench, and Gab scooted onto the floor beside me. All the Christmas rituals had been satisfied. We were ready for the main event.

I never bothered with a wish list. Socks and underwear, masquerading as Christmas gifts, showed up every year. I absorbed the disappointment while waiting for the big moment at the end of the gift exchange. Then, pretending there were no more gifts, Mom produced something unexpected and wonderful.

I nearly burst with anticipation waiting for Mom and Dad to finish opening gifts of handkerchiefs and ties. At last, at long last, Mom stood. "I wonder what else we might have?" she said in turning and walking toward the kitchen and connecting washroom. I prepared for the main event, the grand finale.

The washroom door opened and closed. Mom's footsteps neared. She entered the front room carrying a Flexible Flyer nearly as long as she was tall. This sleek, greyhound of a sled with honed runners of Gillette blue blade steel and a lacquered oak surface was the Cadillac of coasting, the king of the nearby hill blocked off for winter fun.

Gab and I shared a used rattletrap of a sled Mom rescued from a wartime scrap heap and, in an effort to make it more presentable, painted cabinet green. On Christmas morning of 1944, Gab and I were thrilled to have a sled, any sled. The war raged and American troops, including Colonel Ned Moore whose mother lived a block away, were surrounded at Bastogne. Now, with the war over and new sleds available, we were embarrassed by our high-riding model with bent runners, a steering bar frozen in rust, and broken and missing slats.

Thoughts of the ugly green sled disappeared as I took a deep breath and soaked in the awesome sight of the Flexible Flyer. My own Flexible Flyer! I would take it for a test run that afternoon. I would take it to bed with me that night.

"Here, Gary. Merry Christmas!" Mom handed the flashy new sled to Gab. He smiled a full-tooth grin. His eyes glistened with excitement behind his gold-rimmed glasses. Mine moistened too, but not from happiness.

Mom turned toward me. "And I've got something special for you. Just hold your horses."

Mom returned to the washroom. I assumed she would return with another Flexible Flyer. She couldn't carry two at once. I was the youngest and used to getting the last turn at everything. I didn't mind waiting a little longer to have a Flexible Flyer of my own.

Mom's footsteps approached. She entered the front room. She held no Flexible Flyer, no sled of any sort. Instead, she carried a small tan suitcase.

"Here, Carroll Ray. This is for you. Merry Christmas!"

I bowed my head in an effort to keep threatening tears out of sight. Eight-year-old boys, the kind adults call "little man," do not cry. Mom set the suitcase on the floor before me. Forced into the ritual of pretending happiness, I opened it. A new brass cornet reflected Christmas tree lights into my watery eyes. To please Mom, I removed the instrument from its crushed velvet bed. I worked the valves. I blew a couple of notes. The new King cornet was nice, very nice. Mom must have spent a lot of sewing money on it. But it wasn't a Flexible Flyer.

***

I could depend on Mom being home when I returned from school. She sat by the window at her sewing machine, a welcoming view while crossing our vacant lot. This day, however, a week after Christmas vacation, she wasn't in the window.

I entered the kitchen and called for her. "Mah-um." My voice echoed through the house. "Mah-um." No one responded. I moved toward the family closet where I was supposed to hang my coat and saw a note taped to the door: "Helping at church. Back by five. Love, Mom."

I sensed an opportunity. Mom's rules required changing immediately from school to play clothes and practicing my cornet for thirty minutes. From outside, I heard throngs of happy kids testing Christmas sleds on the ice slick Main Street Hill. I had time to change into my snow clothes, take a quick trip down the hill, and still practice my cornet before Mom returned. If I hesitated, the sunlight would disappear along with my chance for a quick run. I changed hastily, went to the back porch, donned my four-buckle overshoes, and reached for my sled.

Gab's sleek new Flexible Flyer, leaning against the wall next to my green eyesore, stood proud, ready, and alone. My brother wouldn't mind, I was quick to conclude, if I took his sled down the hill just once. We shared a sled before. This would be no different, and if I hurried, he wouldn't know anyway.

The Flyer followed its rope effortlessly across our snow-packed yard like a thoroughbred ready to run. Judy Riaski, dressed in snow clothes, stood on the corner across the street. "Wanna go coasting?" I called.

"Where'd you get that neat sled?" she asked.

"For Christmas . . . er . . . kinda. Wanna ride?"

"Yeah."

Three blocks of climbing took us to the top of the hill, next to the Redfern house. When I went coasting with my pals, we went down the hill lying on top of each other. Mom, for an unknown reason, told me not to ride that way with girls. I sat down in front and invited Judy to get on behind.

I had never guided a sled in a sitting position. I steered the green machine by dragging the toes of my overshoes while lying on my stomach. The steering bar of the Flexible Flyer made it possible to sit, Mom's required position with girls, and guide the sled with my feet and the rope in my hands. Judy climbed on behind, wrapped her legs around me, and rested her feet on the inside of the runners where they tipped upwards.

"Ready?" I asked.

"Yep," my passenger replied.

"Giddy up," I shouted, and pushed off into falling snow that dotted my glasses. The sled gathered speed quickly, and more speed, and more speed than I could handle. We were out of control, hanging on desperately, and heading into the unknown at breakneck speed. I had a girl clinging to my back and screaming in my ear, glasses blurred by melting snowflakes, a nose and ears freezing in the raw wind, and no brakes. We careened down the steep slope, tipping on one runner and then the other, swerving side to side, and scattering screaming climbers as we shot past.

We zoomed past the Knauer house, the Lewis house, and headed toward Sam Duttler's dehorning machine, a narrow wooden cart that held steers in place for horn removal. A slip to the right, where Mr. Duttler's machine was parked, would give us a dehorning we did not want. I leaned to the left, pushed hard with my right foot on the steering bar, and avoided the Duttler cart. But now we were heading for the ditch on the left. I corrected to the right and shot straight at Jack Laughery. He ran for the ditch, his sled sliding into our path. We went over his sled and into the air, flying toward a telephone pole. There was no guiding now. I leaned to the right and saved my head from a collision with the wooden pole. The Flexible Flyer wasn't so lucky. It took the pole head-on, right between the runners. The lacquered oak of the sled crumbled beneath me as I caromed off the pole and slid across the snow-cleared sidewalk on my chin.

I lay stunned, collecting my senses and afraid to look at the Flexible Flyer or Judy. She had flown over me and landed on her back in deep snow. She was laughing. I didn't feel like laughing. I was too dazed to feel anything. My jaw hurt, and so did my conscience when I rolled over and saw the scattered kindling wood and two shiny runners that were once a Flexible

Flyer. Gab's sled, true to its name, had shown it could fly, but did not prove to be flexible.

Blood-red drops fell to the snow beneath me. "Your chin!" Judy screamed. I touched my tingling jaw with a mitten, felt the wool dampen, and discovered a hand full of blood. Without a word, I left Judy and the remains of the Flexible Flyer behind and stumbled along the block of cleared sidewalk that separated me from home. Mom had returned to our house and saw me making my way, a mitten over my chin, through the foot-deep snow of our vacant lot. She ran to meet me at the kitchen door.

"What happened?" she cried. I didn't respond. I didn't have to. The blood and tears on my face said enough. She pulled the bloody mitten away from my jaw and shrieked at the sight of shreds of skin dangling over my exposed chin bone. "Oh, my God, we've got to get you to Doc Thornburg's right away," she gasped.

I knew my injury was serious when Mom said I needed a doctor's attention. I hadn't been under a doctor's care since the day Doc Thornburg delivered me in the upstairs den. If Mom's Epsom salts or physics didn't do the job, she called in the family medical consultant, Grandma Phippen. Grandma, born in a log cabin, learned "doctoring" from the frontier folklore of her youth. She knew when to starve a fever and how to make a hot toddy. If we were bypassing Grandma, I was in bad shape. Mom grabbed a coat and my hand and hurried me along the three-block route to the doctor's office.

"What happened, my son?" Doctor Thornburg asked. "My son" caught me off guard. Dad never called me son. I liked the sound of Doctor Thornburg's kind words.

"I slid across a sidewalk on my chin."

Doc Thornburg smiled. "Don't you use a sled for sliding?"

"Yeah, but it kinda stopped against a telephone pole." A confession to the doctor in front of my mother seemed like a good first step for climbing out of trouble. "It was my brother's," I murmured in an attempt to remove a burden from my conscience.

"I don't suppose," the doctor continued, "the sled is in any better condition than your chin. I'll put a clamp on to hold the skin together. It'll heal in no time. You're lucky you didn't break the bone."

During a very quiet walk home, I thought about the consequences of stealing and destroying Gab's sled. Since Judy was laughing, I assumed she didn't get hurt. Her parents, however, might not be happy to learn I drove their daughter into a telephone pole. Dad would be upset about a doctor bill, Mom was probably counting how many of the Ten Commandments I had broken, and I wouldn't dare be alone with Gab.

Dad, under a cold eye from Mom, quietly seethed at the supper table that evening. She never revealed what was on her mind. Gab, as it turned out, had bigger problems than a smashed sled. Mr. Dowd had paid a visit to Dad's business that afternoon and presented him with a thirty-two dollar soda fountain bill Gab had run up. My brother's generosity in treating his pals to malts and sundaes had endeared him with his friends, but sent Dad into a tizzy. Fortunately for me, Gab's problems diverted our father's anger. A stealing, sled-busting son with a bandaged chin came lower on his list of scorn than one who foolishly treated friends with money he didn't have. Gab was in no position to complain about the loss of his Flexible Flyer. He kept mum.

At school the next day, my chin heavily taped and the object of many questions, I learned Judy wasn't injured and didn't tell her parents about the accident. I was relieved on both counts.

APRON STRINGS

I thought my new King cornet might be returned and the money used to replace Gab's sled. I was Mom's last hope for a musician in the family, however, and she seldom intervened when I supplied my own punishment. I continued to follow without complaint Mom's rule of thirty minutes a day of cornet practice. I had gotten off cheap and knew it. Gab and I went back to sharing the homely green sled, also without complaint from either of us. In a way, he traded his sled for soda fountain treats and my dream of a Flexible Flyer disappeared at the bottom of a telephone pole.

The two-inch gash on my chin left a jagged scar and, as I saw it, a sure sign of manhood. I didn't cry – much. No doubt the lack of tears came more from being knocked senseless than from a display of courage. Whatever the reason, I was pleased to survive the family ordeal, proud to shake off the injury, and extremely happy to go unpunished.

Chapter 9

Sparrow in the Treetop

I had a new scar and new-found pride. Like a good boxer, I took one on the chin and got back on my feet. I measured my maturity by the frequency and quantity of tears, and amazingly few appeared during the entire chin-grinding episode. Even when Doc Thornburg washed my wound with an alcohol-soaked cotton ball, I fought off crying. I felt tougher, worthy of being called "little man," and was ready to learn more about the world of big men.

Both of my grandfathers, Henry Phippen and Joe McKibbin, died years before I was born. Mom told Gab and me at an earlier age and in a hushed voice that Bud, my only uncle living in Guthrie Center, was a woman. I didn't understand then, but had learned since, that uncles are supposed to be men and aunts women. I didn't care who was a man and who was a woman, but Bud didn't play baseball or shoot pool. That was important.

Darrell ran the projector at the Garden Theater, spent time

at high school events, and, when home, worked on his radio-building hobby behind closed doors. Gab shared his man knowledge, but he was only three years older and a lot of his information needed more than one grain of salt. Dad worked six-day weeks, ten-hour days, and showed no interest in spending time with me. My mother and I thrived on being together. She was loving, understanding, supportive, forgiving, and often saved my neck. Mom had only one drawback – she wasn't a man.

My mother would never go into a beer parlor or a pool hall, and didn't know how to drive, cuss, smoke, hunt, fish, or play baseball. She didn't even know how to spit. Her stories didn't include traveling salesmen, and she replaced barber shop words with bust and bottom and breaking wind. She called toilet paper "T.P." and used "do-do" and "bobo" for my trips to the bathroom. When I learned the Philadelphia Athletics had a pitcher named Bobo Newsome, I wondered how he could be named after *that*.

"Gab," I asked. "Why would Bobo Newsome's parents name him, ya know, *that*?"

"Oh, they didn't. That's his nickname."

"Where'd he get the nickname?"

"From other players."

"But why *that*?"

"They don't think he can pitch for shit."

***

Mom's words and interests weren't those of a man, and I didn't share her enthusiasm for sewing and cooking. My future was not at her Singer sewing machine or her Westinghouse stove, but on the Cleveland Indians' pitching mound where I planned to become Bob Feller's teammate. He went into the big leagues while still a high school student in Van Meter, forty miles down the road from Guthrie Center. If Bob Feller could make the jump from local baseball to the Cleveland Indians, so could I. In the meantime, I wanted to learn about other man things like the pool hall, fishing, and hunting.

The alley route to McKibbin's Garage, lined on the business district side by the raw brick backs of two-story buildings with unpainted staircases and smoldering, smelly incinerators, included the back entrance to Hansen's Billiard Parlor. Mom told me repeatedly not to go into the pool hall, but didn't mention looking inside. With my conscience free and my curiosity mounting, I opened the door to a loud scene of big boys and men.

"Your ass sucks butter milk when you sit in the sand," a high school boy shouted to the laughter of others. I understood the naughtiness of his words, but not the meaning. I smiled and sized up the setting.

The pool hall was long and narrow with green-topped tables two abreast, like miniature football fields, counting 2-4-6-8 from front to back. Players used long, slender sticks to poke white balls at other balls of various colors, some with numbers and some with stripes. The object of the game was clear: to knock balls into the holes on the sides.

Smiling men slumped on benches along a stark and cracked plaster wall, smoke curling upward from their cigars and cigarettes. A heavy, gray haze lingered over the low-hanging table lights like an early morning ground fog. Spittoons, as permanent as tombstones and caked with years of spit, sat on the wooden floor at the end of each bench. Foul smelling and tarnished, the brass pots stood as monuments to manhood and neglect.

Thump-thump-thump. A man pounded the rubber-tipped end of his long stick, what players called "cues," against the wooden floor. "Rack 'em, Curly," he shouted. A slight man wearing a carpenter's apron around his waist darted from behind the candy counter, herded pool balls into position with a wooden triangle, and scooped up a dime from the table rail. He dropped the coin into his apron pocket on the run as a player at another table hollered, "Rack 'em, Curly."

My eyes glowed with excitement. I wanted to enter this hall of happiness where players called each other sharks and pigeons, and men leaned across tables on one leg, like ballet dancers in bib overalls, to shoot combos and bank shots. I saw Gab thumping his cue on the floor and shouting, "Rack 'em, Curly." That night I asked him about getting in on the fun.

"Gab, how d'ya get in the pool hall?"

"Not too tough. You walk in the back door."

"Mom said not to."

"Yeah, sure. She'll never know."

"Couldn't she see you go in?"

"Haven't ya noticed, sonny boy, women don't go down alleys and they don't go in pool halls."

Gab had a point. The next day I made a beeline for the alley entrance to Hansen's. The door was open and inviting. If I stepped inside, so I could hear better, I wouldn't be breaking Mom's rule very much. Welcomed by the ripe smell of cigars and spittoons, I entered the pool hall brotherhood of older boys and men.

A few feet away, a lonely table with scattered, colored balls lured me closer. Two long cues leaned against a side pocket. No one was watching. I grasped a black ball with an "8" in a white circle and sent it rolling across the green table top. It clacked against other balls and knocked one in a side pocket. What fun! I rolled another ball across the table, and then another, and another.

"Hey, you little fart, what're you doing!" Two high school boys, Phil Bailey and Don Tallman, rushed at me. The taller one, Phil, grabbed his cue, raised it high in the air, and brought it crashing down on my head with a knee-buckling *whop!* My eyes went out of focus. Pain shot through my head. I staggered out the back door and didn't return to the pool hall for a long time. Mom said pool halls spelled trouble. As usual, she was right.

***

The bump on my head only temporarily slowed my interest in the manly arts. I turned next to fishing. I didn't care much about fishing, but wanted to spend time with my dad and talk about catfish and carburetors and catching a baseball. Dad liked to fish, and the money barrier that separated us wouldn't interfere with a free fishing trip. Maybe, so I hoped, I could even ride beside my dad in the front seat of his Hudson. I waited for an invitation. When none came, I approached Mom. "D'ya think Dad would take me fishing?"

"Why, I'm sure he'd love to take you along," she answered with a smile. "Why don't you ask him?" Mom's encouraging words and my experience didn't match. I was afraid to ask Dad for anything. Sunday after Sunday, I stood at my bedroom window, my nose pressed against the glass, watching Dad load his Hudson with fishing gear and drive away.

When I heard Mom and Dad talking downstairs about a fishing trip, I laid my ear on the floor register and listened. "Eldon," I overheard my mother say, "can't you take Carroll Ray with you. He said he'd like to go."

"He don't know nothin' about fishin'. He'd just be in the way."

"Well, he certainly won't know anything about it if you don't teach him. Why don't you give it a try?"

A long pause followed. "Oh, don't guess it'd hurt nothin'."

I jumped up from my eavesdropping position when I heard Mom coming up the stairs. The door swung open. "Carroll Ray, hurry up and get into your play clothes, your dad wants you to go fishing with him.''

Ten minutes later and dressed in patched jeans and a T-shirt, I waited by the door of the narrow garage while Dad backed out his Hudson with the care of a surgeon. I stood on the passenger side as a hint I wanted to ride in front. The car stopped. Dad leaned across the seat and opened the door. Taking the opened front door as an invitation to slide in beside my dad, I stepped onto the running board, a smile on my face, and moved toward him.

"Get'n the back," he commanded.

I did as told and assumed the required church pew position on the brown wool upholstery. Dad, with no explanation offered, went back into the house. The car windows were up and I wasn't allowed to roll them down. The summer sun blazed. Sweat rolled down my forehead and burned my eyes. I didn't want to get out of the car and risk being left behind. I sat and sweat.

Finally, Dad reappeared, said nothing, and backed the car up the alley and into the street. I knew the way to the Panora dam where Dad fished; it was the same direction as Uncle Arch's farm. We went the other direction, however, and, three blocks later, pulled up in front of the green doors of McKibbin's Garage. Dad opened the big doors like a regular business day and raised the hood of the Hudson. I sat and sweltered.

Dad went back and forth between his shop and car with cans of Pennzoil and a fistful of tools, administering to the needs of his favorite child. I hated Dad's Hudson. A week before, I just about wrecked it. I recalled, while continuing to wait, those frightening moments.

I had accompanied my parents on a day trip to visit Uncle Grant and Aunt Addie on their farm. While our parents chatted in the house, I ushered my cousins, Alice May and Marilyn, into the back seat of Dad's Terraplane. I slipped into forbidden territory behind the steering wheel and began making the "boodin-boodin" sounds of a running engine. Just like Dad, I turned the steering wheel side-to-side. "Boodin-boodin," I chanted. I pushed a pedal. The car began to roll backwards down the driveway. Alice May and Marilyn screamed. The Hudson rolled faster. I held on tight to the steering wheel. Parents came running. My foot slipped off the clutch and brought the Terraplane to a halt – only a few inches from a tree. Dad tugged at my door, accidentally but fortunately locked, his eyes wild with anger. Mom edged between him and the car.

"Did you forget to set the emergency brake, Eldon?" she asked. Dad's mood changed, the door was unlocked, and I slipped into Mom's arms. I was starting to wish she was with me now.

"Damn that thing!" Dad's angry words from under the hood jarred me back to the moment. He was getting upset, time was passing, and I was soaked in sweat. I considered jumping out and making a run for home, but that would be the end of all fishing trips. I stayed put and wiped my wet brow with the pulled up front of my T-shirt.

Dad walked into the garage to his upside-down faucet, gave a twist to the handle, and gulped sideways at a spout of water. He turned the faucet off and wiped his dripping mouth with a forearm. I watched with envy.

Cousin Eugene, beyond high school and a regular among Dad's shop cronies, crossed the alley toward McKibbin's Garage, apparently on an afternoon stroll. When he saw the doors open, he stuck his head inside. "What're you up to, Mac?" he asked.

"On the way to go fishin' at the north dam. Wanna go?"

"Why the hell not? Got an extra pole?"

"You betcha." Dad was so certain and positive talking to Eugene, saying things I wanted to hear and feel. I liked the friendly cousin, but didn't want him taking my pole and time with Dad.

"Don't have a damned thing better to do," the tall young man with a dangling cigarette replied. "What's wrong with your jalopy?"

"Nothin'. Just changin' the oil and gappin' the plugs. Be done in a minute. Why doncha take a seat in the garage. Pretty hot in the car."

When Dad finished caring for the Hudson, he closed the hood, called "let's go" to Eugene, and shut the garage doors. The two men got in the car, Dad behind the wheel and Eugene, cigarette and all, on the passenger side. I was sure Dad, who wouldn't allow Gab and me to drink pop or eat anything in the car, would tell Eugene his cigarette wasn't allowed. He said nothing.

We backed out of the drive. The Hudson was finally in motion. We were on our way fishing. But not yet. Dad drove the car across the street and up the gravel drive of Henry Smith's filling station. A gray-haired man pulled himself up from a straight-back chair in the shade of his red shanty and sauntered our way. "What'll it be, Mac, regular or ethyl?"

"Gimme five gallons of ethyl, Henry." *Of course*, I thought, the Hudson required the most expensive gasoline. Nothing too good for Dad's pet.

Using a hand lever, Henry Smith slowly pumped five gallons of amber-colored gasoline into an elevated glass cylinder, inserted the nozzle into the Hudson, and let gravity finish the job. When the Terraplane's appetite for gasoline was satisfied, we started out again. This time we passed the high school, climbed Tank Hill, and headed for the city limits beyond. At last, at long last, we were going fishing.

Hints of a slight breeze from the wing windows reached the back seat when we picked up speed. I leaned forward for a breath of fresh air and to become a silent partner in the front seat conversation.

"Don't need no home runs," Dad said. "Three bases is plenty for anyone." I was excited to hear Dad talk about baseball, even if I didn't follow his logic. Indeed, I was excited to hear Dad talk about anything. He never said much at home. And now he was telling a joke! "Want my name changed the man told the judge. What's your name? Joe Stinker. What d'ya wanna change it to? Bill." Eugene chuckled politely and flipped cigarette ashes out his wing window. I got the joke and laughed out loud to please my dad.

We cleared the top of Tank Hill, passed the city limits and Truman Nagel's house, gaining speed as we went. We were on the open road and on our way fishing. Excitement and anticipation filled my thoughts, along with visions of Dad holding my hand on a rod and showing me how to cast. Absorbed in my imagination, I settled into my seat to enjoy the fifteen-minute ride.

"What's over yonder?" Dad asked. His voice was uncertain, hinting at trouble.

I leaned forward and looked toward the hill we approached. Parked cars lined both shoulders of the highway. People on foot milled about in the middle of the road. Dad let up on the gas and coasted toward the crowd. He stopped and rolled down his window when he saw a friend. "What happened, Homer?"

"There's been an accident. Mrs. Harmon Brady got killed. Her head went clean through the windshield. Nearly cut it off." I covered my ears. I didn't want to hear any more.

I didn't know Mrs. Harmon Brady, but wondered why, even in death, she didn't have a first name. Men had first names, but women, at least married ones, didn't. Mom called our neighbor "Luella;" I called her "Mrs. Ely;" but in the newspaper, she was "Mrs. J.E. Ely."

Dad slowly wove his Hudson through the crowd, waving limply at people who returned the gesture but didn't smile. At the crest of the hill, a black Model A was parked on the side of the road. We passed by the Ford at the pace of a walk, my forehead against the side window. I saw everything. A jagged hole in the windshield was ringed in blood. The driver's door stood open. Two black shoes, a woman's shoes, pointed upward and extended toward me from the front seat of the Model A. Tan stockings covered motionless legs from the shoes to the hem of a print dress. A bloody sheet covered the rest of Mrs. Harmon Brady.

The Terraplane's passengers remained silent for the rest of the short trip. My earlier enthusiasm turned to sorrowful emptiness. We did fish that day. I caught a little carp. Few words were spoken. When we got home, I went to my room, laid on my bed, and tried to erase a dreadful vision from my mind. I couldn't.

Mom said curiosity killed the cat. Curiosity didn't take my life that day, but it did leave a lifelong horrible memory. If my mother had been with me, she would have covered my eyes, offered soothing words, and saved me from many nightmares.

***

I had taken my first and last Sunday fishing trip with Dad. He didn't show any interest in spending time with me, and I lost interest in fishing. Hunting was another matter – that involved guns. I had never held a real gun, but wanted to. Soldiers had guns. Policemen had guns. Hunters had guns. In my mind, nothing was more manly than pulling a trigger.

I was issued a wooden cutout of a rifle as a member of the Schoonover Battalion during the war. Fred Schoonover, our commander and a World War I veteran, taught his troops how to shoulder their make-believe rifles and do "left face," "about face," and all the other faces. When the war ended, the

Nips became Japanese, the Nazis became Germans, and both became our friends. The Russians, our brave allies during the war, were now our enemies. I was confused about who I should shoot, but still wanted to be a soldier and carry a real rifle.

Mom didn't like guns and wouldn't allow me to have one, not even a BB gun. She repeated at every opportunity how a neighbor boy, Elbert Ely, lost an eye in a BB gun accident before I was born. Years later, I learned Elbert didn't lose his eye in a BB gun accident. Mom invented the story to discourage her sons from wanting one.

I didn't have to own an air rifle to fire one. Bruce Thomas, a neighborhood friend, had a variety of sporting goods equipment, including a recently acquired Daisy BB gun, stored in an alcove inside the front door of the Thomas house. Bruce's parents ran a hardware store during the day and left their home unlocked. I often knocked at their door and, if no one responded, borrowed a basketball or football for a short time. The addition of a BB gun to items that might be borrowed caught my attention. Following Mom's instructions, I didn't touch the Daisy air rifle.

A sunny afternoon presented a good opportunity to play basketball. My knock on Bruce's door went unanswered. I opened the door and shouted, "Anyone home?" No reply. The Daisy BB gun leaned against the wall in its usual position. Overcome with temptation, I seized the opportunity and the gun. The sound of BBs rolling about in the rifle added to my excitement as I ran to the backyard for an out-of-view inspection of the weapon.

The gun had a long steel barrel, a wooden stock, and a lever beneath the trigger. The trigger was limp to my touch, but became stiff when I cocked the lever as I had seen in cowboy movies. I squeezed the trigger and heard "snap." A small piece of turf kicked up in front of me. I swelled with excitement over firing a gun. The weapon I held was not the phony rifle I marched with in the Schoonover Battalion. This time, I was a real soldier.

The trunk of a nearby tree provided an easy target. I pumped the cocking lever, felt the trigger tense, placed the stock against my shoulder and looked down the barrel, just like in the movies. I fired. Ping! A piece of bark flew.

I pumped the lever and again aimed down the barrel. A sparrow landed on a limb of the small tree. The tiny bird of dull grays and browns had neither the beautiful color of a cardinal nor the pretty song of a meadowlark. Sparrows were worthless, scruffy nuisances, flitting about soiling cars and park benches. I sighted on the light gray breast of the unsuspecting puff of a bird as it jerked its head and twitched its tail.

I pulled the trigger. The air rifle popped. The tiny creature fell from the tree and bounced on the turf. A rush of accomplishment gripped me. I had bagged a bird on my first try. I ran to inspect my trophy.

The sparrow lay on its back in the thick grass, a round pellet, like a steel Adam's apple, lodged in its throat. Trembling and fighting for life, the little bird opened and closed its bill in agonizing, mechanical movements, as though pleading with me for help. The trembling stopped with one last shudder. The sparrow laid still. It's open and accusing eyes stared deep inside me and asked: "Why?" I didn't have an answer.

I escaped from the scene, returned the BB gun, and ran home – trying to erase the icy stare of the sparrow from my mind. I felt alone, very alone. I had no one to talk to, nowhere to seek consolation. Dad and Darrell hunted and killed animals. They wouldn't understand. Gab would laugh at me. Mom would let me grapple with my conscience. "Let your conscience be your guide," she often said. Mine was guiding me headlong into the depths of shame.

I sat in the porch swing. The sparrow's image stared at me through the rose-covered trellis. I went inside and listened to Stella Dallas on the radio with my eyes closed, but could still see and feel the eyes of my victim. I knew about death and wartime terms like "killed in action," but I had never witnessed the last moments of life. Visions of the frantic efforts by the little bird to cling to life gnawed at me. I could think of nothing else. I was a murderer, a killer, an assassin. I had to make amends. A proper burial came to mind.

I had seen impressive military burials in newsreels, complete with flag-draped coffins, buglers playing "Taps," and gun-firing salutes. I could make a coffin and a flag, and maybe hum "Taps," but no salute would be fired at the burial of the sparrow. I was through with guns.

An empty match box found in a wastebasket served as a casket. I lined it with sheets of Kleenex to create the soft look of a coffin lining. The flag was made from a white paper napkin colored with red and blue crayons.

With the casket prepared, I faced the responsibilities of an undertaker. I couldn't bring myself to touch the dead bird. I needed something to handle the deceased and to dig the grave. Dad had plenty of possibilities in his tool cupboard, but that was off limits. He didn't let anyone touch his tools – ever. At his shop he posted a sign telling would-be borrowers not to ask. At home, I had been warned many times to stay clear of Dad's tools. But this was a special circumstance. My guilt was present and torturing me. Dad was busy at work several blocks away. I opened the forbidden equipment locker in our cluttered storage room. Dad's tools were shiny and plentiful, each one neatly stored in a marked spot. A trowel seemed perfect for my purposes. I took the tool, closed the door to Dad's off limits chamber, gathered up the coffin and flag, and returned to the scene of my crime.

I had hoped the sparrow would recover and fly away, and give peace of mind to both of us. No luck. The bird remained lifeless, lying on its back and staring at me. I slid Dad's tool under the deceased with fitting reverence and placed the little feathered form in the Kleenex-lined casket. I slid the top of the box quickly into place, removing the fixed stare of my victim from my sight and, hopefully, from my conscience. I covered the box with the napkin flag and, acting as a one-man honor guard, began the funeral procession toward home. The body rocked back and forth in rhythm with my strides, creating eerie movements that made the bird seem frighteningly alive. I quickened my pace and, one downhill block later, arrived at the burial site I had selected: Dad's peony patch.

Dad's flower bed was a perfect graveyard. The soft, bare dirt around the pink peonies would make digging easy and leave no trace of a fresh grave. Later, I could construct a cross from popsicle sticks as a tombstone. Plenty of flowers would mark the spot as the peonies bloomed every summer. And, quite importantly, Mom's sewing chair by the bay window faced away from the burial location. I didn't want anyone to know of the funeral.

I knelt at the grave site and began my work. Dad's pointed tool removed the soft soil easily, and I soon had a hole large enough to accommodate the flag-covered coffin. Amidst sniffles, I packed loose dirt around the casket and covered the hole. With the flat of my hand, I smoothed the dirt to conceal the location of the tomb of the unknown sparrow. With the burial completed, I felt better – not so much about myself, but for making amends in some fashion. My conscience was not so easily satisfied. It tortured me with nightmares of chilling scenes of dead sparrows.

Mother and son in a familiar pose.

Dad and Mom in their usual attire.

Our house with extra lot on the corner. Mom sewed by the big window and my bed was next to the window above. The tiny building to the right was the garage for Dad's Hudson. St. Mary's Church and its steeple can be seen on the left.

Darrell, my ingenious and oldest brother, in a high school photo.

Gab, my ornery brother in Mom-made undies.

I am beside my first girlfriend, Joy McDonald, in the children's church choir. Our Methodist Church where I unintentionally set off an air raid siren.

The beckoning knife sign of Rowley Hardware.

Downtown Guthrie Center. Rowley Hardware and its knife sign can be seen on the right, Dowd's Drug is three stores beyond, and the Garden Theatre at the far end. Ferguson's Bakery is in mid-block on the left.

Dad at his shop workbench.

McKibbin's Garage, Dad's business location for nearly sixty years.

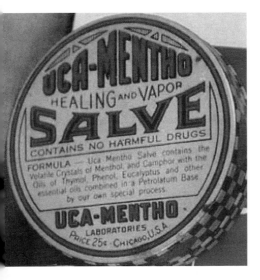 

The salve I sold door-to-door in a big money venture. Two good customers were Grandma Phippen (above right) and Grandma McKibbin in front of her little brown house.

Bill Sanger (left) was a wise and friendly barber who understood little boys. J.R. Compton (right), the local bandmaster who started me in music and directed the Tonette Band.

The Guthrie Center Grade School where I started kindergarten while World War II raged.

The Garden Theatre, where the rest of the world came to Guthrie Center.

This 1932 sign was a Guthrie Center landmark and the site of Sue's Lunch.

My cousin Leonard, the only McKibbin in the war. He lived in Washington State. I didn't know him until after V-J Day.

Howard Ely, my first hero, was a sergeant in the Army Air Force.

I am standing (left) on our front porch in my Victory jacket. Note the hedge haircut and V pockets. I was the only McKibbin (right) in Guthrie Center to wear the khaki. Mom cut one of Howard Ely's uniforms to my size. Below is my official certification as a "Paper Trooper" for collecting waste paper. Mom sewed the PT shoulder patch (out of view) on my Victory jacket.

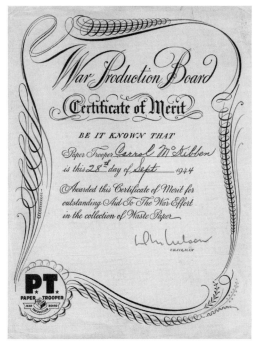

My first reading of the local newspaper included ads like the above.

"Hitler's Children" was a terrifying movie I wished I hadn't seen.

-188-

Dad's beloved 1937 Hudson Terraplane with me in the back — windows up.

St. Mary's Church on our corner. Father O'Sullivan's residence is behind the tree on the right and between our house and the church.

The Guthrie County Courthouse as seen from the west. We saw it from the east, a block away.

The Civil War monument has been a Guthrie Center landmark since 1913. The original courthouse, destroyed by fire in 1963, was to the left and the jail behind it. The expansive lawn behind the statue is where I broke into baseball as a pigtail.

IN MEMORY OF
OUR COMRADES

The bus I boarded in front of the Cottage Hotel
for a hair-raising trip to Hamlin.

The Ludwig home in Exira, my destination on the ill-fated bus trip. This is
the view I had while waiting for the feeling to return to my hand after learning
the game of "burnout."

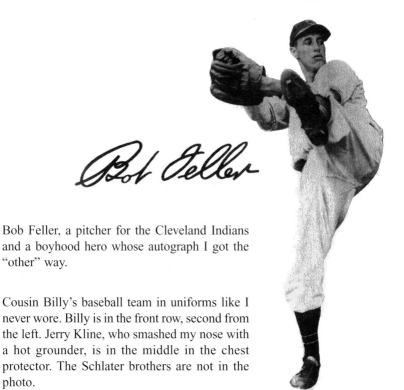

Bob Feller, a pitcher for the Cleveland Indians and a boyhood hero whose autograph I got the "other" way.

Cousin Billy's baseball team in uniforms like I never wore. Billy is in the front row, second from the left. Jerry Kline, who smashed my nose with a hot grounder, is in the middle in the chest protector. The Schlater brothers are not in the photo.

Mom said church attendance was important for peace of mind, something I needed desperately after murdering an innocent bird. Sunday couldn't come quickly enough. I sat in a pew beside my mother waiting for my conscience to clear and for the promised peace of mind.

"Please turn in your hymnal," Reverend McDonald announced, "to page 236, 'His Eye is on the Sparrow,' verses two and three." God knew! That didn't surprise me, but why did He have to tell our preacher? And why were we starting with the second verse instead of the first? I found the answer in the beginning words: "Let not your heart be troubled." My heart was troubled all right, and even more so when we finished the hymn with: "His eye is on the sparrow, and I know He watches me." I felt watched by more than God. My conscience also kept a close eye on me and was now joined by Reverend McDonald.

I felt deserving of punishment. The reminder in church of my sin was painful and understood. I was glad Reverend McDonald didn't mention the dead sparrow when he shook hands with my parents after the services. Apparently, God, the minister, and I were the only ones who knew of my wicked deed. The matter was closed, if I could get my conscience to let up.

The family returned home, changed out of church clothes, and settled into the quiet activities of a Sunday afternoon. Mom sat at her piano playing "Beautiful Ohio." Gab remained in our upstairs bedroom, and I sat at the kitchen table with Darrell while he enjoyed his favorite snack, a square of cornbread in a glass of milk. A gentle breeze floated through the kitchen screen door. I didn't know where Dad was. I soon found out.

"Who the God-damned hell left my trowel in the yard!"

I jumped to my feet and saw my enraged father storming my direction. Mom and church reminded me: "We pay for our sins." I had sinned. I had killed. I had broken the Sixth Commandment and accepted my punishment at church. Now, Judgment Day was rushing at me in the form of a fuming father.

Our eyes locked through the screen door, his filled with fury and mine with fear. Did my guilt show, or was I simply the closest, most available son for relieving Dad's anger? I stood paralyzed with panic. A giant, grease-grained hand yanked at the latch of the screen door and sent it banging against the porch wall. The other hand swung at me. I ducked and crumbled to the floor in a ball, protecting my head with arms and hands. Dad towered over his cowering, crying son. Fists, released with grunts, pounded at me and then grabbed the back of my belt and hoisted me into the air like a rag doll. A kick sent me crashing into the screen door, knocking a hinge loose and smashing me headfirst through a lower panel. I lay draped through the screen, half inside and half out, stunned, trembling, and crying.

My mother came running and screaming, "No, Daddy! No!" She threw her shielding body across my shuddering form, still screaming, "No, Daddy! No!" She and I lay in a heap, sobbing and shaking together. "No, Daddy, no," she whimpered.

Mom and I lay clutched together as one, crying for minutes that seemed like hours. The warmth and protection of my mother's body soothed my shock and absorbed my pain. Dad's footsteps shuffled across the kitchen toward the washroom. The door opened and closed. The eruption was over.

Mom lifted me from the smashed screen door and, with an arm around my shoulder, led me, still trembling and sobbing, into the bathroom. "Are you okay?" she gasped.

I nodded a "yes" I didn't feel. I couldn't talk through chattering teeth. My senses were numbed. Mom's presence felt good. I felt nothing else.

My mother cleaned my face with a damp, warm wash-cloth, her other hand caressing and rubbing my back. I tried to gain control over my unceasing and unmanly sobbing. Mom dried my face and held me close. I buried my head and emotions in her embrace.

"I wanna go to my room," I stammered.

Mom released her hugging arms. I walked past a stunned and silent Darrell and went upstairs. Gab, lying on his bed, gave me a sympathetic look and left the room. I slumped across my bed, my chin resting on a pillow I dragged onto the bordering window sill. The towering pine trees of our vacant lot waved and sighed in the gentle summer breeze. Air flowed through the open window and dried my tears. I remained motionless and quiet, feeling hollow, numb, and betrayed. Teddy, my loving companion of many years, reported for active duty from a shelf behind my bed. I hugged the little brown bear tightly.

Below my window I heard Dad's drill and hammer at work repairing the screen door. I hoped it would take him a long time, make him sweat, and cost him lots of money. Visions of flies flooding into the house and getting on his nerves almost made me smile.

An odd feeling of pride gripped me. I had taken a beating, but didn't feel defeated. I felt vacant, detached from my father, and strangely superior. His outburst was beyond punishment, beyond control, and more animal-like than human. The sparrow and I had something in common: we were both victims of a senseless, violent act. My conscience punished me. I hoped Dad's did likewise.

I skipped supper that evening and no one objected. Mom, her eyes still red, came to my room with a plate of "sick toast," Grandma Phippen's cure-all meal of buttered toast covered with warm milk and cinnamon. I relaxed in Mom's presence, but had no appetite. She stroked my arm, rubbed my back, and held me tight. She said nothing. I understood her feelings and recalled an earlier time when she said: "Love doesn't need words."

The door was repaired that afternoon. Time repaired my bumps and bruises, but not my inner wounds. I never understood Dad's occasional outbursts of violence. I wanted him to say, "I'm sorry," and give me a hug. It never happened.

Mom was incapable of any form of aggression. When upset, she sulked or shed tears or went into spells of depression. She never laid a hand on me, even when I deserved it. She never shouted at anyone, or even raised her voice. Why, I wondered, were Mom and Dad so different?

Some of the answer might be found in Dad's childhood. He was a second-grader in a one-room country school when his father died in their backyard from an apparent heart attack. Grandma stayed on their share-cropping farm and raised her four children, each of whom assumed adult-level responsibilities at an early age. Dad, at age nine, spent three days in their barn when a blizzard marooned the rest of the family in town. After moving the livestock to shelter in the barn, wind-blown snow kept him from returning to the house. He stayed in the barn, using the grain of an oat bin as a blanket and food, and drank out of a horse trough until his family returned.

Dad's school attendance varied with household needs. In fifth grade he dropped out entirely. His responsibilities increased when one older brother, and then the other, married and moved away. When his younger sister did the same, Dad and his mother walked the seven miles to town and started a new life, she as a dishwasher and he as a handyman in a livery stable turned horseless carriage repair shop. The year was 1920, and he had just celebrated his twentieth birthday.

Dad learned minor automobile repairs over the next several months, installing batteries and changing wheels, before arriving for work one morning and discovering the door was locked. The landlord came by and told the young mechanic the garage operator had skipped town to avoid paying overdue rent. He offered the business to Dad and McKibbin's Garage was born.

My father turned down the Chevrolet dealership in 1924 because he wasn't sure the horseless carriage had a future, and then, in the midst of the Great Depression, became the local Hudson dealer. He only sold one car, to himself, when the original buyer backed out. Meanwhile, his wife and first-born son were nearly killed in a heating stove explosion. Their year of bedfast recuperation required frequent medical care from Doctor Thornburg and a live-in nurse. Medical bills mounted, the bank closed and took Dad's savings, and he was stuck with an expensive Hudson he could not afford. Dad and money began a lifelong struggle that spilled over frequently into the lives of his family.

At McKibbin's Garage, Dad was master of the ship and seen as hardworking and congenial. In other settings, including at home, he was often shipwrecked: marooned, unhappy, and lost. I respected my father for his bread-winning efforts, his honesty, and moral habits, but I never cut through his complicated exterior to form a personal relationship. A Sunday afternoon thrashing at age eight ended my efforts.

I began to look for things I could do with older boys and on my own. Baseball provided an opportunity for the former and going to the county fair by myself – the ultimate thrill – an opportunity for the latter.

Chapter 10

Fair Play

A fter striking out at pool, fishing, hunting, and spending time with Dad, I turned my attention to the manly pursuits of baseball and going to the county fair on my own. Mom promised I could roam the midway by myself if I saved enough money. I pulled weeds for grandmothers, ran errands for jailbirds, and passed up more ice cream cones than I wanted to remember in an effort to save a couple of dollars for the September fair. Meanwhile, I prepared for my future as a big league baseball player.

Bill Sanger taught me to read box scores in *The Sporting News* and Emerson Ely allowed me to listen to afternoon Chicago Cub games with him "if I kept still." Bob Feller was the talk of the Ideal Barber Shop and the starting pitcher for the American League in the All Star game at Fenway Park in Boston. I read in the local newspaper that the Detroit Tigers were scouting Don McCarty, our high school catcher, and Judy Riaski told me her dad went to school in Omaha with Mel Harder, a Cleveland Indian teammate of Bob Feller. Big-time baseball was all around me. It seemed only a matter of time before I joined Bob and Mel on the Indians' pitching staff.

I read and re-read *The Kid from Tompkinsville,* the story of a teenager, Roy Tucker, signed by the Brooklyn Dodgers from a small town team in Connecticut. Roy won fifteen straight games on a pitching staff that included Fat Stuff Foster and Rats Doyle before hurting his arm and ending his pitching career. The Kid made a comeback as an outfielder and saved the winning World Series game with a catch that sent him bouncing off the left field fence and off the diamond on a stretcher. When Bob Feller's *Strikeout Story* arrived at the city library, I turned my reading interest from the fictional Roy Tucker to the real Bob Feller. He and I had much in common. We were from small Iowa towns, born in November, played the cornet, attended the Methodist Church, and were on track to become teammates. One difference I needed to correct – Bob had a baseball glove.

"Mom," I asked. "Do you s'pose I could have a ball glove?"

My mother placed her iron in its metal holder and her hands on my shoulders. "I might be able to take care of that. Let's go see if there's a glove in your dad's garage locker."

The opportunity to peek inside Dad's black metal locker with a Pennzoil emblem on the front excited me almost as much as owning a ball glove. Gab said Dad hid a sack of gold coins in his wall cabinet with the large padlock.

Mom and I entered the garage and edged between the Hudson and a wall that included doors to coal and corncob bins and a picture of William S. Hart, Dad's favorite cowboy from silent picture days. The locker protruded over the hood of the Terraplane in the crowded garage, requiring a long reach by Mom to unlock the padlock and swing the top-hinged door open. I tried desperately to see the glitter of Dad's gold, but Mom and the lid obstructed my view. She found the ball glove, handed it to me, and re-locked Dad's hiding place as I inspected my prize. Designed more for the days of Home Run Baker than Joe DiMaggio, the shell of cowhide had no padding, no webbing, and was stiff as a shoe sole from years of neglect. My new equipment looked more like hand wear for Frankenstein than a baseball glove.

"Well, what do you think?" Mom asked when we returned to the house.

"It's okay, Mom, but it doesn't have no padding and the thumb isn't laced to the big finger."

"I can fix that easy enough," Mom replied.

"Could ya make it softer so the fingers bend?"

"I'll take care of that. Now go play and let me see what I can do."

Mom knew nothing of baseball, but a great deal about sewing. She decided her youngest son would have the best padded glove in the neighborhood. Dad's worn-out long johns provided the cream-colored fabric for the lining, and with a few layers of cotton batting and a lot of Mom's handiwork, I had a baseball glove – of sorts. Instead of a pocket in the palm, the glove bulged. The webbing Mom fashioned with a white shoe string was not the standard leather lanyard and contrasted oddly with the dark brown cowhide. Her attempt to make the glove limber by rubbing sewing machine oil into the leather was mostly futile and left a slick and oily surface.

I now owned a large, heavy, useless baseball glove, but a glove nonetheless. I would at least look the part when I ran to join the older boys playing baseball on the courthouse lawn. They were shouting and arguing when I arrived.

"First bat! First bat!" they cried in unison.

"I said it first," they hollered, also in unison.

When the commotion died down and the batting order for a game of "work-up" was decided, I approached the biggest boy, Gene Devilbiss. Gene was six years older and a foot taller than the eight-year-old standing before him with an outsized, over-padded glove reaching nearly to his elbow.

"Can I play, Gene?" I asked.

"Sure."

The tall ball player's response seemed too easy, too accepting. "What position?" I asked.

Gene looked at my makeshift glove and smiled. "Kibbie, I think pigtail is about right for you."

Pigtail? I knew about shortstops and catchers, but nothing of pigtails. No teammate of Bob Feller played that position. Yet, I didn't want to turn down an opportunity to play with the big boys. "What does a pigtail do?" I asked.

"When we're playing work-up, you stand behind the catcher and chase fouls and loose balls. If we're playing 500, you play deep and do the same thing," Gene explained.

"Do I get to bat?"

"We'll see."

I knew Gene's "we'll see" response too well. I heard it often at home. It meant "no." Batter or not, I was in the game. I ran to my position behind the exposed tree root used for home plate and took my first step toward the big leagues – as a pigtail.

I learned two games that summer: work-up and 500. In work-up, players moved up a position, starting with right field and ending as batter, each time a hitter made an out. I had a lock on the pigtail position for work-up, seeing only the back-sides of hitters that never included me.

For 500, the batter tossed a ball in the air and hit it toward a group of players standing in front of a red brick backstop, the south wall of the county jail. Fly balls counted one-hundred points, one-bouncers seventy-five, two-bouncers fifty, and all others twenty-five. When a player reached 500 points, he became the batter.

I preferred 500 to work-up because I got to face the batter like other players. I didn't bat in either case, and though I pretended to be disappointed, I didn't want to be the one swinging the "lumber." I didn't know how to throw a ball in the air and hit it, and suffered from poor eyesight. Dr. Lee, the local optometrist, said I had a "lazy eye," meaning my left eye didn't work without the aid of the right and left me with minimal depth perception, a term I didn't understand at age eight. I did know baseballs came at me in a strange way. They seemed to hang in the air, and then strike like a rattlesnake. I didn't figure to make it to the big leagues as a hitter. I would be a pitcher like Bob Feller, who couldn't hit a lick, and Mel Harder, who had terrible eyesight.

When the 500 batter hit a fly ball, players clustered and competed for the catch by elbowing and pushing, their gloves waving overhead like corn tassels in a July breeze. "I got it! I got it!" they shouted.

I stood on the outside of the huddle, my glove hoisted high, and joined in the shouting. "I got it! I got it!" I cried. But I didn't "got it," and I didn't want it. I couldn't even see the ball through glasses that glared in the sun. The raised gloves of Rex Covault, Larry Towne, Bob French, Jim Knauer, Tom Tucker, Bill Riaski, and Gene Devilbiss protected me like barrage balloons. The *thomp* of the ball in someone's glove brought relief. "Good catch," I called.

I was content to scamper after ground balls others missed or ignored. "Twenty-five points," I shouted proudly before returning the ball to the batter with a quick scamper and an underhand toss.

Hard hit balls rebounded off the jailhouse wall where prisoners cheered and jeered from behind rusty bars. "Hey, DiMaggio, get that hot one," one shouted when I pounced on a ball after it rolled to a stop. Another called my bloated glove a "cow tit" and teased, "Are ya gonna milk that thing or catch a ball with it?"

The jailbirds, as Mom called them, were my fans, calling me "curls," or "hot shot," or "DiMaggio" or whatever else occurred to them. "Hey, Suntan," they shouted at the bronzed Gene Devilbiss, "when're ya gonna let Curls bat?"

I accepted the taunts and laughter of the inmates as involvement with real, bad or not, grown-up men. As with the older boys who let me recover loose balls, my friends behind bars found my services useful. I had something they didn't – free legs that could run to Sue's Lunch and buy them a package of Wings cigarettes in return for a nickel reward. With the county fair approaching, I needed as many nickels as I could lay my hands on.

Bob Feller and I had a good summer in 1946. He went 26 and 15 with the Indians and set a new season strikeout record of 348. I played first-string pigtail with the big boys and once, when they were short of players, filled in as right fielder. I never got to bat, but worked on my hitter's grip at home with Mom's rolling pin.

I picked up word at Mr. Sanger's barber shop that Bob Feller was coming to his hometown of Van Meter, a short distance from Guthrie Center, for an exhibition game after the major league season ended. A "barnstorming" trip Mr. Sanger called it. Whatever it was called, I wanted to watch Bob Feller pitch and get his autograph. My main thought of the moment, however, was the September fair and my first solo trip on the midway.

The Guthrie County Fair was the last gasp of summer, a gloriously happy time when the dormant fairgrounds came to life with the calliope music of the merry-go-round, the thumping hooves of racing horses, the roaring engines of the thrill show, the twirling neon lights of the Ferris wheel, the tempting aroma of cotton candy, and shouts of "bingo" from the American Legion tent. The Seven Deadly Sins and other church rules were given a furlough during the four-day fair while bets were placed on horses, men went into tents where barkers announced they would "see it all," and kids gorged on taffy, root beer, and lemonade. I could hardly sleep at night thinking about being on my own on the midway. It was like Christmas, the 4th of July, Halloween, and a birthday party all rolled into one. In Gab's words, a real "blowout."

When cornfields turned yellow-brown and black and orange box-elder bugs crept inside to escape cool evenings, I knew the county fair would soon follow. I had saved a fistful of nickels and dimes and was ready for action. The moment merry-go-round music soared from the fairgrounds and announced the arrival of excitement, I ran to my mother. "Mom, Mom, can we go? Can we?"

Mom set aside the dress she was hemming. "Looks like it's that time of year, sweetie. Go get cleaned up and get your school clothes on. Don't forget your money."

I soon returned with hoarded nickels and dimes that Mom tied in a handkerchief. "Put this in your pocket. Don't lose it and don't spend it all in one place."

Losing the tiny bundle of coins I grasped deep in my pocket was out of the question. And how, I wondered, could I spend such a large sum in one place?

Mom and I marched off the distance to the fairgrounds, well beyond my normal boundary of the Garden Theater. We walked under the marquee and kept going westward, past Ivan Rutherford's Deep Rock service station, past Mitchell Park, across the bridge over the South Raccoon River, and to the tiny ticket booth at the entrance to the fairgrounds. In the background, the race announcer shouted "they're off," a barker hollered "step right up," and someone yelled "bingo." Dust rose over the horse track as thundering horses rounded the nearby turn. I breathed in the aroma of popcorn and cotton candy. We had arrived at the fair.

"How about a ride on the Ferris wheel," Mom suggested. Mom's joy was my dread. Ferris wheel rides were scary. I mired my anxieties in manly silence and replied, "Sure, Mom."

We walked past booths of raw planks and 2x4's covered with gray canvass roofs. One sold lemonade from giant jars with floating chunks of bright yellow lemons. Another, the "Goodie-Goodie-Cream-Chewing-Candy" stand, offered white or pink strips of taffy.

I listened to horse race spectators cheering from their seats in the wooden amphitheater and to the non-stop background music of the merry-go-round. When we neared the tent of "Ali Baba's Harem Girls," Mom nudged me to the other side of the midway.

After a hundred yard journey of pure excitement, Mom and I arrived at the Ferris wheel. I looked upward at green seats dangling high in the sky. If Mom knew I was afraid, she might think I was too young to solo at the fair. I coaxed my courage while we waited our turn.

The sturdy black boot of a tattooed man steadied a swaying seat. He pulled open the safety bar that hinged on one side and latched on the other. "Next, please," he said.

High overhead, thrill-seeking, screaming teenagers rocked wildly in their seat. Might it fall and hit us? Would this giant Erector Set hold together? Mom constantly cautioned about safety, and now she was "treating" me, as she put it, to this wheel of misfortune.

The tattooed man pulled a tall lever shaped like a cattail plant. Chug-chug. The motor with the long belt of a threshing machine pulled us backward and up, up, up. Mom waved and smiled at friends below who became smaller with each chug of the Ferris wheel motor. I closed my eyes when we neared the top and didn't open them until I felt us moving downward. That became my pattern, closed eyes and tension going up and open eyes and relief when we came down. Round and round we went. I hoped with each cycle it was our turn to get off.

We jerked to a halt. I opened my eyes with a smile, thinking our time had arrived. Instead, we were on top and rocking. Mom felt my shudder. "Look," she said while pointing. "There's your uncle Glen down on the midway."

I saw my uncle in his familiar straw hat. "Yeah, I see him. Look, he's going in Ali Baba's tent."

"That wasn't him," Mom said with a sharp voice. "That was another man."

"That other man was wearing Uncle Glen's hat," I replied.

Mom pointed in the opposite direction. "Look over there. You can see the top of Flanery's Grain Elevator."

Flanery's Grain Elevator? With all the excitement below, why would Mom point out something so ordinary? Elevators or uncles, it didn't matter. We were on our way down and the man with the tattoos was jerking levers and opening safety bars, seat by seat, and letting people out. Our turn came. Mom took my hand and ushered me down a short wooden ramp that led to the solid, comforting feel of earth under my feet. "Wasn't that a good time?" she said.

All thoughts of the Ferris wheel, scary or otherwise, were in the past. I was ready for the big time. My first stop would be the "Goodie-Goodie-Cream-Chewing-Candy" stand for a stick of warm, juicy taffy. I remembered it well from the previous year. The next stop would be a mug of root beer. My favorite pop tasted better out of a barrel, and we didn't have root beer barrels in Guthrie Center. Then I planned to go by Ali Baba's to see why Uncle Glen went into a tent Mom didn't want me to see. From there, I would look around for whatever I could find. One possibility was the digger machines, though Mom had warned me to stay away from them.

Going alone at the fair required my most grown-up behavior. I understood and accepted that responsibility. I was eight and ready to go. From kindergarten on, I walked to school by myself and wandered about town, going in and out of stores and attending Saturday matinees. Guthrie was a giant day care center. People knew me, watched out for me, and knew who to call if I got in trouble.

The fair was different. Tattooed strangers and gypsies, who were rumored to steal kids, came to town. I remembered Mom crying when I got lost at a previous fair, and watched Gab "urp" – Mom's word – after he disobeyed her warning about eating "a lot of junk." I understood the county fair was filled with temptations for a small boy with loose change. I could be trusted. I could take care of myself.

"Are you ready to go on your own?" Mom asked.

Ready? I prepared for this moment and counted days all summer. I nodded my head.

"Okay then, I am going to play bingo a bit and then go home and finish up the dress I'm working on. You'll have to walk home by yourself. Think you can handle that?"

"Sure, Mom."

"If you need anything, you'll find your Aunt Monica at the bingo tent. Don't eat a lot of junk and don't go near the digger machines. That's gambling."

"Is bingo gambling, Mommy?"

"No, that's a game to benefit veterans."

Mom's distinctions on gambling were not clear, but I was too anxious to get underway to ask questions. I wanted to be on my own. Grown-up. A man. I raced down the midway to the "Goodie-Goodie-Cream-Chewing-Candy" stand, untying on the run Mom's coin-filled handkerchief.

I found the taffy-pulling machine hard at work in its glass cage, its metal arms stretching silky white strands one way and then another. Strips of pink and white taffy, the size of Hershey bars and wrapped in wax paper, were aligned in neat rows on a cookie sheet. I faced my first decision: strawberry or vanilla?

A nickel bought a pink stick that I unwrapped and poked and pushed into my mouth. Mom cautioned: "One bite at a time." I had a different opinion. Anything as good as taffy should be enjoyed to its fullest, meaning gorging my mouth to the point I couldn't move my jaws. Sticky, sweet syrup oozed from the corners of my smile. I couldn't chew or lick or even keep my mouth closed. I was in heaven.

The wad of taffy eventually melted enough to allow chewing and swallowing. A couple of swipes of Mom's coin bank hanky across my lips returned me to respectability. Next stop: the root beer stand.

County fair root beer was not the same as the bottled Hires type at Everett Tague's filling station. This was the real thing, right out of a barrel. Thick glass mugs on a wooden counter covered with red gingham oilcloth glittered in the sunlight and beckoned.

"A mug of root beer, mister," I demanded with authority.

"That'll be a nickel, sonny."

I watched foaming root beer gushing from the barrel spigot into a large mug. I savored the sight of the huge, brim-full tankard of root beer set before my anxious eyes. How could I drink so much? I accepted the challenge and hoisted the heavy mug to my mouth with both hands. Foam touched my lips and tickled my nose. I tipped my head backward until I felt the cold soda cross my lips and please my tongue. Gulp-gulp-gulp. The tasty flow stopped. The mug was empty; the root beer gone. The thick glass and hollowed bottom gave the appearance of a lot more pop than reached my stomach. With other midway stops in mind, I didn't have time to worry about being duped by a root beer mug. I moved on to "Ali Baba's Harem Girls."

Mom steered me clear of Ali Baba's when we passed by earlier, a sure sign she didn't want me to know what was going on inside. Uncle Glen was interested in the tent with pictures of dancing girls. So was I.

A shouting man in a straw hat with a red band stood on a small stage at the entrance to the large, buff-colored tent. He waved a cane above his head. "Come right in, my friends. Only fifty cents. See things you've only imagined. Straight from the Iowa State Fair. Forget Sally Rand and her fan dance. Forget Evelyn West and her treasure chest. This is the real thing."

A crowd of men edged closer to the stage. "You'll see Sahara do the famous tassel dance," the man with the waving cane continued. "She has a tassel over first base . . . she has a tassel over second base . . . and, my friends, she has a tassel over home plate!"

Something connected with baseball was going on inside Ali Baba's tent. The man in the straw hat didn't know much about the game. He left out third base.

A woman came out of the tent and climbed the stairs to the stage. She wore a red sequined top, loose filmy pants, and nothing over her stomach. A red jewel, lodged in her belly button, moved back and forth as she swiveled her hips slowly to thumping music.

"Hey, sonny, come on up and help this lady dance," the man in the straw hat called.

Was he talking to me? I tried to lose myself among the mass of attentive men. My friend, Pinky, mounted the stage, much to my relief, and faced the crowd. His short, red hair, waxed upward in a butch style, glowed in the soft September sun. His ears pointed outward like open car doors. His heavily freckled face parted in a gap-toothed grin. He was a perfect prop for the barker.

"Okay, little man – your name's Pinky, right? – time to get friendly with Sahara," the cane-swinging man bellowed.

The dancing lady, still swinging her hips to the beat of the music, put her arms around my buddy, rubbed his chest, and kissed his cheeks. Pinky stood with his hands in his pockets and a big smile on his face. I was impressed with his cool confidence and how he blended with the lady and the moment.

"You see, my friends," said the barker, "you can be just like Pinky. Get in on the action. Get on inside. Only four bits. Step lively now."

He turned to my pal. "OK, Pinky, go on inside with the young lady and help her get undressed for the show." Arm-in-arm, my red-headed friend and the dancing lady disappeared into the tent.

Wow! I had to see what was going on inside Ali Baba's. Knowing I wouldn't be allowed in the front, I slipped around to the back of the tent, looking for an opening where I could peek inside.

The rear of Ali Baba's canvas structure stood ten yards from a far corner of the race track, out of view and a perfect spot for spying. Unfortunately for my intentions, the root beer in my belly had other plans. I had to go bad. The men's privy was at the other end of the midway. I unzipped in haste and used the lawn.

"Hey, you little shit, stop that!" The dancing lady stood at the back of the tent, a cigarette hanging from her plastered lipstick.

I whirled away and trailed a stream across my shoes. "Bad aim," the lady mocked. She took a long puff on her red-tipped cigarette, blew smoke slowly out her nose, and smiled. "Don't look like you've got much to aim with anyway, sonny boy."

I finished the embarrassing call of nature, zipped up, and ran away behind a string of tents separated from the horse track by a grassy strip. I stopped to catch my breath where the midway ended and the livestock barns began. A man wearing an embroidered cowboy shirt and leading a pony by a rope approached.

"Hey, kid," he hollered. "Wanna earn a dime?"

"Sure, mister. What do I hafta do?"

"Just walk this pony while I go make a phone call. Don't let him get near that mare. He'll try to jump her." He pointed to a gray pony hitched to a nearby post.

The man in the Roy Rogers outfit handed me his rope and disappeared into the midway. I had never walked a pony or a horse, or held the reins of either. I understood the instructions to keep clear of the gray pony, but the one I was leading had other ideas. He started dragging me toward the pony the man called a mare. I expected him to try to jump over the back of the other pony at right angles, like a circus act. Instead, he came from behind and reared, but didn't clear the pony in front. He stayed on the back like a car being towed. I pulled on the reins as hard as I could, but he wouldn't budge. Instead, he showed his teeth like a mean dog and let loose with a high-pitched whinny.

"Didn't I tell you he'd try to jump her?" The cowboy had returned and was angry. He yanked the reins from me and tugged hard at the snarling pony. I disappeared into the midway crowd without my dime.

A stand with huge teddy bears, almost as big as me, caught my eye. "Hey, junior," a man hollered, "wanna win a bear?" Everybody's a winner. You win every time." The man in the shadows behind a counter of floating plastic ducks looked as tough as the tattooed man at the Ferris wheel.

"How much does it cost, mister?"

"Only a dime, my boy, and you win every time."

"How does it work?"

"Nothin' to it. You give me a dime and pull a duck out of the water. There's a number on the bottom that tells me which bear you won."

"Is it like those big teddy bears there?" I asked while pointing to the large stuffed pandas suspended from one end of the stand to the other.

"You bet. Maybe a little smaller, but just like 'em."

The man extended a tattooed forearm with an open palm. "Here, put a dime there and let's see which bear you win." I dropped a dime into his hand. "There you go. Now pick up a duck and see what your lucky number is." I grabbed the first yellow duck that floated past and handed it to the man. "Hmmmm . . . number 14. That's a double seven. Pretty lucky. Let's see what you won."

The whiskered man pulled a small plastic bear, no bigger than his thumb, from his pocket and flipped it onto the counter. "Next," he bellowed. "Step right up, everyone's a winner."

"A fool and his money are soon parted," I had heard Mom say, usually to Gab who was quick to spend anything in his grasp. Now I had joined him. It wasn't a good feeling. I flipped the tiny bear into a garbage can and continued my stroll on the midway.

The strawberry taffy was a nickel well spent. The root beer tasted good, but disappeared much too quickly and didn't mix well with a stomach full of taffy. I earned a dime I never got and lost another on a worthless plastic bear. I still had change in my pocket for taffy and lemonade and merry-go-round rides and . . . thoughts of the digger machines hung on my mind.

Mom said not to go near the wagon with little cranes in glass cases. She had gone home by now. Maybe it would be okay if I went kinda near the digger machines to watch the action. I dashed and twisted through the crowd like a halfback on a touchdown run and stopped five feet short of the digger machine stand. Mom said not to go "near." Five feet didn't seem that close.

The wagon had glass cases filled with prizes around the outside and an operator in the middle. A rotating handle on the front of each machine allowed players to operate the derrick inside and, hopefully, snag a reward. I watched customers cranking away, squealing in delight and groaning in disappointment.

The operator, a man in a dirty T-shirt with a pack of cigarettes rolled up in his sleeve and a stained ten-gallon hat on his head, barked at the crowd: "Step right up. Win big prizes for only a thin dime. Lookie there, the gentleman just won a seventeen-jewel Bulova watch."

I inched closer to peek inside the glass case in front of me. A gold Gruen lady's watch with a thin strap lay in the right front corner. In the left corner a man's Bulova beckoned. Other prizes nestled in golden corn kernels included an oversized set of red dice, a ring, and a bracelet. On the back right, a tray of piled dimes awaited the arrival of the crane's claws, and on the back left an open chute stood ready to deliver rewards to waiting hands below.

Players drew the attention of the operator in the cowboy hat by reaching high overhead and tapping a dime on top of the machine they wanted to play. The man grabbed the dancing dimes, left and right, and dropped them into the wide pocket of his carpenter's apron, never once hesitating with his sales talk: "There goes another watch, folks. And look over here, the young lady just landed a bracelet." I couldn't see all the machines at once and took the word of the operator that dizzying numbers of expensive prizes were sliding down chutes and into the hands of lucky winners.

I had dimes. One game wouldn't hurt. I would play once and move on. I strained on tiptoes to reach the top of the digger machine. Tap-tap, tap-tap. A rough hand snatched my dime. Click! A small light came on inside the machine. A voice spoke from above: "There you go, sonny. You're ready for action."

I looked inside the glass case where the miniature dragline waited to snatch treasures and slowly began to turn the handle. The crane swiveled from its position over the chute on the left toward the front of the machine and on to the rear right above the dime tray. The derrick stopped. The teeth of the scoop opened wide and hungry, then dropped and bit into the pile of coins. The steel jaws closed and clenched dozens of dimes. The machine grasped a small fortune, my small fortune.

I turned the handle, slowly and carefully, and watched tiny chains hoist the jawful of silver treasure. A coin dropped here and there, but most remained firmly grasped. The derrick pivoted toward the chute and jerked, causing more dimes to fall. *Slowly*, I told myself, *easy does it*. More gentle handle turning followed, to the background of a pounding heart, until the crane finally reached the chute and dropped its contents. A torrent of dimes came sliding into my eager hands.

I anxiously counted my profits. One dime went in and twenty-two came out. At that rate, I would be rich before the day was over. I reached high above, tapped a dime, and felt it leave my fingers. The light came on in the machine. I was ready to dig up another fortune. This time, however, the machine didn't move to the tray of dimes. Instead, it stopped short and above a large green die. I preferred coins to a gambling object I would have to hide from Mom, but liked the challenge of snaring the cube with the dots on its sides. The jaws of the toy dragline fell clumsily on top of the die, tipped it aside, and clamped shut. When the derrick returned to the chute it had nothing to drop.

Tap-tap, tap-tap. I was ready for another try. This time the derrick went a bit further, but not as far as the tray of dimes, and returned to the chute with only a scoop of worthless corn kernels. Another dime and another turn, and the machine still refused to send its jaws into the stack of dimes. I was losing one dime after another, but on each stop the derrick was getting closer to the tray of treasure. If I could just get the machine back to the dimes, I could regain my fortune.

More tapping dimes disappeared. I was certain the next stop would restore my dwindling fortune. Instead, the derrick restarted its cycle above Cracker Jack prizes and far from the sparkling stack of dimes.

In less than an hour, I spent all my winnings and all my savings at the digger machine. I was defeated and discouraged and trying my best to stave off tears. I couldn't go home ahead of time or Mom would ask questions. Fairs without money weren't much fun, and I hadn't even tasted the vanilla taffy.

The VFW operated a horizontal wheel of fortune on a raised table above the eyes of children. The horse races were over and the amphitheater empty. I slipped inside for an elevated view of the VFW table and discovered players with stacks of coins scattered about. Perhaps, I thought, an unnoticed nickel or dime might fall from the table.

I went to the wheel of fortune table and hung about, staying out of the way and looking for falling coins. My patience paid off. A dime fell from the table, a dime that never hit the ground. I snatched the coin in mid-air and ran full speed to the taffy stand and bought two sticks of vanilla candy. I had run so fast my conscience couldn't keep pace. It caught up with me, however, and ate at me before I could eat the taffy. I started home. On the way, while crossing the fairgrounds bridge, I threw the taffy, my favorite candy, into the river.

I stopped at Mitchell Park, stalled for time in a swing, and reviewed my limited options. Telling Mom I lost all my money at the off limits digger machines was out of the question. I didn't have the price of admission for the remaining three days of the fair and couldn't miss going without revealing my foolishness. When I got home, I avoided Mom and turned to Gab for advice.

"Gab, I lost all my money in the digger machines. I don't want Mom to find out and I can't go to the fair without money, and . . ."

"Slow down. I gotcha. Look, kid, don't pay for anything at the fair you can't eat or ride." Gab was giving advice he didn't follow, but seemed willing to help. "You're covered for tomorrow. It's Children's Day and you get in free. The last two days you can use the stepping stones across the river to sneak in."

Only the first day's solution appealed to me. Crossing the shallow river like Gab and his pals raised the possibility of reporting home in wet clothes and doubling my problems. I decided to take advantage of Children's Day and work my way from there. I returned to the fair the next day looking for free things to do and wondering how I would deal with the two remaining days.

I watched Jimmy Lynch's Death Dodgers through the fence. Blue cars roared around the dirt track and over ramps and up on two wheels, performing the "race of death" and the "dive bomber crash." I went into a March of Dimes semitrailer and talked to a polio victim in an iron lung. I went by the freak show with the painted poster of an alligator lady with a long snout. When she came out and stood beside the barker, she had green scabby skin but no snout. "Can't keep her out here too long, folks," the man announced. "She'll die if she's kept out of water."

I wandered over to a law enforcement exhibit that featured the bullet-riddled black Ford left behind by Bonnie and Clyde when they escaped a 1933 shootout at Dexfield Park, south-east of Guthrie Center. Clyde's brother, Buck, was killed and his wife blinded and taken into custody, but Bonnie and Clyde stole a car at Marvin Fellers' farm and made their getaway.

A large poster of Bonnie Parker with a foot on a car bumper, a cigar in her mouth, and a pistol in her hand was beyond my imagination. "Pistol Packin' Mamma" was a popular song of the time. Bonnie Parker was real, not a song, not someone in the movies, and unlike any woman I knew or could imagine. The "crime does not pay message" of radio's "Mr. District Attorney" struck me hard when I moved to the next poster, this one showing the dead bodies of Bonnie Parker and Clyde Barrow hanging from a car peppered with bullet holes.

I left the grisly Bonnie and Clyde exhibit and moved on to the "Goodie-Goodie-Cream-Chewing-Candy" stand to watch the taffy-pulling machine. A "Help Wanted" sign was attached to the stand. I approached the owner. "I could work for you, mister," I declared.

"I need someone to sell taffy on the midway. You seem a little young."

"I can do it, I'm ten." I was always too young for something. Adding two years to my age didn't stretch the truth much and might serve a good purpose.

"Okay, I'll give you a try. I'll put a dollar's worth of taffy sticks on a cookie sheet. You can go walk the midway and sell them for a nickel apiece. When you return with the empty tray and the money, I'll give you a dime and a stick of taffy. Okay?"

I had fallen into a deal, an opportunity to pay for the last two days' admission while eating taffy. Along the way, I sold a couple of sticks to Fizz Reed and his dad and received an invitation to go with them to Bob Feller's exhibition game in Van Meter. I was making rags to riches round trips faster than I could count.

After my first day at work and adding a couple of dimes to

my empty pocket, I told Mom about my new job. She never learned of my misadventure at the digger machines, and I never played them again, at least not at that fair.

I hated to see the fair end and school resume, but looked forward to watching Bob Feller pitch and getting his autograph. A few weeks later, I sat in the back seat of Lawrence Reed's car with Pink and Fizz and rode to the Bob Feller game.

The day was crisp and the game exciting. Bob Feller didn't pitch very long, and I was disappointed to see a Van Meter batter get a hit off him. My hero had thrown a no-hitter against the Yankees earlier in the year. How, I wondered, could he strike out Joe DiMaggio and give up a hit to an amateur?

When the game concluded, Fizz, Pink, and I joined dozens of other young fans clustered outside the locker room waiting for Bob Feller to appear and sign scraps of paper, programs, and baseballs. I stood near the front of the crowd, no more than three steps from the gym door. I held a blank sheet of paper in one hand and a pencil in the other, ready to receive the written endorsement of the man I planned to join one day on the Indians' pitching staff.

The door opened and my hero appeared with a large, inviting smile. He seemed younger, smaller, and a little softer than I expected. He was six feet tall and in good condition, but I had in mind eight feet of muscle. A rush of raised hands and pencils greeted him.

"Okay, fellas, take it easy. I've only got a few minutes," the pitcher announced.

A shoving match pushed me backward. I watched Bob Feller signing things from an ever-increasing distance. I was losing ground, losing patience, and losing the opportunity to get my hero's autograph.

"Gotta catch a plane, fellas," the Indians' star announced.

"I'll see you next time." Feller opened the gym door and disappeared.

When would *next time* be? I doubted he had plans to come to Guthrie Center, and I would never get to Cleveland.

The lucky boys in the crowd compared their Bob Feller autographs. I had lost contact with Fizz and Pink. I didn't know if they got a Bob Feller signature or not. I couldn't face my two friends without an autograph. I slipped away from the crowd to a nearby picnic table, sat down, and wrote B-o-b F-e-l-l-e-r. There! I had my idol's autograph just as I imagined he would write it.

On the ride home, Pink and Fizz compared their Feller autographs. When I didn't show mine, Fizz asked, "Hey, where's yours?"

I pulled a wrinkled sheet from my shirt pocket.

"That's not Bob Feller's autograph. That's your own writing. Hey, look, Pink. He signed Feller's autograph himself."

"It says the same thing," I offered meekly.

My Bob Feller autograph did say the same thing. When I returned home, I added autographs from his teammates: Ken Keltner, Lou Boudreau, Jim Hegan, right down the roster. Then, for good measure, I added President Truman, Babe Ruth, John Garfield, Joe Louis, and General MacArthur. I was learning more about spelling than any involvement with the famous, but for a disappointed eight-year-old boy, my method saved the day.

I made important strides toward a big league career during the 1946 season. I played a lot of pigtail, learned to play catch, worked at developing a batter's grip, and "met" Bob Feller. I couldn't wait for another summer of baseball.

Chapter 11

Of Mitts and Men

During the off-season, I made my stage debut as "Mr. Tell-Us-A-Story-Man" in a third grade Christmas pageant and played in the Junior Band, but my mind was on baseball. The school year came to a close, the days grew warm, and I resumed training for a big league career. An unforeseen and special opportunity came with a telephone call. I raced to the kitchen when the phone rang. Mom beat me to it.

"Oh, hi, Annie. How are you?"

Mom was talking to Aunt Annie, her oldest sister who lived with Uncle Bill and four cousins in Exira, a small town a half hour's drive from Guthrie Center.

"He's in Bible school right now. When did you have in mind?"

They were talking about me. I attended several Bible schools, one after the other, starting with the Methodists and ending with the Baptists.

"Two weeks? Yes, I think that would be fine. He'll be done with Bible school by then. Hold on, he's right here. I'll ask him." Mom cupped her hand over the speaker and turned to me. "Would you like to spend a week in Exira with Billy Dean?"

Billy and I were the same age and size, cousins, and shared an interest in baseball. Our games at family gatherings were cut short when farm relatives broke up the party at four o'clock to go home and do "chores." An entire week of baseball with Billy Dean made me tingle with anticipation. I beamed and nodded.

"Yes, he'd like that . . . I could put him on the bus two weeks from tomorrow . . . Okay? . . . Sorry I can't make it this time . . . He's big enough now to travel that short distance by himself."

Apparently, I was going to Exira on a bus. I had never been away from home by myself and never traveled alone. Mom's vote of confidence made me feel older than my nine years.

"Okay . . . I'll put him on the bus at eight o'clock. You can pick him up in Hamlin."

Mom hung up the phone and turned to me. "It's all settled. I'll put you on the bus in two weeks. Bill and Annie will meet you in Hamlin. Do you think you can handle the trip by yourself?"

"Sure, Mom."

"Why don't you run and play. I have a little sewing to do. Then, I'll go downtown and buy you a new pair of jeans for the trip. We'll have two weeks to get you ready."

While Mom's plans for my journey to Exira focused on clothing, mine turned to baseball. I was long on interest but short on experience. I played catch with friends and served as the neighborhood pigtail, but had no batting experience beyond a few imaginary swings with Mom's rolling pin. What would my Hall of Fame plaque say? "Carroll Ray McKibbin. Position: Pigtail. Batting Average: .000 (it never happened). Fielding Percentage: 1.000 (never muffed a stray ball)." For the moment, however, I was more concerned about going to the plate in Exira than my Cooperstown credentials. I needed batting practice.

Hitting a baseball required a ball and a bat. I had neither. I used a pink rubber ball, the size of a plum, to play solitary baseball in the house. Mom thought I owned a baseball, one she gave me for perfect Sunday school attendance, but her model was a refugee from the war years, rock hard, and covered with yellow canvas with printed stitching and a warning: "Not Recommended for Hitting." How, I wondered, was I supposed to learn to be a batter with a ball marked "Not Recommended for Hitting?"

"Why don't you play with the baseball I got you?" Mom asked. How could I tell her I was ashamed of the yellow thing? It was the wrong size, the wrong weight, and the wrong color. It had a flat spot and couldn't be used for hitting. Mom's baseball was a useless embarrassment that I kept out of sight.

"I'll be gone for an hour," Mom said. "I'll pick up your jeans and run a few errands."

After Mom left, I went to the kitchen, opened a cabinet drawer, and grabbed my rolling pin bat. With my version of a Louisville Slugger in one hand and the yellow ball in the other, I went to the front porch for practice. I placed the yellow ball on the railing, flat side down, and took several vicious practice swings before stepping to the plate.

Across the street, Emerson Ely's radio blared a Cubs' game: "A beautiful day here at Wrigley field. We have two down in the bottom of the eighth. Andy Pafco's on second, Peanuts Lowry on first, and Phil Cavarretta at the plate."

At 605 Main Street, Carroll Ray McKibbin was pinch hitting for Cavarretta and waiting for the pitch. I would bring Peanuts and Andy home with one swing. Bert Wilson called the play: "Heeere's the pitch." I reached back for every inch of power, gritted my teeth, closed my eyes, and let fly a powerful swing.

"*Kabonk!*"

Wood met wood as the rolling pin collided with the porch railing and sent a brain-rattling jolt down my spine. I stood at the plate, my bat lying at my feet, recovering my senses and massaging numbed hands. The yellow ball remained unmolested on the railing. The fake stitching mocked me with a curved smile. "Not Recommended for Hitting," the ball noted. At least I hadn't broken that rule. But I wasn't through yet. I was going to play baseball in Exira and needed batting practice. Besides, that was only strike one.

When my head cleared and my hands regained feeling, I picked up the bat. From the Ely radio I heard: "Runner on first, one down, and the pitcher at the plate. He squares to bunt . . ." *Good idea!* I'm a pitcher. I need to learn to bunt. I nudged the stationary yellow ball with the rolling pin. It teetered off its flat side and fell into a rose bush below. I retrieved the ball at the price of several long scratches down my pitching arm and returned to the batter's box. Satisfied I had mastered the art of bunting, I returned to my power stroke.

"This is a big moment," Bert Wilson called. "The Cubs are down to their last out. Looks like they're gonna bring in a pinch hitter."

That would be me. I took two practice swings and stepped to the plate. The yellow ball rested peacefully in the strike zone, but not for long. I planned to win the game with one mighty swing and send the ugly ball out of sight over the Ely house.

From my "Stan the Man" crouch, I lunged at the sitting

duck baseball, put my back into a smooth swing, and connected dead center. Sawdust flew. The ball didn't. It plopped off the railing and fell into the rose bush again. With one swing of the bat, I had converted the yellow baseball into a torn, sawdust-leaking bean bag. Mom's baseball had failed to survive one "not recommended" hit.

The short life of the homely, useless baseball didn't bother me. Telling Mom about it did. I had to get rid of the evidence and think up an excuse for the ball's disappearance. A sewer drain provided a solution to both problems.

The curbside opening had gobbled up assorted balls that strayed from our yard and rolled along the gutter of the Seventh Street hill. Sometimes we retrieved the runaway ball before the sewer got it, and sometimes we didn't. It was a tricky maneuver because Main Street had to be crossed in a hurry. If I followed the rule of looking both ways twice before crossing the street, I would also look at the rolling ball disappearing into the storm sewer.

My plot hatched quickly. I would say I was playing with the nice baseball Mom bought for me. A wild pitch sent it rolling down the hill and into the storm drain. I had dutifully looked both ways twice before crossing the street. In the meantime, while I was carefully following the rules, the sewer swallowed the rolling ball.

The flattened, sawdust-leaking ball was in no condition to roll anywhere. I plucked its remains from the thorny rose bush and headed for the hillside gutter. I carefully crossed the street, making that part of the story true, and chucked the limp ball deep into the open mouth of the storm sewer.

The remaining part of my scheme called for working up a good cry to convince my mother I had been victimized by the greedy gutter. But first, I would hide out in my bedroom until Mom returned to listen to "Portia Faces Life," her favorite radio program. When Mom was confronted with a son's problem while seated at her sewing machine and listening to Portia, she looked for quick solutions. She believed her three sons could do no wrong in any case, and bent facts to fit her wishes. Gab's capers kept her busy. In comparison, my efforts at mischief were embarrassingly innocent. I hardly qualified for the excuse that "boys will be boys."

I disliked telling stories to Mom, but the alternatives that came to mind were even less pleasant. I waited for the end of the Post Bran Flakes commercial and the resumption of Portia's efforts to make things right in Parkerstown.

"Mommy, Mommy, my yellow baseball rolled into the Hasbroucks' gutter." Two manufactured tears rolled down my cheeks. "By the time I looked carefully both ways before crossing the street, it was gone."

Mom turned her attention from Portia's problems to mine and wrapped her arms around me. "Now, now, don't you worry." I tried to work a quiver into her receptive hug. Mom was easily deceived. She lived in a world colored in vivid rose. Even during the war, we were not allowed to say "hate." People who misbehaved, from high school boys bent on mischief to Hitler, Mom labeled as "pills."

My mother's caressing hands and love pats calmed my conscience and granted a pardon for the loss of the ball. Her capacity for soothing and my need to ease my conscience were a good match.

"I'm sorry, Mommy."

"That's all right, sweetheart. I'll get you another one."

Another one? My plan had worked perfectly to this point, both excusing my misdeed and providing a cover-up. Now, my scheme had backfired. I didn't want another freaky non-baseball made of war-shortage materials. I faced inventing yet another story.

"That's all right, Mommy. I can use my rubber ball for a baseball."

"We can settle that later. I want you to try on your new jeans and a surprise I got for you."

Clothes were of little interest to me, but what could the surprise be? Mom handed me a narrow box. Inside, I found a pair of black tennis shoes with white rubber ankle patches inscribed "B.F."

"Do you like them?" Mom asked. "They're for sports. They came from the B.F. Goodrich Company in Ohio."

"Isn't Cleveland in Ohio, Mom?"

"Why, yes. Why do you ask?"

"I was thinkin', if the Cleveland Indians are in Ohio and the shoes came from Ohio, maybe Bob Feller wears shoes like these."

"He probably does," Mom said with a smile. "Maybe 'B.F.' stands for Bob Feller."

Mom's offhand comment spurred my imagination. *That's it!* I'll be wearing Bob Feller's autographed shoes to play ball in Exira and make an awesome impression on Billy and his friends.

Mom interrupted my thoughts. "Let's try them on and see how they fit," she said. "I'll help you lace them."

Moments later, I stood in front of Mom's fitting mirror admiring my new Bob Feller shoes. Mom pressed her fingers along the toes. "Do they feel comfortable?"

"Yeah, they feel super."

I threw my arms around my mother's neck. "Thanks, Mom. The shoes are really neat. And the new jeans . . . uh . . . I like too."

"You better slip out of your new pants and get your play clothes on. You can leave your shoes on if you're careful. You should break them in before going to Exira."

Back in my play clothes, I took my sports shoes for a shake down trip of running and jumping. My Bob Feller shoes looked and felt wonderful, and propelled me to new speeds and greater heights. I couldn't wait to show off my new shoes in Exira.

To my dismay, Mom reopened the baseball issue at the supper table. "Eldon, we really need to do something about that sewer drain by the Hasbroucks. I don't know how many balls the neighborhood boys have lost down that thing. Carroll Ray lost another one today."

Dad didn't reply. He was more of a sounding board than a talker, but his involvement in any way troubled me. I never knew what, if anything, was going through his mind.

Mom continued her monologue: "Tomorrow morning I'm going to the Hasbroucks and have a talk with Gertrude. Maybe the city could put a screen or something over that opening."

I listened nervously. If city workers became involved, the ball might be retrieved in its bean bag condition. My fib would be exposed and Dad might be asked to pay for the cost of their efforts. That was dangerous territory.

I wondered if I should come clean before I got into deeper trouble. Matters were getting out of hand and creating new problems faster than I could deal with the old ones. "One lie leads to another," Mom had warned. I understood, but wasn't yet prepared to reveal my fibbing.

The next morning, Mom crossed the street to visit Gertrude Hasbrouck. I sat in my porch swing spying position, this time with my attention directed at the Hasbrouck house. Time passed. I listened to both "The Breakfast Club" and "Back-stage Wife" before I heard Mom say "good-bye" to Gertrude and head my way. She was carrying something in her hand, something round and dirty-white. She crossed the street, climbed the three steps to the front porch, and handed me a baseball. A real baseball! It was scuffed and dirty, but a regulation ball with "Spalding" printed on it.

"Gertrude said you can have this. Jay and Dick are at college and don't have much use for it anymore. But be careful. Don't knock the stuffing out of this one."

She knew! But how? If Mom figured out my lost ball scheme, what else did she know? My plot had worked better than expected. I got rid of the yellow baseball, escaped punishment, and ended up with a real baseball. Pretty neat, except the episode reinforced my fear that Mom could read my mind and knew my every move. I didn't need another conscience. I had enough difficulty dealing with the one I had.

***

The baseball games on the courthouse lawn halted temporarily when four "teammates" won a *Des Moines Register and Tribune* paperboy contest and a free trip to Chicago to watch the Cubs. While envying their good fortune, I took advantage of their absence to think about my baseball career. The little boy position of pigtail no longer interested me, and I didn't like having my glove compared to a cow's udder and told to "milk it or suck it."

I was tired of chasing loose balls and no longer interested in wearing the misfit glove. But I wasn't done with baseball. I replaced my rubber "baseball" with the Hasbrouck model and continued my practice sessions, throwing the regulation ball against the back of the davenport and fielding it on the bounce next to Mom's sewing machine. She tried to listen to her soap opera lineup while I pitched to a lineup of New York Yankees.

The new ball was larger, heavier, and had a stiffer bounce than the rubber ball. The soft rhythm of the past was replaced by a "boing-bonk-bonk" that vibrated the hard linoleum floor. And while the smaller ball settled comfortably into my bare hands, the larger and heavier new ball was awkward. I needed a store-bought glove with a pocket and web.

I knew where to look for ball gloves. My trips downtown included a mandatory stop at Charlie Booth's combination cafe and sporting goods business. In the back of the store, hamburgers could be ordered from a row of counter stools. In the front, the sporting goods section, a large table displayed baseball gloves in open boxes. Mitts and gloves with "Wilson" or "Rawlings" written on them invited a hands-on test. I tried out the gloves, one after another, feeling the soft leather interior and slapping one of Mr. Booth's baseballs into the pocket. I inhaled the sizzling aroma of hamburgers and the leathery smell of ball gloves in one sustained, happy whiff. I didn't have the money for either, but both smelled good and sparked my imagination.

Boing-bonk-bonk!

I began another session of indoor training with the davenport in preparation for my trip to Exira while dreaming of the day I might own one of Mr. Booth's gloves. That day came sooner than I thought.

"Carroll Ray, I see where Charlie Booth is having a sale. I thought maybe you could use a new ball glove for your trip to Billy Dean's."

Was I dreaming? It wasn't my birthday or Christmas. Mom really could read my mind. This time it didn't bother me. I wanted a glove more than I worried about her reading my thoughts.

"We could go to Charlie's this afternoon and see what he has." I knew what he had: every glove, every lace, every strap, every rivet. But I also knew something about Mr. Booth I couldn't tell Mom – I had robbed his store.

A few days before, on my way home from a picture show, I made the usual stop at Booth's. While trying out gloves, I spied a small box of wooden matches lying on the floor beneath the cash register. The tiny box of matches sold for a penny, but seemed free for the taking. I snatched the box, dashed out the door, and didn't stop running until I reached the bandstand north of the courthouse. Kneeling among the white park benches, I struck match after match. My conscience went AWOL while I watched the yellow flames, but reappeared in full force when the last match turned to charcoal. I had stolen, a violation of the Eighth Commandment, and played with matches, a violation of Mom's Number One Commandment. Any mention of fire in our home had a sense of warning that I understood and felt, and had ignored. I had run across Fourth and Fifth Streets without looking both ways twice and disobeyed Mom's direction that I come "straight home" from the movie. Now, I had to invent a fib to cover my late arrival from the Garden Theater. I was a thief, an arsonist, and a violator of Mom's and God's Commandments. I trudged on home.

Mom's absence removed any thought of a confession. My conscience gnawed at me. I couldn't unburn Mr. Booth's matches, but I could take a penny, return to the sporting goods store, and pay off my debt to Mr. Booth and my conscience.

With a penny in hand from my Sunday school shoe "bank," I began my return to the scene of the crime. I still needed a way, short of a confession, to transfer the copper coin to Mr. Booth. I thought hard about that problem as I rounded the corner at Sue's Lunch and headed down the two-block slope to the sporting goods store.

Presto! The solution appeared in the form of Mr. Booth. He was sweeping the sidewalk in front of his store and wearing a half-length apron tied around his waist. His back was turned. My plan began to unfold. I would run past Mr. Booth, drop a penny in his apron pocket, and continue a straight line sprint with my back to him so he couldn't see my face. A quick right at the Gamble Store corner would take me completely out of his view and provide a clear run for home. Mr. Booth would be paid in full, he wouldn't know the identity of the thief, and I would be right with God and Mom, at least on the stealing issue.

I made my move when I reached Al Cornish's beer parlor and picked up speed passing Rowley Hardware. Mr. Booth still had his back turned. I dropped the penny in his apron pocket and raced around the Gamble Store corner and out of sight. I ran all the way home, arriving breathless and sweating.

I avoided Mr. Booth's store for a few days out of fear he might recognize me. Now, to get the desperately wanted baseball glove, I had to risk Mr. Booth putting the finger on me and telling my mother her youngest son was a thief. If I begged off and gave up the prized glove, Mom would be suspicious.

I had to return to Booth's. I did want the glove. If something else came up, I would have to deal with it on the spot. My brain numbed trying to figure out every possibility.

"Carroll Ray, are you ready to go?" Mom's voice caught me off guard. Plotting and conscience mixed in my mind and reached no conclusion.

Mom and I walked together, my hands becoming sweaty in my pockets as we approached the Booth store. I didn't know how to handle a face-to-face confrontation with the owner and had no plan to avoid it.

When we entered, I stayed close to the ball glove table near the front door, keeping my head down and my back turned to where Mr. Booth was frying hamburgers in the rear. Mom looked at ball gloves, especially at price tags. Her interest went as far as satisfying her ball-playing son while holding down the pressure on her sewing money. I understood.

Pitchers wore fielders' gloves, and that was what I had in mind. A Ken Keltner model caught my eye. Mom's attention was drawn to the $3.98 price tag on a Johnny Mize first baseman's mitt, about one-half the cost of my choice. She pulled the mitt from its box. "What do you think of this one?"

What could I say? Mom's budget was under pressure and so was I. Mr. Booth might recognize me at any moment. Besides, I was thrilled to have a ball glove of any kind.

"Yeah, that one's real neat." I handed Mom the box for the Johnny Mize mitt. "If you wanna take care of it, I'll just wait outside."

Through the front window and with my head turned, I watched Mom out the corner of my eye. She handed Mr. Booth several dollar bills. He didn't seem upset. He smiled at my mother. I turned my back to the window and smiled to myself.

Mom appeared and handed me a red and blue box. I removed the lid to admire my new mitt. It looked like a large, flat mitten with an extra big thumb. The name of the Giant's first baseman was tooled into the heel of the glove: "Johnny Mize."

With a new glove and a real baseball, I intensified training for my baseball debut in Exira. The back of the davenport and I continued our games. It was the batter, the third baseman, or whatever teammate I needed. I played every position the sofa didn't.

We started with grounders. The fingers of my left hand nestled into the soft leather of the Johnny Mize mitt; the fingers of my right gripped the raised stitches of the regulation ball. The back of the davenport provided the spring of a bat and bounced the ball across the linoleum floor and into my outreached glove. Seated nearby, Mom worked at her Singer.

The sound of her machine and my baseball game joined. *Whir-whir-boing-bonk-bonk!*

Sometimes the davenport and I combined into a double play combination, it playing shortstop with me at second. As the opposing batter, the couch sometimes bunted and made me charge from the mound to scoop up the ball and fire it to first. The sofa and I played every infield position when on the same team. When we opposed each other, always on friendly terms, I won every game.

Boing-bonk-bonk!

Mom sat at her sewing machine, a dress draped across her knees while she hand-stitched the hem. She tried to listen to the radio and Belle Jones, Lorenzo's wife, through my baseball game.

I didn't hear the baseball springing from the davenport and bouncing into my hands. I heard only the crack of the bat and the cheers of the crowd. Mom's Singer whirred away. A string of soap operas paraded from the kitchen radio. I paid no attention. I concentrated on my game and turned an unassisted triple play – only the second in major league history.

When I returned from Bible school the next day, I discovered the davenport and my baseball diamond had been moved from next to Mom's sewing machine to the front room. A new throw rug in front of the couch subdued the hard sound of bouncing grounders from a "bonk" to a "phump." No difference to me. I was back in business. Play ball!

Boing-phump-phump!

The new playing field worked better than the old one. Three windows on two sides of my diamond, two behind the couch and one to the side, provided improved sunlight for day games. A light fixture overhead made night games possible, if Dad was working late. With additional space, I no longer worried about chasing grounders among the six legs of Mom and her sewing machine.

Boing-phump-phump!

I gained range and confidence as the sofa and I practiced together day after day. I learned to go deep into the hole at shortstop, dig out a hard grounder, and nip the batter at first. From third base, I backhanded a drive down the line and fired a rifle shot to first, doubling off the runner.

Boing-phump-phump!

Manager Boudreau called me in from third to pitch to Joe DiMaggio. It was the bottom of the ninth and Scooter Rizzuto was on first with the go-ahead run. I tried to keep the ball low and away to the Yankee slugger. He laid down an unexpected bunt. I charged the ball, scooped it up with my bare hand, and flipped it hard toward first.

Krash!

The ball never reached the first baseman. My hurried peg smashed through the window behind the sofa and left a jagged hole. The ball lay among broken glass two feet below, between the inside window and the storm window. I climbed onto the sofa to see how I might retrieve the ball and hide the evidence.

"Don't reach in there!" Mom shouted as she rushed into the room. "You'll cut yourself. You'll have to wait 'til your dad comes home and removes the broken glass."

Dad and broken glass were not a happy combination. He worried about our ball games on the lot next to the house. A bay window beside Mom's sewing machine allowed her to sew and keep an eye on us. Balls of various types sometimes bounced off the large window with the stained glass panel across the top, but it had survived so far. An inside window between the front porch and the living room hardly seemed vulnerable to a baseball game. But now it was broken. Dad wouldn't be happy.

Mom surveyed the damage, her arm around my shoulder. "I'll pay for it, Mom," I blurted while thinking more about Dad's reaction than where I could raise several dollars.

"Don't worry about it," she consoled.

But I did worry about it. Dad had warned about breaking windows while playing ball. I went to my room and awaited my punishment. When Dad arrived, I laid my ear on the floor register and listened.

"Eldon, Carroll Ray had an accident this morning. He threw a baseball through a window in the living room."

"Livin' room? How the dickens did he do that?"

"He was bouncing the ball Gertrude gave him off the back of the couch and accidentally threw it into the window."

"Baseball? In the house?"

"He offered to pay for it, but he doesn't have any money. I'll pay Emerson to fix it."

Mom's solution was perfect. If Dad didn't have to supply the money or labor, he was satisfied. He said nothing. I took his silence to mean I could reappear.

I soon had my baseball back and went unpunished for breaking the window. Two for two. A good day for any ball player.

The davenport and I called it a season. I moved outdoors with my pink rubber ball, bounced it high off the windowless wall next to the front porch, and developed my outfielding skills. With my baseball trip to Exira coming up, I needed the practice.

***

"Carroll Ray, you'll be leaving for Exira in a couple days. Have you decided what personal possessions you want to take? I'll pack your clothes. You won't have to worry about that."

Mom was a planner. She always had trips figured out in advance. When we traveled in the Hudson, she filled two large and battered thermos jugs with ice water, fixed sandwiches, prepared car games, set out maps, and assembled an array of eating equipment. Once, she forgot the plastic silverware. No problem. She ripped paper plates into pie-shaped pieces that became our spoons. I had no doubt my paper bag suitcase from the United Food Market would have all the clothes I needed.

What "personal possessions" did I have? The words seemed too important for the few things I called my own. All my things, mostly clothing, were on a shelf in our bathroom metal cabinet or hanging in our bedroom closet. The white metal cabinet, with Mom's usual floral decals on the doors, was as tall as Dad and the width of a yard stick. The top shelf was for medications, including the remaining inventory of my UCA salve venture. Darrell had the second shelf, Gab the third, and mine, as with everything, was on the bottom. Sunday school clothes occupied my two hangers in our closet.

My "personal possessions," as Mom called them, were few in number. I possessed a baseball, a new mitt, a Bob Feller autograph of sorts, and Teddy, my faithful stuffed bear. My knife and top were long removed from my attention and interest.

My baseball would not go to Exira. It could be lost too easily. My Johnny Mize mitt was a must. Impressing Billy and his friends with my new glove, still smelling of fresh leather, added to my enthusiasm for making the trip. My home-made Bob Feller autograph would be replaced by my B.F., presumably Bob Feller tennis shoes.

The remaining decision concerned my teddy bear. He and I had once shared a bed, his fuzzy brown coat nuzzled against my cheek. Teddy was the most faithful, the most understanding, the most accepting friend I had. We fought World War II together. When I awakened from a nightmare of a Zero strafing our playground, he was there. Teddy and I had a frightening dream of the scary fireball and mushroom cloud of the A-Bomb, waking up in each other's arms. We slept under the covers together on a night when a bat was loose in our room and made flapping sounds diving around our bed. Teddy and I held each other close and made it through that night. And when Mom tried to break me of sucking my thumb by sewing mittens to my pajama sleeves, Teddy let me use both of his.

I felt grateful to Teddy, and I also felt shame. My misdoing had blinded him in one eye. During a short-lived attempt to run away from home, I left Teddy unattended on the front porch while I told Mom good-bye. In my absence, a mean dog bit off Teddy's left eye. I postponed my departure when I discovered my friend, his eye missing and bleeding stuffing, needed emergency aid.

"Can you fix him?" I cried.

"He'll be good as new," Mom promised.

With needle and thread and the skill of a surgeon, Mom deftly closed Teddy's wound while I stood by sobbing. She then spread the contents of several jars of buttons over the linoleum floor to ease our search for an eye transplant for Teddy. We found buttons suitable for everything from Eisenhower's jacket to FDR's cape, but no match for Teddy's flat plastic eye with the roving pupil.

"How about an eye patch," Mom suggested. "I could make it for him. You could say he lost his eye in the war. I could even make him a Purple Heart."

I didn't want an eye patch for Teddy. Pirates and Nazis wore eye patches. "How 'bout something like Charlie McCarthy wears?" I suggested.

"Oh, you mean a monocle. I'm afraid that's a bit complicated."

I finally settled for a gray cross-stitched button for an eye that at least covered Teddy's wound. I felt guilty every time I looked at Teddy with his one good eye and a button substitute for the other. I knew what it was like to have a bad eye, and I had caused the same misfortune for my best friend.

Teddy and I no longer slept together. He was nearby, however, on a shelf behind my bed and available in case of an emergency. I didn't know if Billy Dean had a teddy bear. I decided mine should stay home.

***

"Carroll Ray, do you know what day it is? You'll be on your way to Billy Dean's this evening." I didn't need Mom's reminder. Wednesday, July 23, had arrived. We learned to read calendars during the past year in third grade. I noted the passage of time on Mom's kitchen calendar out of pride and growing anticipation over the trip to Exira.

My baseball training had moved outdoors since breaking the living room window, and I had no opportunity for batting practice beyond my imagination. But with my new Johnny Mize mitt and Bob Feller tennis shoes, I felt ready for the big time and ready for Exira.

The day dragged, the clock dragged, and I waited. I picked at my dinner and supper with little appetite. My paper sack suitcase sat next to the door. Finally, Mom called, "Are you ready to go, Carroll Ray? We should be heading for the bus depot."

I lifted the United Food Market suitcase into my arms, my ball glove on top, and joined Mom for the five-block trip to the Cottage Hotel. Mom paused at the open expanse of the courthouse square and looked toward the west. Black and purple clouds billowed upwards beyond the horizon. Patches of faint green tinged the mounting mass.

"Looks like rain for sure," Mom said. "Maybe hail as well.

That can happen when you see a little green in a thunderhead."

Among Mom's lengthy list of talents was weather fore-casting. She and other grown-ups typically included comments on the weather in their conversations. The Iowa climate didn't suit any of them. Either it was too wet to work in the fields or too dry to plant seeds, or too cold to work outside or too hot to work inside. I paid no more attention to comments on the weather than I did to church sermons.

We continued our march to the bus stop. We passed the Square Deal, Hugh Price's grocery store, and Pauline Dudley's Ready-to-Wear, all closed and quiet for the evening. I knew the route well. It also led to the comic books of Dowd's Drug and movies at the Garden Theater. Mom steered me around the corner at Jack Myers' dime store and toward the Cottage Hotel, a short distance south of the three-block string of familiar stores. My bag wasn't heavy, but it was bulky and limited my vision. I wagged my head side to side to see my way, leaving little opportunity to admire my new shoes.

"Wait here a minute while I buy your ticket," Mom said when we arrived at the hotel. I set my sack on the concrete sidewalk of the curbside bus stop, making sure my mitt was safe. Mom went inside through the front door with its inscrip-tion: "O.K, or No Pay."

I stood alone. An unwanted tremor challenged my lower lip. I wanted to get on the bus and be on my way. Delay was stirring doubts.

Mom soon returned. "Here's your ticket," she said. "Look, here comes your ride."

A boxy, square-cornered bus wobbled over the wavy brick surface of Prairie Street. The gray and blue body of the vehicle seemed too large for the undercarriage, making it sway like a gypsy wagon. "Swing and sway with Sammy Kaye" went the orchestra leader's slogan. The Davis Line coach seemed to follow that motto, rocking back and forth in its approach.

The bus stopped next to me with a spine-jangling, chalk-on-blackboard screech. I stood at eye level with the Ford insignia, a blue oval on the radiator. The Davis bus was a lot bigger than Dad's Hudson.

The driver jumped out and stood beside the open door in his gray uniform and matching eight-cornered cap. With round eyes, opossum smile, and an extra chin that draped over his necktie-tight collar, he looked like Gene Autry's sidekick, Smiley Burnette.

"Boooooard," he drawled.

The driver's formality and adult-level attention to his only boarding passenger gave me confidence. Mom licked her hankie, washed something from my forehead, and kissed my cheek.

"You'll have a good time," she encouraged. She handed me a hankie with a few coins tied inside. "You'll need this in Exira. Don't spend it all in one place."

The excitement of traveling on my own and playing ball with Billy Dean was challenged by unwanted feelings of doubt. Mom gave me a love pat and a gentle boost onto the first step of the waiting bus. "You'll have a good time," she repeated.

The driver punched my ticket. "Sonny," he said. "You can take any seat you want." Any seat I wanted would be next to Mom, but she was outside waving at me. I liked the freedom of choosing my seat, but already missed the comfort of my mother's presence.

The stark interior of the bus was the shape and size of Aunt Monica's chicken house. Hard bench seats, covered with blue plastic cloth, contrasted with the soft, cushioned uphol-stery of Dad's Hudson. Five rows of seats allowed for twenty passengers, but I saw only two others when I took the window seat behind the driver. Mom told me not to stare at others, but I could look freely and without notice through the rearview mirror.

A young man in an army uniform, his khaki duffel bag beside him, sat on the opposite side near the back, staring vacantly out a side window. He seemed as alone as I felt. A chest full of colorful campaign ribbons told me he had seen a lot of action. I wanted to join him, but lacked the courage to move beside the corporal looking into space.

A nun sat behind me. We didn't have ladies who dressed like that in Guthrie Center, but I had seen Ingrid Bergman in a similar outfit in a movie, "The Bells of St. Mary's." I thought the story was about the St. Mary's on our corner and was disappointed that Bing Crosby took Father O'Sullivan's place. When I returned from the movie, I bombarded Mom with questions.

"Why do nuns have to wear such uncomfortable clothes, Mom?"

"Oh, they don't mind. They are so committed to their faith they hardly notice."

The one I was eyeing in the rearview mirror looked committed, but not comfortable. The white band around her face made her cheeks pouch. Sweat streamed down her forehead. She looked straight ahead through her rimless glasses.

The driver entered the bus. "Hi, folks, I'm your bus driver. Name's Bob. Looks like there's a bit of weather ahead of us. Nothin' to worry about. Just sit back, make yourselves comfortable, and I'll take care of the rest."

I liked being included in the driver's greeting of "folks," a term used for adults in general and parents in particular. That made me a folk, and someone more important than a kid.

I was alone with strangers, a new experience. I took another look in the rearview mirror. The nun seemed deep in thought, like she was on a mission. The soldier's mission seemed finished. He continued to look out the window, his head tilted to the side. He didn't appear to care where he was going.

The driver was happy. He hummed "Whistle While You Work," a song I recognized from "Snow White and the Seven Dwarfs."

Bob took his seat behind the wheel, closed the levered door with a handle to his right, and started the motor. I felt comfortable in the midst of a worker for God, a soldier for Uncle Sam, and a driver for the Davis Bus Line. They all wore uniforms. I wore new B.F. Goodrich tennis shoes that I admired with a downward glance.

I looked outside and waved at my smiling mother. I wanted to get underway before my courage ran out and I did likewise.

The bus began to move. My mother walked along side waving at me while we picked up speed. The waving image of my mother grew smaller. The lump in my throat grew larger. An unwanted sniffle erupted.

The driver leaned his head toward me. "Are you okay?" he asked.

"Uh-huh," I managed.

A left turn on State Street took us past the Garden Theater, its marquee announcing the latest Bowery Boys movie. On the left, Clink Hinton's Ford garage displayed the same blue Ford logo found on the front of our bus. We were still in familiar territory. We passed Ivan Rutherford's yellow and blue Deep Rock station on First Street, the grassy green lawn of Mitchell Park, and the fairgrounds amphitheater before reaching the city limits at the foot of Fairgrounds Hill.

The bus tipped upward for its long climb. On the horizon, dark and angry clouds churned, forming thunderheads that reached high into the approaching nightfall. A nickel-sized raindrop slapped against my window. The amphitheater below grew smaller, its oval horse track shrinking to rubber band size. St. Mary's steeple disappeared slowly into the sweeping twilight.

The bus chugged and groaned, backfired and balked. Bob's feet moved about the steel floor pedals. His left hand steadied the steering wheel while the other worked at the ball-handled rod of the floor shift. Gears grated and the engine roared as our driver coaxed the lumbering four-wheeled machine upward in "I think I can" jerks and jolts. I began to wonder if the ever-slowing, over-the-hill bus could make it up this one. Bob seemed unconcerned. He continued to hum and whistle as we chugged up the steep slope.

I thought about my family clustered around our radio laughing at the latest crashing cave-in from Fibber McGee's closet. I wasn't there. I was alone on a bus. My mother, my home, my existence remained at the base of Fairgrounds Hill. I was going the other direction into a gathering storm and the uncertainties of a week in Exira. Adventure has a price. I was paying for mine with silent tears that matched the raindrops trickling down my window.

The sky draped us in the dark blanket of nightfall. I took one last glimpse at Guthrie Center, its evening lights twinkling like stars on a clear winter night. The familiar and predictable were vanishing behind me. The future gorged my emotions with excitement, wonder, and doubt. Many unknowns awaited me on the other side of Fairgrounds Hill – more than I could ever imagine.

Chapter 12

Ernie at the Bat

KEE-RASH!

An explosion of thunder shook the bus and gave me a jolt. A crooked dragon tongue of lightning crackled and slashed across the sky. Huge raindrops splattered against the windshield. With his left hand gripped hard on the steering wheel, Bob used his right to operate a manual windshield wiper suspended from above. His arcing motion of the wiper lever reminded me of J.R. Compton conducting our band. Bob "conducted" the windshield wiper as he drove. I smiled at the comparison.

CRACK-CRACK. KEE-RASH!

I quit smiling. The crackling flash of lightning illuminated the faces of the soldier and nun in the rearview mirror. The corporal still stared out the window, seemingly unaware of the mounting storm. The nun, equally unconcerned, looked straight ahead from her bus pew. The peace of mind of my fellow passengers was reassuring. Our driver's efforts were not. Bob struggled to make the windshield wiper, gearshift, floor pedals, and steering wheel work in harmony. The bus glanced off the curb of the narrow highway. Steamy mist clouded the windows. Bob leaned forward and wiped at the glass with his shirt cuff. The neckline of his collar had turned dark with sweat.

CRUNCH-KEERACK-BANG!

I clutched my grocery sack suitcase. Its contents offered the reassurance of the familiar. Second thoughts emerged over leaving Teddy behind. His dependable companionship, unfailing support, and fuzzy hug would help. My mistake. I chose pride over security.

CRACKLE-BANG-KEERASH!

I had endured thunderstorms of this magnitude before, but never alone. When thunder claps shook our house and lightning showed the way, I ran to my mother, violated the "do not enter our room without knocking" rule, and crawled in bed beside her.

"Don't worry," she whispered. "It's only the angels moving their furniture." I no longer took Mom's explanation seriously, but the cozy warmth of her embrace calmed my shaking and eased me into slumber. At church, we heard of the comforts of "thy rod and thy staff." I didn't know the meaning of "rod and staff." I did know of the comfort of Mom's presence. Now, I was alone and getting nervous.

A fog bank, like a mountain of gray cotton candy, wrapped the bus in obscurity. I could see nothing beyond the murky blanket that clung to our windows. Bob shifted gears and slowed the bus.

Bang-ping-pang!

Golf ball-size hail crashed against the flat metal top of the bus and collected on the highway. The tires fought the ice, slipping and struggling to maintain a grip on the pavement. Bob cranked the wheel one direction and then the other. He wiped sweat from his forehead with a quick swipe of his shirt sleeve. The bus was not responding to his frantic efforts. I watched in stunned silence.

Thomp!

The bus bounced over the right curb and came to a shaking stop half on and half off the highway. Bob sat frozen in place, his hands clutching the steering wheel, his wide eyes fixed in a stare. A pause followed before he switched on the interior light. Turning to his passengers, he mouthed unheard words pounded into silence by hammering hailstones. The soldier leaned forward trying to hear the driver. The nun touched her forehead, her chest, and then one shoulder and the other. I slid away from the window, afraid crashing hailstones might break it. My teeth chattered. I no longer thought of pride, manhood, or self respect. I was scared. We four, originally united only in our efforts to get to Hamlin, were enduring the wrath of a frightful storm. We sat in anxious silence as the bombardment continued.

The banging ice and bus-rocking sheets of wind-blown rain lasted a seeming eternity. Finally, the hail stopped and the fog lifted. An eerie stillness hung over us. Bob pulled his hat from his head and a large bandana from a trouser pocket. He loosened his tie and wiped his face and under his collar. He stood up and faced us, forcing an awkward smile.

"Folks, that's as nasty a storm as I've ever run across. Looks like it's letting up now. Let's get this buggy back on the road."

Bob's self-assurance restored some of my beaten confidence. I heard hailstones crunching under the bus tires as we pulled back on the highway. Our driver resumed his conducting of the windshield wiper. We were underway again.

Lightning lit the sky like shell bursts, silhouetting houses and barns on the horizon before turning them back to darkness, and then repeated the process with another burst. We passed the road to Uncle Cecil's farm and traveled across the long, straight stretch of Simmons Flat. I began to calm as we approached the M&M store. I thought the business was named for one of my favorite candies.

"Mom," I asked. "Do they make M&M's at the store west of town? You know, the one with the baseball team."

"No, honey, that stands for the M&M Divide, the point where water runs one way to the Missouri River and the other to the Mississippi."

My disappointment over learning M&M's did not come from the store of that name was relieved by their sponsorship of a baseball team. The M&M Cardinals played at the fairgrounds diamond in Guthrie Center. St. Louis Cardinals or the M&M Cardinals, Stan Musial and Marty Marion, or Hugh Secoy and Bing Miller, it was baseball and all the same to me.

Our bus passed the road to Adair where Jesse James pulled his first train robbery, climbed over a few more hills, and came to a stop where Highways 64 (now 44) and 71 intersected. We had arrived in Hamlin, a town of little more than a filling station and a general store. Ahead, the bus lights shined on a slope-backed car parked at the bus stop. Uncle Bill's Ford was a welcome sight.

I fled the bus the moment we stopped, protecting my paper suitcase from the rain with wrapped arms. The door of the black Ford swung open. Aunt Annie leaned forward, pulling the back of the seat with her so I could slip quickly into the rear between Billy Dean and Donna.

"How'd the trip go?" Aunt Annie asked.

Dammed emotions gushed like the cloud burst I had experienced: "We were in a hail storm and the fog came and we hit a curb and almost wrecked and, and . . ."

"Sounds like you had quite a ride. When we get home, you can relax with some hot chocolate."

Aunt Annie's gentle voice soothed my nerves. The promise of cocoa and an opportunity to unwind sounded good. Donna grasped my hand and added her soft warmth to my comfort. She was blond, beautiful, and going into eighth grade. Holding hands with her boosted my sense of importance.

Billy sat silently on my other side. Our quiet friendship needed few words. We liked and understood each other.

Uncle Bill lit a cigarette and started the engine. Ten minutes later, we pulled into the gravel drive of the Ludwig house, perched on a corner knoll on the south end of Exira. Their home was much like ours with its white clapboard siding, linoleum floors, and lived-in look and feel.

Aunt Annie turned to me when we entered the house. "I'll fix that cup of hot chocolate I promised. Bet you're ready for that."

Mom's sister was the eldest of ten children, as much a mother to her siblings as a sister. They adored her, and I understood why. Her humble and pleasant manner shed grace upon those around her. She had a glow of serenity, as though encircled by a halo. If I couldn't have Mom with me, Aunt Annie was my next best bet.

I soon tasted the warmth and sweetness of a cup of cocoa. Donna sat beside me at the dining room table, her Camay complexion and blue eyes drawing my attention. She had visited our home several times as part of Mom's system of rotating nieces to replace the daughter she never had. A parade of girl cousins came to visit for a week of baking, sewing, and pampering before returning home with lacy creations from Mom's sewing machine.

On one of Donna's visits, she and I sat together in the Garden Theater holding hands and waiting for the start of the picture show. I was thrilled to be seen with an older woman, a blond beauty who had just finished sixth grade. The theater darkened. We laughed at a Woody Woodpecker cartoon before the newsreel started. The narrator told of the Chicago Cubs' drive for the National League pennant while we watched Stan Hack circling the bases after a home run. The scene and the narrator's voice changed. "The first views of the Atomic Bomb explosion over Hiroshima," he announced in solemn tones. A gigantic explosion roared on the screen. Circles of fire-filled clouds billowed outward and upward, leap-frogging each other before rising into a towering column that expanded at the top into a huge mushroom-shaped cloud. I had watched quietly when newsreels showed B-29's dropping hundreds of bombs that exploded in a series of flashes. The Atomic Bomb was different. It didn't seem fair; didn't seem human. It scared me beyond fright. The nuclear explosion in the newsreel lifted me out of my seat and shot me out of the Garden Theater, leaving Donna behind. I needed to be home and near Mom. Donna must have understood. She never raised the issue. I sat beside her again, absorbed and charmed by her quiet presence.

A car roared up the gravel driveway and ground its tires to a crunching stop. Darwin, the eldest of the four Ludwig cousins, had arrived. The first born in our extended family all had grown-up, important names like Darwin, Dale, and Darrell. The last born got stuck with pansy names like Billy Dean, Frankie Dee, and Carroll Ray. Billy Dean and I never talked about being short-changed on names. We suffered that indignity in silence and turned our attention to playing ball.

Darwin, more interested in cars than baseball, entered a room like he drove his Ford, hard and fast. "Hey, Carroll Ray, you tryin' to eat us out of house and home?"

A sprig of dark wavy hair dangled on Darwin's forehead. His abundant confidence flashed in a sly, slightly twisted grin. Darwin was considered ornery in family circles. At a picnic he challenged Uncle Gilford, a squat muscular man who once separated two fighting bulls by hand, to a wrestling match. Buttons flew and the air filled with grunts, groans, and blue words before the two quit from sheer exhaustion.

Glen, the middle Ludwig son, stood behind Darwin. Blond and equally capable of mischief, Glen was quieter, more observing, and more calculating than his older brother, perhaps because he was smaller and they sometimes settled their differences physically. Darwin was larger than life and took a lot of space. Glen settled for what was left in quiet reflection.

"How long you gonna be here?" Glen asked.

"A week, I think."

"Mom, hide the cookies. Carroll Ray's gonna be here a whole week," Darwin chided.

Uncle Bill interrupted Darwin's jibes when he entered the dining room carrying a pair of dark maroon boxing gloves. "Okay, McKibbin, let's see how you handle your dukes," he challenged. No one called me by my last name. My brothers nicknamed me Ked. Others called me Carroll Ray or Carroll or Kibbie or Mac. I had lots of names. Boxers were called by their last names. Maybe that was what Uncle Bill had in mind. The announcer for the Friday night fights on the radio always repeated last names: "And in the near corner, wearing purple trunks, the defending world champion, Joe Louis. Louis."

"You can go a couple of rounds with Billy Dean. You're about the same size," my uncle declared.

Whoever coined the phrase "opposites attract" must have had Uncle Bill and Aunt Annie in mind. He was as feisty as she was serene, as outspoken as she was quiet, and endowed with bad habits she wouldn't even think about. He smoked openly, said naughty words, and, as rumor had it, drank beer. Slight in stature and wiry in build, Uncle Bill wore round, gold-rimmed glasses and combed his salt and pepper hair straight back like the Katzenjammer kids.

Billy Dean removed his shirt and donned boxing gloves that Glen laced tightly. He pounded his gloves together and practiced his footwork, darting about the living room bobbing, jabbing, and weaving. He knew what he was doing. His not so worthy opponent didn't. I had come to Exira to play baseball, not box. I was Bob Feller, not Joe Louis. The only mitt I wanted to wear was my Johnny Mize model.

"Wanna take your shirt off?" Darwin asked.

"Uh-uh."

I feared removing my shirt almost as much as boxing. My skinny chest of protruding ribs and two large moles – Gab called me "chicken chest" – was embarrassing. Leaving my shirt on would save me that much humiliation. I could hear the ring announcer: "And in the far corner, wearing a shirt to cover his scrawny chest, Carroll Ray McKibbin. McKibbin."

I had thrown only one punch in my life, a right hook that flattened Ruth Ann French after she yanked my curls with both hands. I could bill myself as "One Punch McKibbin," but that was a number of years ago and involved a little girl. I kept my mouth shut.

Darwin laced and tied my gloves. I danced about punching at imaginary chins, imitating a professional boxer I saw at the county fair. He offered twenty-five dollars to anyone who could last three rounds with him.

"Heck," Pepsi Conrad boasted, "I can run that long." He climbed into the ring planning to convert his winnings into cases of his favorite beverage. But that night Pepsi tasted only the leather of his opponent's gloves. He got his bell rung almost as quickly as the one that opened the match. He didn't last a round.

I also saw the results of boxing. Jiggs Shelley, a former

boxer who lived in Guthrie Center, had a tic that yanked at the right corner of his mouth, jerking it downward and exposing a large cord in his neck. "He took too many punches," people explained. I believed them. I didn't want to end up with Pepsi's headache or the jerking mouth of Jiggs. Willing or not, I was about to fight an unwanted, unintentional match for which I had no experience, no talent, and no desire.

"Better take his glasses off," Uncle Bill told Darwin. I felt my glasses slipping from my nose and heard someone say "gong." My lazy eye, without the aid of glasses, leaned into my nose. Billy Dean, with the aid of a left hand, leaned into my chin with a haymaker that scrambled my curls and rattled my brain. I windmilled my arms in front of my face to protect my chin. Unfortunately, that left my midsection open. Billy noticed.

Thud! My cousin buried a fist in my belly that went clear to my backbone and emptied my lungs like a blown out tire. I dropped to my knees, the most upright position I could manage, and tried to recover my breath.

Uncle Bill kneeled and thumped me a couple of times on the back. "You'll be all right in a minute," he said. "You only had your wind knocked out."

Only! Easy for him to say, I thought to myself while trying to clear my head and fill my lungs.

Uncle Bill was correct. I did, after a mercifully short interval, resume breathing. The boxing match did not resume. It went into the books as "no contest."

"Time for bed," Aunt Annie called.

I hated bedtime. At home, I used every ruse possible to avoid "climbing the wooden hill." Visits to the bathroom, a question that needed answering, something I had forgotten – anything to avoid going to bed. But now, thoughts of a peaceful and quiet bed, far from hailstorms and boxing matches, appealed to me. I wanted nothing more than a night of blissful, uninterrupted sleep.

In a bedroom next to the living room, Billy and I shared a double bed. Aunt Annie and Donna slept in the same room in a bed separated from ours by a nightstand. Uncle Bill, Darwin, and Glen passed the night in a second bedroom at the other end of the house.

Billy snickered at my pajamas. He obviously found my seersucker night clothes with little red hearts sissy stuff, but said nothing. He crawled into bed in his skivvies.

"Lights out," Aunt Annie announced.

I welcomed the end of a punishing day. In the quiet dark, a soft, sweet breeze of washed air drifted through the screened window beside our bed. Crickets serenaded us from beyond. I soon eased into the depths of heavenly slumber.

"Help! Oh, help me! Please! Please! Oh, Jesus, they're gonna get me!"

Billy sat up in bed, crying and shouting and trembling. I sprang up beside him like a jack-in-the-box. My heart pounded. Where was I? What was going on?

"Oh, no! Oh, no! Oh, God! Keep 'em away from me! Help me, Mom, help me!"

Was there something in the dark I couldn't see? I tried to get a hold of Billy, as much for my comfort as his, but flailing arms kept me at a distance. I felt like joining him in a good scream.

"I'm right here, honey. Just calm down. You'll be okay."

I recognized Aunt Annie's gentle voice. She sat on the side of the bed and held Billy in her arms.

"There, there. There's nothing to be frightened about," she soothed.

I needed the words as much as Billy and could have used the hugs as well. My shaking cousin calmed down. I tried to.

Aunt Annie whispered to me: "Billy has these fits sometimes. He doesn't know what he's doing. He'll be okay. Are you all right?"

"I guess so," I replied without conviction.

"Good, then. Let's all get back to sleep."

Aunt Annie eased Billy back on his pillow. He resumed his sleep. I didn't. But I gained some consolation knowing my cousin had his demons, too. Perhaps I was uneasy about being away from Mom, reluctant to leave Teddy behind, and frightened of thunder and lightning and hail and boxing. But I didn't throw fits in my sleep. Score tied.

***

The next morning, Donna cupped a hand over my ear and whispered that Billy not only threw fits in his sleep, he also went for nighttime walks. They once found him a block from home in the wee hours of the morning. Aunt Annie sometimes tied Billy's feet together at bedtime to keep him from unconsciously taking a midnight stroll and hurting himself. Donna asked that I not bring up this delicate subject with her younger brother. I didn't, but knowing of a flaw in my cousin, the one who kayoed me the night before, gave my damaged ego a boost.

My thoughts turned to the main purpose of my trip to Exira: baseball. My favorite sport provided the heartbeat for this town of 1,000 players and fans. They boasted of a state champion high school team, a semi-pro team, an American Legion team, and a midget team for the smallest boys. Bob Gibson, a 1981 inductee into the Baseball Hall of Fame, set a major league record in 1968 by allowing opponents an average of only 1.12 runs per game. But as a youngster two decades earlier, he and his Omaha Monarchs gave up ten runs to the Exira midget team and went home a 10-2 loser. Baseball was more than a pastime in Exira – it was the lifeblood of the community.

Billy and I went to the side yard near the kitchen door for our first round of catch. His lack of reaction to my new glove and tennis shoes disappointed me. Perhaps he wasn't interested in a first baseman's mitt with his aspiration of becoming a pitcher. I shared that goal, but figured major league scouts wouldn't care what kind of glove I wore when they saw my lightning fast ball.

Thump. Billy's first throw landed solidly in my new mitt. It felt good. I felt proud.

Thump. Another throw and another catch. I loved the feel of my Johnny Mize mitt.

Screeech! Locked wheels, a skidding stop, and a whirlwind of dust announced the arrival of Darwin in his Ford. His car had the same slope-backed shape of Uncle Bill's, but no hood. I had never seen a car motor publicly exposed. Dad would never allow his Terraplane to suffer such an indignity.

Darwin emerged from the dust. "How 'bout a game of burnout?" he hollered.

I was prepared to go along with any game involving a baseball. I didn't know the game he mentioned, but didn't want to embarrass myself by asking.

"Carroll Ray and Billy Dean, you two guys go down by the tree. I'll throw from up here by the cellar cave."

Darwin was eight years older, shaved, and owned his own car. He was tough. He played baseball with bare hands.

Billy and I stood beside each other under a tall elm tree at the top of a high bank that dropped abruptly to the gravel road below. Darwin would be throwing downhill to us, about a pitcher's mound distance away.

"Billy, you're first," Darwin announced.

With a full windup and a high kick, Darwin hurled the ball with all his strength.

Whop!

Billy winced but caught the ball. He paused for a moment, went into a stretch windup, and unleashed his best fast ball.

"Good throw, Billy," Darwin shouted as he caught the baseball with a bare hand.

"You're next, Carroll Ray."

I caught on. Darwin was about to fire his best fast ball at me. If I didn't catch it, I was "burned out" and lost. Darwin went into his windup.

My lazy eye tried desperately to follow the blazing ball coming at me like a bullet. I stood my ground and relied on my Johnny Mize mitt to do the rest.

Splat!

Amazingly, I found the ball in my glove. The meaty sound of its landing came more from the flesh of my hand than the leather of my mitt. A skillful first baseman catches the ball in the web, sparing his hand the agony of a direct hit. The pain in my hand told me I didn't do it quite right. Tears threatened. This was not the time, in front of Billy and Darwin, to give in.

My left hand throbbed. In my right, I held the means of getting even with Darwin. I wanted his hand to hurt as much as mine. I wanted to throw the baseball through him. I wanted to end this game of burnout with Darwin surrendering to the pain I was about to inflict. I reared back as far as I could, until my knuckles almost touched the turf, and launched my powerhouse throw.

"Very nice," Darwin teased as he plucked my high, hard one from the air with his fingertips.

Whop!

Billy winced again, but held onto the ball. The alternating throws allowed time for me to think. With the assistance of a pulsating left hand, I reached several conclusions: (1) This game is dangerous. (2) Pride will not allow me to back out. (3) I am not going to risk my hand to another of Darwin's pitches.

The ball rocketed toward me. I stood to the side, made a phony swipe at it, and watched it bounce down the bank and land in the ditch beside the road. "I'll get it," I announced grandly.

Down the steep bank and out of sight, I removed my mitt and rubbed my red, pulsing palm. I saw the baseball in the ditch, but ignored it for a few moments while I tried to recover the feeling in my hand. When I returned to the top of the bank, I flipped the ball to Billy and trotted toward the house. "I have to go to the bathroom," I said over my shoulder.

Behind closed doors I ran cold water over my throbbing hand and took my time, plenty of time. When I heard Darwin's voice inside the house I knew it was safe to come out.

***

With feeling returning to my glove hand and lunch under my belt, I waited on the front porch for Billy to dress for his team's afternoon practice. Exira was organized for baseball, including a Baseball Council, but lacked the population to divide by age groups below high school. Boys big enough to carry a baseball glove, but too young for senior high, were divided by Main Street into two teams. Billy invited me to practice with the South Team.

My cousin had shown no enthusiasm for my new baseball equipment. But now, fully decked out in my new B.F. Goodrich tennis shoes, my Johnny Mize mitt, a gold baseball cap with a black "G" for "Guthrie" above the bill, my baseball jeans, and a white T-shirt, I assumed Billy would be overcome with awe. I marked time, shifting foot to foot, anticipating his arrival and waiting for the right moment to bowl him over with the news that the B.F. on my shoes stood for Bob Feller.

The screen door swung open. "Ready to go?" Billy asked.

My teammate was wearing a white T-shirt, just like mine. But that was all we had in common. He had baseball shoes, real baseball shoes with cleats, tied together at the shoestrings and thrown over his shoulder. He had baseball pants, real gray flannel baseball pants with elastic that secured his uniform just below the knees. And leggings. He wore real red and white striped leggings, just like a major leaguer.

"Nice uniform," I forced.

"My jersey's at the dry cleaners. I'll get by with a T-shirt today."

I turned my head away and looked at my reflection in a nearby window. Before Billy's arrival, I admired the image of a proud baseball player. Now I saw little more than a hobo. I had more in common with Sack Shoe Sam than my baseball-clad cousin.

"Clothes do not make the man," Mom said. She made a lot of clothes, so I figured she knew. But Billy looked so good and I felt so bad. I would have to make up for the shortcomings of my "uniform" with big-time plays on the field. Yes, I would dazzle Billy and his friends on the baseball diamond. And I could still look forward to the day I wore a Cleveland uniform with the smiling Indian on the sleeve. On that day, the Indian and I would have the last laugh.

***

Billy and I walked the several blocks to the baseball diamond, making a point of using the middle of the freshly graveled street as our path. With the rules of our mothers far from our minds, we reached an unspoken agreement that we were big enough to do as we liked. We reveled in the freedom of running zigzags through furrows of gravel, playing kick-the-can, and testing our marksmanship with rocks thrown at trees and poles and signs. As we neared the park, I heard the sounds of bats striking balls, baseballs thumping gloves, and the shouts and jeers of boys eager to play ball.

I was awed at the sight of the Exira baseball field. Compared to our diamond on the courthouse lawn, it looked like Yankee Stadium. They had a pitcher's mound topped with a regulation white rubber. We had no mound and our pitcher's "rubber" was a scuffed place in the sod. Their bases were white and angular. We used anything we could find for bases: a brick, a rock, an unused baseball glove, or anything that wouldn't blow away. They had a regulation home plate; we had an exposed tree root.

I had figured Exira to be a one-horse town compared to Guthrie Center. After all, we were a county seat with a population double that of Billy's town. We had two dime stores to their one, two drug stores to their Bredahl's Pharmacy, and our Garden Theater was a palace compared to their cracker box Kozy Theater. But I was overwhelmed by their baseball park, and even more so when I saw Billy's teammates warming up. Their stylish uniforms contrasted painfully with my T-shirt and patched jeans. Red letters spelling E-X-I-R-A adorned their chests. I hoped my new Johnny Mize mitt and B.F. Goodrich tennis shoes would draw their attention away from the shortcomings of my uniform.

Billy introduced me to a few friends as his "cousin from Guthrie." His team played catch and participated in drills that Billy called "pepper games." No one called him "Billy Dean" or "Billy." In this baseball setting among teammates he was promoted to "Bill" or "Lud."

None of Billy's teammates had curls like those hidden under my cap. Their hair was short and even, like it had been cut with a lawn mower. They were all business, baseball business. While I was learning the books of the Bible, they were learning to pitch and hit. They thought Mathew, Mark, Luke, and John was a baseball lineup, with John batting cleanup.

"Kiss my ass!" someone screamed.

"I'd rather kiss that than your face," came the reply.

The Exira boys not only used bad words, they shouted them at each other. Gab said naughty things in the quiet darkness of our bedroom, and we giggled as we slipped into the forbidden. Billy's teammates used those words like they were school-learned vocabulary. Profanity that froze my mouth flowed out of theirs as easily as water over a spillway.

Billy and I played catch in front of the first base dugout. We were the youngest and smallest. Bigger and bigger players began to arrive. And then the biggest of all stepped forth – the fearsome Schlaters. This was a twosome to the core. Brothers and battery mates, they were also matched by unbending bravado. Darwin, tall and lean and big enough to be in the army, was the pitcher. Deanie, a year younger and his brother's catcher, had the squat build of his position. With cigarettes dangling from the corners of their mouths and gloves clinched under their arms, the Schlaters strutted past their parting teammates and took their positions as if by divine right.

Darwin Schlater dropped his cigarette and snuffed it out with his pitcher's toe plate. Tall for his fourteen years, he stood on the mound like a giant.

Deanie snapped on his shin guards and chest protector without removing the cigarette he clenched between his teeth. I had never seen anyone his age puffing on the real thing. My cigarettes were made of white candy that looked like a piece of chalk with a red tip. Deanie blew smoke out his nose and tipped ashes like Humphrey Bogart. He was so public, so bold with his Lucky Strike. He pulled on his mask with his non-cigarette hand, crouched into position, and reinserted his fag. Smoke spiraled upward from the bobbing cigarette jutting through the wire of his catcher's mask.

Mom and our church did not approve of smoking and drinking. Every Sunday I learned of the evils of cigarettes and alcohol. Anyone who used those instruments of the Devil was sure to join him in Hell. The Schlater brothers seemed coolly indifferent to that prospect. I was dumbfounded by their defiance of adult and church rules. Didn't they have a mother? Didn't they go to church?

Pop! Darwin's first warm-up pitch exploded into his brother's mitt.

Pop! Another fast ball jarred Deanie's mitt and knocked ashes from his cigarette. Smoke curled upward into his eyes. How, I wondered, could he see to catch?

Pop! Deanie removed his catcher's mitt and shook his hand. The last ball stung. He pushed the mask away from his chin, took a quick puff, spit, and pulled the mask back into place. He slipped on his mitt and pegged the ball to the mound. "Ready?" he shouted to his lanky brother.

Darwin Schlater nodded with a cap pulled tight to his eyes. He had folded the bill into a sharp "A," his shaded slit eyes serving as the cross bar. The red cap with the white "E" offered the vision of a peep hole. How could he see? With a blind pitcher throwing bullets to a catcher looking through smoke, I feared for the poor sap who batted first.

Darwin Schlater pawed the ground with a cleat, hunched his shoulders, and leaned his head forward like a vulture. He twisted the ball in his dangling hand, searching for the right grip for his fast ball.

"Who gets it first?" he sneered.

"Batter up!" Deanie bellowed.

Baseball games at home, whether 500 or work-up, always started with an argument over who got to bat first. "First bat," a number of eager players would holler, almost in unison. A round of "I said it firsts" followed until someone finally won out.

I waited quietly for the usual shouts of "first bat." No one spoke. An awkward hush hung over us.

"Hey, let Bill's cousin bat first," came an unwanted suggestion.

"Yeah, let the new kid with the B.F. tennies bat first," another shouted.

"Hey, four-eyes, what does the B.F. stand for on your snazzy shoes?" asked a voice.

"Butter fingers," someone volunteered.

"Yeah, butter fingers," laughed another.

I had waited for the right moment to wow Billy and his friends with the news that the B.F. on my shoes stood for "Bob Feller." Too late now. My new tennis shoes, a prized possession of a day before, had become an embarrassment. And I stood in them, planted in them, rooted in shame. My face glowed as red as the letters on the fancy Exira uniforms.

"Hey, butter fingers, stand in there. Let's see if you can hit Dar's fast ball," someone demanded.

Peppered by taunts from nameless tormentors, I sauntered toward a bat rack near the third base dugout. At home, we salvaged broken bats from the high school team and tried to give them a new life with wrappings of black electrical tape. Here, Louisville Sluggers with the names of famous hitters hung in a row. I selected the biggest and longest bat, a Johnny Mize model, to impress my new teammates with the size of the "lumber" I carried to the plate. Perhaps, so I hoped, some magic in my mitt might carry over to Johnny's bat. Besides, I liked the extra length to keep me away from Darwin Schlater's fast ball.

The heavy bat was beyond my strength. I realized my mistake immediately, but returning to the bat rack to select a smaller model was not a manly option. The Johnny Mize bat would have to do. I strode to the plate with the bat on my shoulder, the only way I could support it. I put all my strength into a practice swing, trying desperately to keep the bat level. Instead, the swing started with the bat leaving my shoulder and ended with a *thud* on the ground. The catcher snickered.

The diamond was lined with neat stripes of chalk, including the batters' boxes. I stood so far back in the right-handers' box that my Louisville Slugger hardly reached the plate. That was consistent with my priorities of safety first, appearances second, and hitting the ball a distant third.

"Hey, watch four-eyes miss it," a voice shouted.

"Okay, tennis shoe Ernie, take a swing," a second voice called.

Another burst of laughter erupted as a competition developed for making fun of me and my shoes, the latest entry connecting my tennies to the singer from Tennessee.

Trying to hold my bat up and my tears back, I awaited the first pitch from the towering figure on the mound. Darwin Schlater's narrowed eyes punctured and tested my withering ego.

"How d'ya want it, Ernie?" he threatened. He had the manner and finality of an executioner. I stood at the plate as helpless and condemned as a hooded prisoner tied to a post.

The catcher's cigarette smoke burned my eyes. The catcalls continued. "Waaatch'im miss it," taunted someone.

"No hitter," called another.

"Hey, Ernie, get the lumber off your shoulder," shouted a third.

I was on center stage. Watching eyes penetrated; the teasing stung. In Bible school, I learned about David and Goliath. I felt like David, but without a slingshot. The pitcher had that weapon and was setting it in motion with a high leg kick. A blur of a fast ball rocketed toward me.

Pop!

The ball required an amazingly short time to leave the hand of one Schlater and arrive in the mitt of the other. As Bill Sanger would say, "He could really hum the potato."

"Strike one," the catcher cried.

Bill Sanger said Ted Williams, the Red Sox star, could tell a fast ball from a curve by the rotation of the seams. My eyes, the good and the lazy, saw no rotation, no seams, and very little of the ball. It seemed to hang in a haze and then snap at the last instant.

"Good pitch," Deanie hollered to his brother. "Now give'm your fast one."

The bat remained on my shoulder, as it had from the beginning.

"Ya can't hit what ya can't see," came a voice. The words of the speaker were correct, but I was determined to swing at the next pitch, even if I couldn't see it. Standing with a bat on my shoulder and a puzzled look on my face, while the ball whizzed by, was not good for appearances. To "go down lookin'" was the worst possible humiliation, something like unconditional surrender. To "go down swingin'" was more acceptable. I could do that.

Darwin Schlater went into his windup. I saw arms and knees and elbows and feet, but no ball. He was stepping more toward third base than home. I watched with wonder. A sidearm pitch headed my direction. I leaned back. The pitch came after me. I leaned more. The ball kept coming and zoomed close across my chest. If I had been wearing a shirt with buttons, I would have lost one. I fell backward on the seat of my pants as I watched the ball go back over the plate and into the catcher's glove.

"Nice curve," shouted Deanie.

"Way to hit, Ernie," a voice mocked.

"Oh and two," the catcher hollered.

One strike to go. I might strike out, but I wouldn't go down lookin'. I planned to muster an impressive swing before gladly giving way to the next batter.

Darwin Schlater's windup changed again, the third time in three pitches. He kept his pitching arm behind his back and the ball hidden until the last instant. Then he swung his arm in a high arc over his right ear. I had seen the blur of his fast ball. I had survived his curve ball. What was coming now? Something left his hand that even my limited vision told me was not a baseball. This object, glittering in the sunlight like an icicle in January, cartwheeled end-over-end toward my head. I hit the dirt and heard the crash of breaking glass against the backstop. The remains of a Grapette bottle lay in jagged fragments a dozen feet behind me.

Another ripple of laughter and heckling made the rounds.

"Way t'go, butter fingers."

"Yeah, good hittin', Ernie."

I picked myself up and dusted off my shirt and pants. A two-tone green auto pulled into a shaded parking spot behind the bleachers. Deanie Schlater quickly snuffed out his cigarette. Verne Liddicoat, the coach, stepped from his car. Shouts of "butter finger" and "tennis shoe Ernie" stopped, as did the assortment of four-letter words that filled the air before his arrival. Coach Liddicoat was a tall man, over six feet, with square shoulders and auburn hair. His face was as straight as a drill sergeant. He was all business.

Bill took me by the arm and led me to the coach. "This's my cousin from Guthrie."

"What's your name, son?"

"Ernie," volunteered a voice.

Too embarrassed to make a correction, and preferring "Ernie" to the other names I had been called, I smiled instead of replying.

"Looks like from your mitt there that you play first base. Is that right?"

I nodded a lie.

"We'll start with your side batting. We'll give you a chance at first later."

The coach turned towards his players. "Okay, men," he shouted. "Take your positions. We're gonna let Ernie bat first."

The coach's intended generosity was unwelcome news and meant facing Darwin Schlater again. He had thrown a fast ball, a curve ball, and a pop bottle at me. I was not eager to see what might come next, but at least the stern coach offered a second chance to prove myself. My mind moved faster than my feet as I shuffled toward the bat rack, plotting how to wise up and outsmart the fire-balling Darwin Schlater.

I could get to first base in any of three ways: a hit, being struck by a pitch, or manipulating the pitcher into throwing four balls. A hit was out of the question. "No hitter!" came the catcalls, and they were right. My lazy eye saw more of my nose than the blur of cowhide that whizzed my direction. Getting hit by a Darwin Schlater fast ball pained my imagination. I rejected that option in an instant. But a walk! That was my best bet, my only bet.

I selected a smaller, more manageable bat, a Luke Appling model. I swung my lumber with one arm and then the other, and sauntered to the plate. I tapped the sides of my soles with the Louisville Slugger, knocking free imaginary dirt from the imaginary cleats of my B.F. Goodrich tennis shoes. The rap of hard wood against soft canvas went to the bone. I winced. My smirking opponents, bent in fielding position more from habit than expectation, remained silent in the presence of their coach.

Mr. Liddicoat took a position behind the mound where he could make calls at both the plate and bases. After launching three mighty practice swings and straightening my black and gold cap, I stepped into the batter's box – barely.

Behind me, Deanie Schlater crouched in his catcher's position. "No hitter, no hitter," he called.

On the mound, Darwin Schlater pulled the creased bill of his cap hard against his beak-like nose. Thin slits of shaded eyes surveyed his prey.

"Ernie, choke up on the bat."

What did the coach mean? I was gripping the wood with all my strength.

"Move your hands up on the bat, Ding Dong," the catcher mocked.

"Ernie, stand closer to the plate," the coach shouted.

I moved forward an inch, emphasizing movement more than distance. The loose and lanky Darwin Schlater glowered at me from atop his throne of dirt, his eyes narrow, his arms long, his pitching hand fingering for a fast ball grip. The now familiar windup of arms and elbows, knees and feet followed. The ball shot my direction.

Pop!

The ball was in the catcher's mitt before I could react. Ears more than eyes produced an embarrassingly late swing.

"Strike one!" called the umpire. "The count's oh and one."

"Good pitch," yelled the catcher. "Put some more heat on the next one."

"He's swingin' like a rusty gate," an infielder jeered.

I had more than rust to worry about. My timing was bad, my eyesight worse. Stepping from the batter's box, I bent, swiped my hands with dirt, and in "Casey at the Bat" fashion, wiped them on my shirt. Two vicious practice swings followed before I stepped back into the outer reaches of the batter's box. Low in the knees in a "Stan the Man" crouch, I awaited my fate.

Another windup, and another speeding blur came at me. The ball bounced in front of the plate, off the catcher's shin guard, and rolled to the backstop.

"Ball one!" cried the coach turned umpire. "The count's now even, one and one."

A sense of momentary triumph swept over me with Coach Liddicoat's announcement of an even count. My thoughts turned to coaxing another ball out of Darwin Schlater. If I leaned in far enough, so I figured, the pitcher would throw wide of the plate to avoid hitting me. The instant Schlater let loose with the pitch, a quick leap backward would protect my health and move me one ball closer to first base. A perfect strategy. My adversary went into his windup and unleashed the ball. I jumped backward as planned. A curve ball, mindless of my strategy, came after me, almost spinning the bill of my cap. I dropped the bat and myself to the ground. A round of laughter erupted.

"Ball two!" I heard from flat on my back. My strategy had worked – to a point. I picked up my bat, dusted off my jeans, and stood again at the plate.

Something happened to the ball on its next trip to the plate. It just hung in the air, absorbing more time than my nervous bat could allow. A hefty swipe at the seemingly stationary cowhide drew nothing but air. I lost my balance, stumbled to my knees, and watched the floating ball tease across the middle of home plate.

"Good change-up," the catcher shouted.

"Strike two!" the umpire bellowed. "The count's two and two."

A high screaming fast ball took the count to three and two. At that point, Casey had pounded his bat upon the plate. I bent and did likewise against the rubber surface, and watched my bat rebound and knock my cap to the ground.

Curls I had carefully hidden sprung forth like coiled springs.

"Hey, guys, look. It's Shirley Temple," the third baseman shouted.

Another round of laughter swept the infield. Let them laugh, I thought, I have another plan for earning a ticket to first. I tucked my curls under my cap, pulled it tight against my head, and resumed my Musial batting stance. I stooped lower and lower until my elbows rested on my knees and reduced the strike zone to the size of a mail slot. Only a perfect pitch could keep me off first. I wouldn't be swinging this time. I was about to become a base runner. I waited, locked in my awkward, but invincible, crouch. I had out-smarted Darwin Schlater.

A fast ball zoomed right down the middle, splitting the plate and my dream of a walk. I turned and took a step toward the bat rack, not waiting for the coach's fatal verdict and the jeers that were sure to follow.

"Ball four!" cried the umpire. "Take your base, batter."

Batter? I had done nothing to earn that title. No matter. I accepted the coach's charity and trotted toward first. The corner of my eye noted with satisfaction a scowling Darwin Schlater. From his position behind the mound, Mr. Liddicoat turned toward me and smiled.

I stood tall on the first base bag. The coach walked to home plate, bent over with his back to me, removed a whisk broom from his rear pocket, and began to sweep dirt from the white rubber surface. Darwin Schlater swaggered my way, a gloved hand on one hip and a gripped baseball on the other. He loomed over me. The "EXIRA" on his shirt nearly touched my nose.

"Hey, Ernie," he sneered. "The ump made a mistake. You're out!"

"I'm not either," I murmured.

"Get off the bag. You're out!" he insisted.

Intimidated, overwhelmed, and my head hanging, I stepped off first base. I felt the slap of the ball across my leg.

"You're out now, dummy," the pitcher gloated.

Laughter echoed about the field. I stood stunned and silent for a moment before trudging toward the dugout. Sniffles fought through my defenses. Tears of humiliation quickly followed.

Coach Liddicoat looked up from home plate, frowned, and took a step toward first base. "Knock it off, Schlater. Ernie's our guest."

Guest? I could only wonder at the coach's choice of words. He looked into my glistening red eyes. "Ernie, get back on first."

I turned around and dragged my feet back to the bag. My heart wasn't in it. I had been shown up on the diamond and my tears were evidence I couldn't take it. I hadn't measured up as a player or as a man. I finished the game that afternoon, somehow, but have no other memories beyond a feeling my major league career was slipping away and my aspiring manhood placed on hold.

Chapter 13

A Nose for the Ball

When Billy and I returned home, I went behind the closed doors of the bathroom, removed my tennis shoes, took a last sneering look at the B.F. ankle patches, and ripped them off. All that remained were scars of dried glue and fragments of rubber. Later, my mother asked what happened to my new shoes. I told her the patches were torn off playing baseball in Exira – only a partial fib.

Billy and I returned to the local field in the evening to watch the Exira Raiders battle their arch rivals from Audubon. The searing heat of the day had given way to the cooling breeze of a summer evening. Comfortable and relaxed and ready to watch the local semi-pros, I sank into spectator obscurity on the bleachers behind home plate. The aroma of popcorn drifted my way. Kids shouted and chased about under the bleachers. I was relieved to be in the stands among fans, and away from a batter's box of fast balls and catcalls.

I was captivated by the atmosphere of a big-time ball park

and big-time players warming up on the field. Guthrie Center didn't have a semi-pro club and our merchants' team had switched from hardball to softball, an embarrassing secret I kept from Billy. With chalked lines, an elevated pitcher's mound, white bases, bleachers, and a grassy, green outfield surrounded by a fence – the Exira ball park was like the big leagues.

Players tossed balls back and forth, scooped up grounders, and chased flies hit to the outfield. Their uniforms were clean and bright: Exira's white with red lettering and their opponents with crimson letters on a gray background. Billy pointed out the King brothers from Audubon: Deb, Don, and Lynn. Don had pitched in the big leagues and Lynn played in the infield of the St. Louis Cardinals' "Gas House Gang" of the 1930's. Billy also pointed out the tall, square-shouldered Raider's first baseman, Bob Shadibaugh. Billy said Shadibaugh was a "hired gun" who didn't live in Exira, but came by on game days. The Exira Baseball Council paid him and other key players. These were professionals.

I enjoyed watching the game tucked away in the crowd. After the cheers faded and the game ended, Billy and I began our homeward walk along a now familiar gravel street. We had only covered a short distance when a car skidded to a stop beside us.

"Jump in!" Cousin Darwin hollered. Armed with a gray slant-back '37 Ford with a "flathead V-8," as he liked to remind others, Darwin was wild to drive. He tapped his fingers on the top of the car to the tune of "Choo, Choo, Ch'Boogie" blaring from his radio. Billy and I scurried to get in on the fun, he leading the way and taking the middle position with his legs straddling the floor gearshift rod. I followed and sat next to the passenger door, the lumpy springs beneath me threatening to pierce the worn upholstery and my rear. The front seat was forbidden and unknown territory in Dad's

Terraplane. Looking through a windshield was a new and exciting experience, although obscured by the lack of a headlight on my side.

My car-riding experience was limited to Dad's Hudson. The Terraplane was neat and orderly, shined and comfortable. Dad drove with both hands on the wheel and eyes straight ahead. He made full stops when required and never exceeded the speed limit. His driving habits were absolute textbook style.

Darwin's rough and tumble Ford looked like a candidate for the battering ram stunt of the Jimmy Lynch Thrill Show at the county fair, better suited for Beck's Auto Salvage than the highway. If Darwin's driving habits came from a book, as I would soon find out, it was the manual for Jimmy Lynch's drivers.

I had seen the exterior of Darwin's Ford. Minus a hood and covered with pock marks of dents and rust, it had an assortment of tires that included one white wall, a knobby, and a couple of booted, almost round, strays. The inside, as seen in the dim glow of an overhead light, had pink pompoms hanging from the rearview mirror, assorted dashboard gauges dangling from wires, and upholstery-less doors exposing lowered windows in mechanical nudity. Darwin's right hand ringed a silver steering knob adorned with a picture of a naked woman.

Our driver's left elbow extended out the open window and locked on the side of the door, his hand gripping the post of the wing window. He moved the grasp of his right hand to the knob of the floor shift while a foot spurred the gas pedal like a bronco rider. The Ford fussed and fumed and kicked. Smoke gushed from the exposed engine, from under the dash, in the windows, and out of Darwin's mouth where an Old Gold dangled in George Raft fashion.

The Ford and Darwin fought it out. The motor backfired in protest. Darwin reacted with the same naughty words I heard that afternoon at the ball park. "Choo, choo, ch'boogie," the radio bellowed.

Darwin and his gray jalopy had much in common. Smoking, noisy, brash, and straining to leap into the unknown. That was Darwin's car. That was Darwin. That wasn't me. Too late now. I was inside and the door was closed.

"Ready for the takeoff?" Darwin shouted over the uproar.

How, I wondered, did he plan to drive? With one hand gripping the window post and the other the gearshift, none seemed available for the steering wheel.

I had no time to reflect on our driver's dilemma. Darwin "dropped the clutch," as he called it. The Ford's back tires spun into the loose gravel, clawing down, down until they struck the solid clay roadbed with a *screeeeech* and shot us forward with whiplash force.

Darwin used his left arm, always locked over the door, as an anchor to the car, his left hand never releasing its grip on the post of the wing window. His right hand shifted gears, guided the car via the steering knob, tipped ashes from his cigarette, adjusted the radio volume, and slapped the glove compartment door shut with a "damn that thing" when we hit bumps and the adhesive tape "latch" lost its hold. Between curses, Darwin sang along with "Choo, choo, ch'boogie" and tap-danced like Bojangles on the floor pedals, almost in time with the music.

The brief stop sign interruptions to the hurling Ford were tire-biting, gravel-grinding slides with the car arriving at the intersection in a variety of angles. I clung to the door and Billy to me as the sliding car threw us at the dash and the following dust caught up and flooded through the windows. Another flurry of gear maneuvers, steering wheel cranking, and pedal dancing followed as Darwin launched us again with a head-jerking squeal. "Dropping the clutch," "peeling out," and "laying rubber" were added to my vocabulary and nervous system.

Billy had told me the story of riding with Darwin on a trip to Uncle Jess's farm. Aunt Annie rode in the front, and Billy, Donna, and Grandma Phippen in the back. When the railing of a narrow bridge showed up too late to avoid, Darwin took to the ditch, bouncing and jostling his passengers around while he steered down one bank, across a creek, up the other side, and to a stop on the gravel road. The backseat had torn loose and caused a topsy-turvy jumble of seat, Grandma, Donna, and Billy. Grandmother Phippen declared that was her last trip with Darwin. She meant it. She never rode with him again.

I began to understand my grandma's decision as we shot down the gravel road toward the Ludwig house. Darwin continued to agitate the Ford, roaring the engine and changing gears and yanking the steering knob one direction and then the other. Billy and I ricocheted about in the old Ford like pinballs. He kept his legs far apart, allowing Darwin maximum freedom to jerk the gearshift about, and with a thought, no doubt, of avoiding a painful mishap.

We sailed across the rise of a bridge, the wheels of the car leaving the ground before we landed in a slide that Darwin corrected with a series of yanks and turns on the steering knob. We were in the home stretch. I could see the lights of the house on the knoll ahead as we raced up the hill.

To reach the Ludwig home a left turn was required at the intersection, followed immediately by a right turn up the steep driveway to the house. A difficult maneuver was not necessary for someone driving at the speed limit and with the car under control. In our case, the former was out of the question and the latter much in doubt.

I thought Darwin missed the left turn. At the last instant, however, he shifted gears and cranked the steering knob hard to the left. The back of the Ford fishtailed in an arc past the corner, but left the front facing east, our intended direction. The car leaned hard in my direction, the sliding Billy pinning me against the door. A rear tire spun and threw gravel in a fighting effort to right the jalopy and move us forward. Darwin, elevated almost to a standing position with his elbow grip on the door, now cranked the steering knob hard to the right. The car shot eastward, going much too fast to make the sharp upward turn into the driveway. Darwin stomped on the brake, cranked the wheel to the right, and threw us into a slide. We were pointed at the driveway but sliding past it sideways. Darwin changed gears again, put the gas pedal to the floor, showered the side of the neighbor's garage with gravel, and catapulted the Ford up the driveway. He ground the brake into the floorboard and brought us to another sliding stop as the trailing dust again caught us and swept through the car. The Ford was still jiggling and settling when Darwin yanked on the emergency brake, hopped out, and bounded into the house.

I had watched the Jimmy Lynch show at the fair with cars speeding around the track, maneuvering over ramps, crashing through flaming walls, and skidding to dramatic stops in front of the grandstand. It looked like great fun. I wondered what it would be like to ride with my favorite Death Driver, Pony Wilson. I found out. It wasn't fun.

The ride with Darwin was far removed from my previous car experience of Dad driving carefully, Mom reminding us to keep our feet off the seat, and Gab and I sitting in the back in church pew position. "Safety first," Mom often said. I saw her point. I remained in place while my nervous system recovered.

"C'mon, I can't get out," Billy pleaded.

***

I climbed into the inviting brass bed without complaint or hesitation, a full two hours past my usual 8:30 bedtime. I found refuge in a soft mattress, a gentle breeze, and the warmth of Billy. Heavy eyes closed out a long day.

"Isn't it about time you boys got up?" Aunt Annie asked from beside our bed. "It's nine o'clock." I rubbed my eyes. Billy squirmed in warm comfort beside me, sharing my reluctance to rise for another day. "I put a pot of hot chocolate and some bread on the table. You boys can make yourselves some toast. I've got washing to do."

Billy and I dressed, moved to the dining room table, and sat facing each other across the oak surface. Aunt Annie's version of "Zip-a-Dee-Doo-Dah," sung to the churning beat of the washing machine, drifted our way from the laundry room. "My, oh my, what a wonderful day," she sang. I certainly hoped so. The trip to Exira had not gone well. I had been punched out, burned out, tagged out, and scared out of my wits. I needed a victory.

Mom boasted to friends that I was a "good eater." Maybe I could make up for my poor showing in boxing and baseball with a triumph at the breakfast table. Like a poker player raising the ante, I pushed the toaster toward Billy.

"Betcha I can eat more toast than you can."

"Betcha can't."

The match was on. We pulled open the bottom-hinged chrome sides and deposited our competing entries in the one-side-at-a-time toaster. At the first smell of browning bread, we seized our half-toasted slice, swiped a knife with butter across the crusted side, added homemade gooseberry jelly, and downed the opening round with a gulp of hot chocolate. And so it went, each round starting when the toaster produced two more slices and ending when we washed down the last bite with another swig of cocoa. The battle continued, slice for slice, round by round until the bread on our plates was eaten and the hot chocolate consumed. After six rounds, I was bloated, sick of toast, and prepared to settle for a draw. Not Billy. He went to the kitchen and returned with a bottle of milk and a fresh loaf of Butternut Bread.

My pride was larger than my stomach. I labored on, slice for slice, gulp for gulp. The pace eased and my interest dragged. By unspoken agreement we slowed the match by toasting the now tasteless bread on both sides. The seesaw battle reached the twelfth round. Billy looked at his toast, put it to his lips, hesitated, and set it back on his plate. He was finished.

A mere slice of toast stood between me and victory. With all the milk consumed, I faced a dry run. Billy showed little interest in my efforts. I bit and chomped and chewed and choked down the parched piece of triumph.

"I win," I declared. But I didn't feel like a winner. The victory was hollow. My stomach wasn't. It bulged and threatened to expel its contents. My head ached. I tried a few steps to relieve the painful pressure on my stomach. Walking didn't help. Jarring, no matter how slight, only made matters worse. I laid down on the sofa. That didn't help either. No position brought relief. Billy remained at the table, motionless and looking ill.

Aunt Annie, her white apron wet from the laundry, stepped into the dining room. "I'm finished with the wash, boys. What would you like for lunch? How about a bacon, lettuce, and tomato sandwich on toast?"

"Mom, I think we'll just skip lunch," Billy moaned.

"Why, what on earth for? You need your energy if you're gonna play ball again this afternoon. Your practice will come before you know it."

Aunt Annie's well-intended reminder increased my discomfort. I didn't feel like doing anything, and certainly didn't mind skipping another belittling session at the ball park. Billy, however, would never miss a practice. He would get to the diamond if he had to crawl, a prospect that, in our condition, could not be ruled out. Ninety minutes later, and only slightly relieved from our eating contest, Billy and I headed for the ball diamond. This time kick-the-can, rock-throwing, and running and dodging were ruled out. Instead, two nine-year-old boys waddled down the gravel street, burping and belching on their way to the Exira baseball field.

I hoped Coach Liddicoat would be at the diamond when we arrived. His presence brought order and gave my abused ego a shot at survival. When I didn't see the coach's car, I began planning protective measures. If offered the opportunity of first bat, I would suggest politely that someone else be given that honor. If threatened with again facing Darwin Schlater on the mound, I would excuse myself to go to the bathroom, a distinct possibility given the quantity of toast and cocoa I had consumed. In the meantime, I would shrink into the background.

Darwin Schlater was on the mound whipping fast balls across the plate. I looked for an opportunity to disappear among the fielders before anyone mentioned batting. Second base, seemingly the least menacing position of the infield, was open. Only lefties were likely to hit that way, and first base was close. I could throw a baseball that far. I took my position at second, leaned forward, and placed a gloved hand on my left knee and my throwing hand on the right, like the Raiders' second baseman I watched the night before. I felt better behind Darwin Schlater than in front of him at the plate.

No one paid attention to me and no one called me "butter fingers," perhaps because my shoes no longer included the B.F. initials. My teammates had settled into calling me "Ernie." I understood the make-fun origin of the name, but as long as they didn't precede it with "tennis shoe," I didn't mind. Ernie Lombardi, a catcher for the Giants, was an all-star and former

MVP. I could go along with sharing a name with someone headed for the Baseball Hall of Fame. Now in a supporting role at second base, I chanted, "No hitter. No hitter."

Jack Peppers wiggled his bat at the plate, waiting for Darwin Schlater's pitch. Several fast balls and curves popped into the catcher's glove without a swing from the batter. The slender figure on the mound, yesterday's villain, had turned into an ally as his untouched pitches removed the pressure of fielding. Darwin's second baseman was more of a spectator than a player. That suited me fine. "He's swinging like a rusty gate," I heckled, even though Jack's bat had not yet left his shoulder.

"Hey, Dar, let up on it a bit," Deanie shouted from behind the plate. "This is batting practice."

Mocking his brother's suggestion, Darwin lobbed a pitch toward the plate. Jack smacked a two-hop grounder to the shortstop. Robert Lykke gobbled up the ball and threw out the runner at first. "Round the horn," he shouted.

Round the horn? I wondered what that meant.

"Hey, Ernie," Charlie Schwab hollered from his first base position. "Catch." He threw the call to me. I didn't know what I was supposed to do with it.

"Round the horn," Robert Lykke repeated. "Throw the ball to *me*, Ernie."

I did as asked. The ball then went from Lykke to the third baseman to the catcher and back to the pitcher. I would know what to do next time.

Jerry Klein stepped to the plate. I prepared myself for another out and another "round the horn." Billy told me Jerry was their best hitter. He was square-shouldered and muscular and taking hefty practice swings with the Johnny Mize bat I could hardly lift. Darwin Schlater would not let this batter off easy. He hummed an inside pitch that made the red-headed hitter jump backwards. I watched the drama as Jerry moved back to the plate, unfazed and looking intently at the pitcher.

The next pitch, a fast ball over the plate, met with a "crack" of the bat that sent a hot grounder shooting my way. A smoking trail of dust marked the path of the bullet. I tried desperately to track the ball, hoping to snare it in my mitt. I reached. The angry grounder snapped at me, smashed against my nose, and ricocheted off my forehead. My tin glasses flew skyward. I fell backward, blood streaming from my nose. I was out cold.

"Get 'im off his back," someone hollered as I started to come around. Red sticky liquid continued to flow from my nose. Groggy and dazed, I sensed voices more than I heard them.

"Yeah, roll 'im over on his side so he won't choke on his blood."

"Are you okay, Ernie?"

I didn't know if I was or not. The blood frightened me, but I was too stunned to make sense of anything.

Someone placed a handkerchief under my nose. "You'll be all right, Ernie. Don't worry."

"Hey, guys, let's get 'im outta the sun. Give me a hand." My blurred eyes made out the image of Darwin Schlater. His hands and unknown others lifted me gently and moved me toward the bleachers. "Here, let's lay 'im on the grass in the shade," Darwin directed.

Though reduced in quantity, the flow of blood persisted. I could feel the thick liquid drying and caking around my nose and lips. Red splotches covered the front of my white T-shirt. My nose and head throbbed. Tears without sobs mingled with the blood on my face and drew no reaction from my teammates.

"Don't worry, Ernie. It'll stop bleedin' in a minute."

"Yeah, don't worry."

The tone of the voices soothed my feelings more than the repeated words. A feeling of acceptance stirred my courage. This wounded, bloody heap lying on his side in the grass had become a part of the group. "Butter fingers" or "tennis shoe Ernie," baseball player or not, I had become one of them. What I had not achieved with a bat or a glove, I had accomplished with a bloody nose.

A Good Samaritan in a blue pickup stopped when he saw me lying on the ground. Bob Shadibaugh, the first baseman for the Exira Raiders, stepped out of his GMC. "What happened?" he asked.

"Ernie took one in the nose."

"We gotta stop that bleeding. Do one of you guys have a piece of paper to stick under his lip? That can stop it."

Adults had "Indian tricks," clever ways of dealing with problems, medical and otherwise, that were not found in books. I took the placement of paper under my lip to be such a trick, a method Doc Thornburg was unlikely to use.

When no one responded to his request for a piece of paper, Mr. Shadibaugh opened his wallet. I watched him thumbing through a row of dollar bills. Was he going to use a dollar for his medical treatment? That would surely make me feel better.

A grocery list written on the back of a brown stained adding machine tape was placed under my upper lip. The broad-shouldered Raiders' first baseman helped me into a sitting position. The bleeding had nearly stopped. "Maybe you better go home. I can drop you off."

I looked at my bloody T-shirt and nodded. The Good Samaritan lifted me to my feet and helped me into his pickup. I would soon be under the gentle care of Aunt Annie. Men could not duplicate motherly tenderness, even Good Samaritans with Indian tricks.

The five-minute trip to Aunt Annie's passed silently. "How d'ya feel, kid?" Mr. Shadibaugh asked when we stopped in the gravel driveway.

"Better."

"Looks like you're gonna have a couple of shiners."

I didn't know what a "shiner" was and didn't take time to ask. I wanted to be near my aunt. I thanked the Good Samaritan and entered the house, afraid to look in the mirror. I held a bloody handkerchief against a nose that still oozed. My T-shirt was a crimson mess, my cheeks a mixture of blood and tears.

Aunt Annie dropped the clothes she was folding and rushed to meet me. "Looks like you had an accident," she said in her unflappable manner. "Better get you cleaned up."

My aunt soon had me washed and in a clean shirt. My headache was disappearing. Annie's care was divine intervention.

Billy's mother suggested he and I not sleep together that night, no doubt thinking one of his nighttime outbursts might cause further injury to my nose. Billy and I were in agreement with her decision, but for different reasons. I needed a night of rest without worrying about my cousin throwing another fit, and Billy wanted to try out the jungle hammock he had purchased from an Army surplus store.

The hammock Billy proudly showed me was fully enclosed, with net windows on the two sides to allow for airflow and keep out insects. A long zipper opening with a pull that could be reached from either the inside or outside ran almost the full length under one of the windows.

At bedtime, I helped Billy into his hammock. Tinges of envy tore at me, but I looked forward to a quiet and cozy night in a bed by myself. My cousin looked comfortable and happy as he zipped the hammock shut. I told him to "sleep tight and don't let the bed bugs bite," and returned to the house.

I had trouble breathing through my nose that evening, but freedom from a fit-throwing, arm-thrashing cousin more than made up for my discomfort. I soon fell asleep. Another tough day had passed. Rest was needed and welcomed.

The sweet cooling breeze of an Iowa summer evening passed through my window. Middle-of-the-night shrieking also passed through the window and awakened me with a start. I recognized the cries of my cousin.

"Get me out of here! Oh, please help me! They're after me! Please! Help! Help!"

Billy's nightmares and screaming no longer frightened me, but I did need the sleep. "Here we go again," I said to myself while joining others in running to the aid of Billy.

A jumping and gyrating jungle hammock, almost spinning from the frantic movement inside, greeted our arrival.

"Get me out of this thing! Please! Oh, Jesus! Get me out of here!"

Billy was fighting another battle in his sleep. Moaning and groaning and pleading for help, he struggled and fought demons in his canvas chamber. Unconscious and panicked, he was unaware of the zipper pull.

"They're after me! Help! Oh, please get me get out of this thing!" he screamed.

Uncle Bill was trying to do exactly that but having difficulty in the dark finding the exterior zipper pull of the kicking and bouncing hammock. Finally, he managed to get the zipper open. Aunt Annie reached inside and applied her motherly magic. "There, there, sweetheart. We're going to take you inside to bed."

Billy's solo in the jungle hammock ended along with my opportunity for an unshared bed. I hoped my cousin's quota for fits was no more than one per night.

Billy received no more visits from goblins and slept soundly for the rest of the evening. The next morning, he wanted to know how he started the night in the hammock and ended it in bed with me. He could not believe the details of his middle of the night struggle. "Did I really do that?" he asked.

Aunt Annie asked that I not talk to Billy about his "problem." I knew about problems. That was what Mom called my nail-biting. Throwing fits didn't seem natural. Something was wrong. Grown-ups seemed to confuse silence with a cure.

Aunt Annie had restocked bread, butter, and jam, and again served hot chocolate for breakfast. She said nothing about our eating contest of the previous day. I thought for sure we would get in trouble. My aunt's level of tolerance made Job look anxious. She allowed small boys to learn from their mistakes. Billy and I had learned the drawbacks of an eating contest. We switched to a bowl of Wheaties to go with our cocoa.

Because of my battered condition, Billy and I changed our competition to cards. Donna joined us after breakfast for rounds of "Old Maid" and "Crazy 8" before Billy and I moved outside looking for something else to occupy our time. With me on the baseball disabled list, we turned to the other Exira pastime – mischief. That was not really my nature. It was more of "when in Rome." I was in Exira and the boys there were an ornery lot. To fit in meant to be naughty. Besides, Mom was twenty miles away.

Across the street from the Ludwigs, an old man, Sy Wahlert, operated a machine shop in his garage. A downhill view from atop a steep bank behind Billy's house provided a good opportunity for watching Mr. Wahlert at work. Trees and shrubs provided the means for hiding, and we were far enough from the house that Aunt Annie was unlikely to happen by. Billy and I decided to amuse ourselves by throwing rocks on the tin roof of Mr. Wahlert's shop.

Our first efforts fell short of the objective. We moved down the bank and closer to the shop, giving up much of our cover. Our throws hit the mark this time and rattled down the ribbed metal roofing, making a wonderful racket. We ducked behind a bush. Mr. Wahlert came out of his shop, looked at his roof, and went back inside.

Billy and I launched two more rocks that landed where we wanted and with the noise we hoped for. Mr. Wahlert charged from his garage looking for culprits. I panicked and ran for the house. I didn't make it. I slipped and fell in the gravel driveway and ground rock fragments into the heel of my right hand. Mr. Wahlert gave up the chase when he saw I had provided my own punishment. I stumbled into the house holding a painful and bleeding hand.

Grandmother Phippen, the family physician, had arrived that morning for a visit. "Grandma, I hurt my hand," I cried out. Withholding tears, I showed her my scraped, rock-embedded hand.

"Looks like you took a fall. We'll get that cleaned up and you'll be as good as new." Grandma led me to the sink, rinsed the dirt and blood from my hand and, after holding a match flame to the pointed tongs of tweezers, removed rock and dirt fragments.

"Better wash that with alcohol to kill the germs," she said. I gritted my teeth, but said nothing, while grandma poured the stinging liquid over my wounds. She then took a piece of bacon from the refrigerator, covered it with salt and pepper, and laid the fatty meat across my wound. The salt hurt, but the cool fat of the bacon felt soothingly good.

"The salt will heal your scrapes. The pepper will draw the poison out, and the bacon will keep the wound from getting crusty." Grandma had spoken. She was as sure of her methods as Doc Thornburg.

"We'll hold the bacon in place with some sheet strips and you'll be just fine." I watched Grandma wrap my hand and saw my time on the baseball disabled list extended. I would be left-handed for awhile.

My left hand was as useless as my left eye. I used it as little as possible. It didn't have the strength or skill of my right hand. What could I use my left hand for?

One of my intentions in visiting Billy was an opportunity, away from Mom, to comb the curls out of my hair. Pulling a comb through my hair wouldn't take much skill. I could do that with my left hand after a good plastering of water on my unwanted waves.

In the quiet of the bathroom, I soaked my hair with water and pulled a comb across my head, as flat to the scalp as possible in an effort to keep curls from popping back up. I repeated the process over and over, hoping for immediate success.

While ridding myself of curls, I heard an argument between Glen and Darwin. The dispute grew in volume and intensity until bodies and furniture crashed against each other. I peeked out the bathroom door. The fight had spilled into the kitchen. Chairs tumbled, the table scraped across the linoleum floor, and clenched hands pounded flesh. In the movies, a fist struck a chin with a hard "knock." The real thing sounded different, more like "splat," but the struggle was the same. I watched in amazement as Darwin and Glen thrashed each other about the kitchen.

"Stop that! You boys, stop that!"

Grandma entered the fray. A gritty woman of eighty-seven pounds and an inch short of five feet, the square-jawed Laura Phippen had the look and determination of Mammy Yokum. She stiff-armed her way between her battling grandsons like a referee calling "break" in a boxing match.

"Stop that! That's enough!" she shouted.

A wild fist caught Grandma flush on the chin and decked her. She went down for the count, sprawled and dazed on the kitchen floor.

Unaware their grandmother had been kayoed, Darwin and Glen continued to bash each other while Grandma, flat on her stomach, searched blindly for her eyeglasses and false teeth. Her glasses, smashed into bent frames and shattered lenses, lay scattered about the floor. Her false teeth were intact and under the refrigerator.

I wanted to help Grandmother Phippen, but was fearful of meeting her fate. I watched, saucer-eyed and ready to slam the bathroom door if the fighting came my way.

Aunt Annie had gone to the cave to select canned items for dinner. When she returned, she saw her seventy-year-old mother lying on the kitchen floor, feeling around for her glasses and dentures. Her two sons, still oblivious to the plight of the fallen referee, continued to flail at each other.

I saw something new in Aunt Annie's eyes. Could it be anger? I had never seen a trace of irritation, hostility, or anything approaching violence in this saintly lady of kind words and good deeds.

My aunt surveyed the scene, placed her hands on her hips, and reached deep inside for appropriate words.

"Damn!"

Did that bad word come from Aunt Annie? Glen and Darwin froze with their fists in mid-air. They turned toward their mother, their chins drooping. Had she actually said such a word? Did an angel curse?

Annie seemed more embarrassed than commanding. Darwin helped Grandma to her feet. Glen retrieved the several pieces of broken glasses and lamely handed his grandmother her false teeth.

"We're sorry. We'll buy you new glasses," the two grandsons said in unison.

***

The rest of my week in Exira passed without further injury, but with many activities. I held hands with Donna at the Kozy Theater watching "Maizie Gets Her Man" and got drenched in a downpour on the way home. Billy and I camped out in a pup tent in the backyard of Gary and Charlie Schwab. When I awakened, my cousin was gone. No fit and no Billy. He had walked home in his sleep and woke up in his own bed the next morning. We went on another camping trip, just beyond the edge of town. Aunt Annie made me promise to tie Billy's feet together before he went to sleep. He didn't escape that night. We located an abandoned farm house on the way home and quickly determined it was haunted. We got chills walking through vacant rooms of cracked plaster and broken windows. We created a golf course in the Ludwig yard by planting tin cans for holes, and stroked a golf ball with "clubs" made from slats rescued from the discard bin at Kozy Industries. We played "Crazy 8," "Old Maid," and "Authors" on the living room floor and walked every afternoon to Bredahl's drug store for a fudge sickle.

My week in Exira concluded with Aunt Annie telling me Darwin would drive me to Guthrie Center after lunch. I was battered, bruised, and brimming from my adventures – but ready to go home. Riding with Darwin was a terrifying prospect for which I had no choice. I reported to his Ford with my torn and wrinkled United Food Market suitcase.

"Come on. Get in. Let's go." As always, Darwin was wild to drive.

I placed my paper suitcase with dirty clothes and my ball mitt in the back seat and climbed into the front. Darwin was pumping the footfeed, creating the usual smoke and racket. I slammed the door and he dropped the clutch. We shot backwards, the Ford roaring down the steep driveway like an avalanche. Darwin extended his head out the window and looked to the rear. As usual, his left elbow clamped to the outside of the door, his right hand jerked the steering knob back and forth, and his feet danced on the floor pedals.

At the bottom of the drive, he cranked the silver steering knob hard to the left while standing on the brakes and threw the Ford into a backwards and sideways slide. Before the car quit skidding, Darwin shifted to low. When the car lined up with the road, he jerked his foot from the clutch. The rear tires struggled to stop the slide and move the car forward, throwing gravel and dirt everywhere. The tires eventually had their way. We shot through the cloud of dust the sliding Ford created. We were on our way to Guthrie Center.

The trip home was more exciting than I wanted. Sensations of speed and noise glued me to the seat like a roller coaster ride. Through open windows, the wind passed my ears in a howl. The hoodless engine roared and strained as Darwin pushed for more speed. The Ford shuddered and rattled and poured fumes into the interior through windows, the dash, and a hole in the floor board big enough to watch the pavement of Highway 64 zipping by below my feet.

My level of anxiety was more than matched by Darwin's delight. He was having a good time. He laughed and tried to talk above the uproar. He pushed the footfeed flat against the floorboard and swore at the Ford for not going faster. We passed everything: cars, pickups, trucks, and tractors. Everything. If it was in front of us, we passed it.

In my advanced nervous state, I took a peek at the speedometer. Perhaps, I hoped, the rushing air, noise, and pavement catapulting past beneath my feet exaggerated our speed. Catching a look at the speedometer was not easy as it bobbed about on the end of a cable. I had the impression speedometers didn't go past 50 because Dad never exceeded that number. Darwin's was locked on 80.

Noting my worried stare at the bouncing speedometer, Darwin leaned my way to make certain I could hear. "Don't worry about that damned thing. It's broken. We're goin' a hellava lot faster than that."

The only advantage to the terror of riding with Darwin was the trip went fast, very fast. After bouncing across the tops of the rolling hills of Highway 64 like a flat rock skipping on a pond, we arrived at the top of Fairgrounds Hill. I caught a quick look at Guthrie Center before we plummeted down the hill and up State Street, took a screeching left on Fifth, another to the right on Main and skidded to a stop at 605, the McKibbin house – home.

"You're home," Darwin announced.

I didn't need the reminder. I felt it.

***

Until my week with Billy, I thought Guthrie Center was like every small town. I was wrong. Exira was different, much different.

Exira was baseball and beer, tobacco and taboos. Guthrie Center was sugar and spice and pansy nice. We learned to read books. They learned to read the third base coach's signals. We listened to stories during the children's hour at the library. They listened to the crack of the bat and baseball chatter.

Guthrie Center had churches, Sunday schools, and Bible schools. So did Exira, I guess. But I didn't hear the name of Jesus mentioned in any Mom-acceptable manner during my visit.

The front doors of Exira's taverns were worn and loose, like the back doors of beer parlors in Guthrie Center. Both towns had city councils, but Exira also had a baseball council for the town's more important business. We learned poems about Jack and Jill and Humpty Dumpty. The Exira boys spouted limericks starring an old hermit named Dave and a lady from Nantucket.

Exira was a good training ground for a nine-year-old boy intent on becoming a man. Controlling my tears was essential to that cause. The Exira boys forced the issue. I was looking for a playground, but with two shiners, a bloody nose, a skinned hand, a sore chin, and an aching belly, I found more of a war zone. If I didn't meet the test of manhood fully, I at least survived and was proud of that. I didn't cry very much, didn't call my mother, and didn't ask to go home. A week in Exira converted me from a little boy to a little man.

I also learned families are not the same. Our family existence had a quiet conformity. Mom sewed and cooked, humming as she went. Dad said little, and Darrell marooned himself at his work desk upstairs. Gab was ornery but sly, saving his naughty words for our bedroom. I was mostly an observer, particularly in my earlier years, trying to figure out how to fit in. I no longer worried about that.

The Ludwig home was one of contrasts. Aunt Annie was the eye of a hurricane, calm and serene in the midst of turbulence. Uncle Bill, Darwin, and Glen supplied the storm, Donna joined her mother in the eye, and Billy played baseball.

My major league aspirations came home from Exira in the same condition as my nose. I learned standards of excellence are not based on fantasy and, no matter what point of achievement is attained, there are those who perform at a higher level. I continued to re-read the *Kid from Tompkinsville* and *Strikeout Story*, but more as fiction and history than an outline of my future.

I tugged harder at the knot on Mom's apron strings. I began to comb my hair, making every effort to flatten the curls with a plastering of soapy water. I asked Mr. Sanger to cut my locks shorter and retired Teddy permanently to a closet drawer. Over the years, Dad rebent the bows of my glasses with his pliers several times so they would continue to reach the ears of a growing boy and save the cost of a new pair. Shortly after I returned from Exira, the bows of the glasses I had worn since age two ran out of length and I ran out of patience. One day – lazy eye be damned – I threw the tin-rimmed, corroded glasses in a wastebasket. I didn't wear glasses again for decades.

***

Mom's apron strings never completely untied. I hold them to this day, more than thirty years after a call from a doctor in Des Moines. Gladys Oakley, the department secretary, gently opened the door to my classroom in Oldfather Hall and beckoned with a message in her hand. I stepped her way and took the note. "This came a minute ago," she said. "I told them you would call back when your class was over."

I thanked Gladys and glanced at the pink memo slip. A phone number was followed by a message: "Please call about your mother's condition. Mercy Hospital, Des Moines."

Two days before, I sat in Mom's living room while she played on the floor with my two daughters, Micki and Jackie, her only granddaughters. After three sons and four grandsons, she was thrilled to have girls in the family. In the middle of the play session, Mom got up with tears in her eyes and complained of pain in her side. She went to the phone, called her doctor in Des Moines, and arranged to see him the next day.

I thought little about her call at the time and returned that afternoon to Lincoln. Mom and doctors and hospitals were a combination I had known all my life. She seemed both vulnerable and invincible. She rested on the davenport frequently, took daily naps, and twice remained bedfast for nearly a year. She had suffered from burns, ulcers, breast cancer, a car accident and rounds of knee surgery afterwards, but always bounced back.

When class concluded a few minutes later, I went to my office and called the hospital. A doctor spoke in a solemn voice: "Your mother has ovarian cancer. There is nothing we can do. I'm sorry."

"How long does she have, doctor?"

"Perhaps a few months."

"Thank you," I murmured. I heard a "click" on the line and then a dial tone from the receiver that dangled from my limp hand. I stared out the window of my fifth floor office at the nearby campanile of the University of Nebraska. Tears blurred my vision and streamed down my cheeks. I leaned on my desk with my elbows and sunk my face into my hands. I had to go. I had to be with Mom.

A few minutes later, I was on Interstate 80 and on my way to Des Moines. The day started with my usual drive down Vine Street listening to Dick Perry on KLIN. He always closed his program with a reminder: "It's nice to be important, but it's more important to be nice." Mom would like that, I had thought to myself. Now, I was on the road and four hours from her bedside.

I passed through Omaha and on to the rolling hills of southwest Iowa with the radio off and my thoughts tuned to my mother. Happy memories of times together came to mind. I recalled looking for Mr. Yahoody in the refrigerator, holding hands during matinees at the Garden Theater, swinging arms in rounds of "making candy" on our way to the Square Deal, drinking "green" 7-Up at Cronk's Cafe, and listening to Dr. I.Q. while snuggled against her in bed. I remembered hearing "The Fortune and the Beggar" and smiled thinking about Mom's yellow baseball and bloated ball glove.

I passed the intersection at Highway 71 and noted the exit

for Exira where I had produced more blood than base hits on the baseball diamond. Twenty minutes later, another green sign indicated "Guthrie Center." The mere name of my hometown brought the aroma of Mom's apple pie to my nose and recalled my eighteen years at 605 Main Street.

The house was gone. Dad sold the family home to St. Mary's and the church replaced it with a parish community center. Meanwhile, Mom and Dad moved to a small residence they built on the alley where Grandmother McKibbin's little brown house once stood.

I had walked through the structure at 605 Main one last time the day before the wrecking crew came. The home where mom managed the scrapes on my soul and a bloody one on my chin, where I played indoor baseball and practiced my cornet, was reduced to an empty building of cracked walls and scuffed linoleum floors. Without Mom sitting on the floor, one leg tucked under the other, straight pins in her mouth, and busy converting newspapers to dress patterns, it wasn't a home. I left town that day pained at the thought of a wrecking ball crashing through the bay window where Mom sat at her Singer, bashing the sink where she stood, and ripping apart the house where I was born and raised.

I passed Stuart and Earlham and a sign marked "Van Meter," Bob Feller's hometown. I followed his career that led to the Baseball Hall of Fame, but not his footsteps. I pitched for my high school team, but with a fast ball considerably slower than Mr. Feller's and a curve with the bend of a steel clothes line. No baseball scouts waited at my door as I had waited for an autograph outside my idol's locker room.

My thoughts returned to my solemn journey as Van Meter slipped into the background and I approached the outskirts of Des Moines. A few minutes later, I pulled into the parking lot of Mercy Hospital. A receptionist provided my mother's room number. A ride in an elevator and a long walk down a buffed linoleum corridor led to my mother's room.

A short time before my arrival, a doctor had informed Mom of her terminal illness. When I entered the room she was staring at the ceiling, her eyes filled with fright, and shaking in near convulsions from head to toe. She seemed unaware, incapable of knowing, of my presence. I went to her bedside and grasped her trembling hand. I wanted to offer soothing words and recalled how she had told me, "That's just the angels moving their furniture," when I was frightened by house-shaking, window-rattling explosions of thunder. I searched for words for a moment before recalling those of my mother when cleansing my itching chicken pox with salt water through a long and fever-ridden night. "Why don't you say something, Mommy," I had asked.

"Love doesn't need words," she responded.

I remained silent, continued to hold my mother's hand, and ran soft love strokes up and down her arm. Her shaking slowed, and then stopped. She turned her head toward me and smiled. "Did you have a nice trip?"

THE END

Where Are They Now?

Mom passed away in January of 1974. We were called to her bedside at the Guthrie Center hospital a month before, but she fooled the doctors with a miraculous, if short, recovery. "We just about lost you, Mom," I said when she opened her eyes.

"I wanted one more Christmas," she replied. She lived through what she called "the best Christmas of my life" in a room filled with cards and flowers before leaving to help the other angels move their furniture.

Dad went into a tailspin of medical and emotional problems when Mom died. He continued to work when able, remarried, and lived another ten years. A stroke closed his right hand and the doors to McKibbin's Garage. He passed away months later.

Darrell McKibbin was a scientist for the National Space and Aeronautics Administration for thirty years before retiring to Ukiah, California, where he lives with his wife, Polly.

Gary "Gab" McKibbin spent most of his adult life as a traveling salesman. He is retired and lives in Atlanta, Georgia, with his wife, Mary Lou.

Bill Ludwig was a pitcher in college and for the Shenandoah and Clarinda, Iowa, semi-pro teams. He is a retired high school teacher living in Shenandoah with his wife, Jan.

Darwin Ludwig worked as a carpenter and roofer in Des Moines for many years before passing away in 2003.

Glen Ludwig is the owner of an engineering firm and lives in San Bernardino, California, with his wife, Pearl.

Donna Ludwig Thygesen married and raised a family on a farm northwest of Exira. She passed away in 2004 after several bouts with cancer.

Howard Ely returned from the war and established an auto body repair business in Guthrie Center where he now lives in retirement. In 2005, Howard and his siblings, Lawrence, Elbert, and Norma – all octogenarians – enjoyed a family reunion.

Bob Feller retired from baseball in 1956 after setting scores of records. His story, that of a seventeen-year-old boy who went from an Iowa farm to the major leagues, is one of the greatest in sports history. He lives in Florida with his wife, Anne.

Harry James passed away in 1983. I saw him play once at the Val Air Ballroom in West Des Moines. I listen regularly to his recordings.

Darwin Schlater worked for Audubon County as a road grader operator for many years before retiring. He still lives in Exira.

Dean Schlater remained in Exira and worked in the meat packing industry before retiring.

Verne Liddicoat moved from Exira to another coaching position in Missouri Valley, Iowa, where he remained until his retirement in 1975. He passed away in 1998.

Richard Beane moved from Guthrie Center to Jefferson, Iowa, where he lived with his wife, Sheryl. He is deceased.

Judy Riaski Roberts lives in Tulsa, Oklahoma, with her husband, Jim.

Eldon "Fizz" Reed, M.D., is an anesthesiologist living in Fremont, Ohio, with his wife Monteen.

Jim "Pink" Dowd is a retired businessman living in Merrimack, New Hampshire, with his wife, Lynn.

Father Jeremiah O'Sullivan retired from his post in Guthrie Center and returned to his native Killarney, Ireland. He is deceased.

Ruby Rosenthal is a fictitious name, the only one in the book. The real "Ruby" moved away while we were in second grade. I never saw her again.

Name List

Allen, Ted
Anderson, John W.
Applegate, Jack
Appling, Luke
Arends, Gerald L.
Arends, Leslie J.
Astaire, Fred
Bailey, Phil
Baker, Frank "Home Run"
Ball, John
Barrow, Blanche
Barrow, Buck
Barrow, Clyde
Bateham, Ellsworth
Bauer, Henry J.
Beach, Harold
Bean, Ray T.
Beane, Maxine
Beane, Richard
Beck, Merle L.
Benton, Curly
Benton, Raymond J.
Bergman, Ingrid
Blaubaugh, George F.
Blomquist, Harold
Bogart, Humphrey
Booth, Charlie
Boudreau, Lou
Brady, Joyce (Raygor)
Brady, Mrs. Harmon
Brainard, Doris
Bruner, Jess
Buck, Frank

Buttler, Ralph J.
Buttler, Richard C.
Campbell, Charles L.
Carmichael, John
Cavallaro, Carmen
Cavaretta, Phil
Coffman, Ida Rose Sanger
Compton, J.R.
Conrad, Richard "Pepsi"
Conway, Robert
Cooper, Robert P.
Cordon, Myrt
Cornish, Al
Corrigan, Bill "Zag"
Covault, Gifford
Covault, Rex
Crees, Bud
Crees, Edri
Cripe, Kenneth
Cronk, Dan
Crosby, Bing
Decker, Ned
Devilbiss, Gene
Dickey, Donald D.
DiMaggio, Joe
Dixon, James
Dowd, James
Dowd, Jim "Pink"
Dudley, Pauline
Dunlevy, Brian
Egger, Dean J.
Eisenhower, Dwight
Ely, Elbert

Ely, Emerson

Ely, Howard

Ely, Lawrence

Ely, Luella

Ely, Norma

Emmons, Calvin L.

Eversall, George R.

Feilmeyer, Robert

Feilmeyer, Ronald

Feller, Bob

Ferguson, Bill

Ferguson, Lloyd

Fillman, Richard D.

Fitzpatrick, James A.

Flanery, Charlie

Fleak, Bob C.

French, Lynette

French, Robert

French, Ruth Ann (Newell)

Garfield, John

Garnes, Loren W.

Gephart, Donald E.

Gilson, Cecil

Goodman, Bennie

Grable, Betty

Grandbouche, LeRoy D.

Hack, Stan

Hagen, Leo

Hall, Cecil E.

Hall, Gale H.

Hambleton, Gene L.

Hansen, Andy

Hansen, Frank

Hasbrouck, Dick

Hasbrouck, Gertrude

Hasbrouck, Ivan

Hasbrouck, Jay

Hegan, Jim

Henie, Sonja

Hinton, Barry

Hinton, Clink

Hollar, Joe

Houk, Lloyd

Hubbard, Rosa

Hunt, Colina (Abbott)

Iseminger, James E.

James, Harry

James, Jesse

Johnson, Paul F.

Johnston, Billie R.

Jorgensen, Melvin O.

Jorgensen, Warren L.

Keltner, Ken

King, Deb

King, Don

King, Lynn

Klein, Jerry

Laude, Lyman "Dutch"

Laughery, Gerald

Laughery, Jack

Laughery, Lloyd

Lee, Jack

Lee, Dr. John

Leib, Raymond

Liddicoat, Verne

Louis, Joe

Lowrey, Harry "Peanuts"

Ludwig, Anna

Ludwig, Bill

Ludwig, Darwin

Ludwig, Donna (Thygesen)
Ludwig, Glen
Ludwig, William
Lydon, Leonard C.
Lykke, Robert
Lynch, Jimmy
Mahler, Everett L.
Marion, Marty
Masters, Fred
McArthur, General Douglas
McCarty, Don
McClellan, Estel R.
McDonald, Earl
McDonald, Irma
McDonald, Joy (Nelson)
McDonald, Merton
McDonald, Rev. Lester
McKibbin, Darrell
McKibbin, Dora
McKibbin, Eldon
McKibbin, Ernie
McKibbin, Gary
McKibbin, Hazel
McKibbin, Jackie (Yeager)
McKibbin, Leonard
McKibbin, Lynn
McKibbin, Micki
McNary, Charles E.
McQueen, Delmar A.
Menning, Debbie
Messner, Lew
Miller, James A.
Miller, Lorene
Miller, Richard "Bing"
Millhollin, Frances

Miranda, Carmen
Mize, Johnny
Moore, General Ned
Moore, Ned Jr.
Moraine, Ivyl
Musial, Stan
Myers, Jack
Nagel, Truman
Naughton, Earl B.
Newman, Ralph R.
Newsome, Louis "Bobo"
Nickel, Kenneth L.
Nolan, Mary
Nolan, Patrick
Oakley, Gladys
O'Sullivan, Father Jeremiah
O'Sullivan, Julia Anne
Oswald, Joel
Parker, Bonnie
Parson, Kenneth W.
Pennington, Stewart R.
Peppers, Jack
Perry, Dick
Peterson, Anne
Phippen, Adelyn
Phippen, Alice May (Hall)
Phippen, Dwayne
Phippen, Frank
Phippen, Gilford
Phippen, Glen
Phippen, Grant
Phippen, Laura
Phippen, Marilyn (Kirkpatrick)
Phippen, Monica
Price, Hugh

Raft, George

Rains, Joseph E.

Rasmussen, Harley N.

Raygor, Carrol "Bull"

Reed, Eldon "Fizz"

Reed, Lawrence

Reese, Harold "Pee Wee"

Renslow, Verland D.

Reynolds, Roland E.

Riaski, Bill Jr.

Riaski, Carolyn

Riaski, Judy (Roberts)

Riaski, William

Rizzuto, Phil "Scooter"

Robinson, Bill "Bojangles"

Robinson, Sam

Rogers, Ginger

Roosevelt, Franklin D.

Rowley, Paul

Ruth, George Herman "Babe"

Rutherford, Ivan

Rutt, Donald T.

Sanger, Bill

Saucer, Earl F.

Schlater, Darwin

Schlater, Dean

Schneider, Vanessa

Schwab, Charlie

Schwab, Gary

Scott, Fred

Searl, Ralph D.

Seeley, William A.

Shadibaugh, Bob

Shaw, Artie

Shelley, Lyle "Jiggs"

Sleister, Pat

Spillers, Glen

Smith, George

Smith, Henry

Stammer, James C.

Stephensen, Warren R.

Stiles, John D.

Stoy, Earle

Tague, Everett

Tallman, Don

Temple, Shirley

Thomas, Bruce

Thomas, Cora

Thornberg, Dr. William

Towne, Larry

Trotter, George

Truman, Harry

Tucker, Tom

Tyson, Everett V.

Vincent, Earl

Vincent, Madge

Waddell, Maurice E.

Wahlert, Sy

Walcott, Barbara

Wesack, Everett H.

Williams, Ted

Wilson, Arch

Wilson, Bert

Wilson, Claiborne J.

Wilson, Dale R.

Wilson, Daniel S.

Wilson, Eugene

Wilson, John M.

Wilson, Marion E.

Wilson, Mildred

About the Author

Carroll McKibbin barely followed the footsteps of his boyhood heroes. He didn't join Bob Feller on the Cleveland Indians' pitching staff and didn't play trumpet duets with Harry James. Like Howard Ely, he did wear an Air Force uniform, but not with the stripes of a sergeant and not on active duty. Instead of spending a career at ball fields and ballrooms, the author served as a diplomat after receiving an appointment from President Kennedy and later moved to academia. In that setting, he has held appointments at Kansas University, Drake University, Nebraska University, Cal Poly, Iowa State University, and the University of Pittsburgh. He is now a professor emeritus, a writer, and living in California with his wife, Lynn.